Heidegger, Strauss, and
the Premises of Philosophy

Heidegger, Strauss, and the Premises of Philosophy

ON ORIGINAL FORGETTING

Richard L. Velkley

The University of Chicago Press CHICAGO & LONDON

The University of Chicago Press, Chicago 60637
The University of Chicago Press, Ltd., London
© 2011 by The University of Chicago
All rights reserved. Published 2011.
Paperback edition 2015
Printed and bound by CPI Group (UK) Ltd, Croydon, CR0 4YY

21 20 19 18 17 16 15   3 4 5 6 7

ISBN-13: 978-0-226-85254-6 (cloth)
ISBN-13: 978-0-226-21494-8 (paper)
ISBN-13: 978-0-226-85255-3 (e-book)
DOI: 10.7208/chicago/9780226852553.001.0001

Library of Congress Cataloging-in-Publication Data

Velkley, Richard L.
Heidegger, Strauss, and the premises of philosophy on original forgetting / Richard Velkley.
        p. cm.
Includes bibliographical references and index.
ISBN-13: 978-0-226-85254-6 (cloth : alk. paper)
ISBN-10: 0-226-85254-7 (cloth : alk. paper)   1. Strauss, Leo. 2. Heidegger, Martin,
1889–1976. 3. Philosophy, Modern—20th century. 4. Political science—Philosophy—
History—20th century. 5. Ontology—History—20th century.   I. Title.
B945.S84V45 2011
193—dc22

2011000175

CONTENTS

ACKNOWLEDGMENTS

I wish to express my gratitude to the John M. Olin Center for Inquiry into the Theory and Practice of Democracy, the LeFrak Forum, and the Symposium on Science, Reason, and Modern Democracy, and to Nathan Tarcov and Richard Zinman, conference organizers, for the invitation to participate in the conferences at the University of Chicago and Michigan State University on Leo Strauss's *Natural Right and History* in April–May 2001, which were the occasion for a lecture that became chapter 7. Also I express my debt to Alfred Denker and Holger Zaborowski of the Heidegger-Forschungsgruppe for the opportunities to speak at the 2004, 2006, and 2008 meetings of the Forschungsgruppe in Messkirch, Germany, out of which arose chapters 5 and 6, and to the late Dr. Kurt Pritzl, O. P., dean of the School of Philosophy at the Catholic University of America, for his invitation to give a paper in the Fall 2007 Lecture Series on Pre-Socratic Philosophy, from which my first chapter is derived. My thanks go to various friends and colleagues with whom I have discussed parts of the book: Avner Ash, Fred Baumann, Diego Benardete, Robert Berman, Ronna Burger, Michael Davis, Patrick Goodin, Victor Gourevitch, Richard Hassing, Mark Lilla, Nalin Ranasinghe, Susan Shell, Martin Sitte, Nathan Tarcov, Holger Zaborowski, and Catherine Zuckert. To David Brent and Laura Avey at the University of Chicago Press and Brian Walters I am greatly indebted for help and support with the manuscript, technical and otherwise. It has been a great pleasure to work with Susan Tarcov in the final stage of editing.

Parts of the book have been previously published: chapter 4 in *Logos and Eros: Essays Honoring Stanley Rosen*, ed. N. Ranasinghe (South Bend, IN: St.

Augustine's Press, 2006); a shorter version of chapter 6 in German translation as "Heidegger, Strauss und der Nationalsozialismus," in *Heidegger und
der Nationalsozialismus—Interpretationen. Heidegger-Jahrbuch*, vol. 5, ed. A.
Denker and H. Zaborowski (Stuttgart: Alber Verlag, 2009); chapter 7 in *Review of Politics* 70, no. 2 (spring 2008): 245–59.

Parabasis

To work out the question of Being adequately, we must make an entity—the inquirer—transparent in his own Being. The very asking of this question is an entity's mode of *Being*; and as such it gets its essential character from what is asked about—namely, Being.

MARTIN HEIDEGGER, *Being and Time*

Now questioning has priority over answering. God does not *ask*, but he answers. Questioning is more characteristic of the human intellect than answering. There is no answer without questioning, but there is indeed questioning without answer.

LEO STRAUSS, "Religiöse Lage der Gegenwart"

I

"The crisis of our time may have the accidental advantage of enabling us to understand in an untraditional or fresh manner what was hitherto understood only in a traditional or derivative manner."[1] The time of crisis and of questioning tradition that was the twentieth century saw a number of leading thinkers seeking to reach new insight concerning the roots, the meaning, and the fate of Western rationalism. Of the figures engaged in this inquiry, Martin Heidegger and Leo Strauss were the two to develop the most searching analyses of the philosophical tradition as originating in radical questioning and as undergoing forgetting.[2] The close linking of these thinkers will doubtless provoke resistance in many readers. Heidegger's followers are unlikely to think of Strauss as a comparably penetrating and fundamental thinker. Should they think of Strauss as having any connection with Heidegger, it is as *the* critic of the latter's "radical historicism" and therefore as a hostile voice, not as a sympathetic reader open to the challenge of Heidegger's questioning of the metaphysical tradition. Strauss's followers commonly view Heidegger as an early stimulus to Strauss, which he left behind quickly for a more salutary philosophic endeavor, as Heidegger's philosophy expresses the ultimate decline of the tradition into extreme relativism and nihilism, whose political manifestation was Heidegger's participation in the National Socialist movement. Strauss's mature thought, accordingly, took notice of Heidegger only for critical and cautionary ends, while his own concern with recovery of the beginnings of the tradition bears only a superficial resemblance to Heidegger's effort of *Destruktion* of the tradition. Contrary to such opinions, it will be maintained here that Strauss's reflection on the basic philosophic questions has a radicality comparable to Heidegger's, and that he was to the end of his life engaged with Heidegger as the one contemporary thinker with whom his thought was in essential dialogue.

In one of his last publications Strauss considers the place of political philosophy in three great figures of recent philosophy who helped to shape the direction of his thinking: Nietzsche, Husserl, and Heidegger.[3] The essay contains this statement: "As far as I can see, [Heidegger] is of the opinion that none of his critics and none of his followers has understood him adequately. I believe that he is right, for is not the same true, more or less, of all outstanding thinkers?"[4] The insertion of the personal note ("I believe that he is right") strengthens the suspicion that Strauss applies the general claim about outstanding thinkers to himself as well as Heidegger. He speaks "from experience." If this is indeed one of Strauss's rare self-referential asides, the context is striking and suggests the question of whether Strauss means that the inadequate understanding of Heidegger is related to the inadequate understanding of himself. It is not a question that many readers of Strauss have asked. Although Strauss privately in letters from his early years onward and publicly in lectures and writings of his later years spoke of Heidegger's supreme importance as thinker—"the only great thinker in our time is Heidegger"—only recently have the two figures been linked in a theoretically substantial way.[5] The best-known writing of Strauss, *Natural Right and History*, is now easily seen as directed at Heidegger, but at the time of its publication (1953) Heidegger was unread in the English-speaking world.[6] Yet since Heidegger's star has risen in that world those who study Heidegger and those who study Strauss have been mostly disjunct groups.[7] Even so, Strauss may well have meant with his seemingly casual aside that his work—and Heidegger's as well—would not be adequately understood until his readers had learned to study how his thought relates to Heidegger's.

This claim may strike many as improbable. Strauss's work does not seem to be much concerned with metaphysical questions, and Heidegger's thought lacks close attention to political matters, although notoriously at certain junctures it is politically engaged. Part of the difficulty is that Strauss's work is too often viewed through that of his students (first and second generation) who were on the whole disinclined to undertake study of metaphysical texts and thinkers, and perhaps especially not those of late modernity. Strauss's own writing encourages a certain reserve (albeit solemn and awestruck) before "first philosophy," with his refrain that philosophy begins with reflecting on "the surface" of things, the human experience of the political and moral phenomena.[8] For Strauss, however, the surface of things is the home of problems, not of absolute principles and solutions. In its ambiguity it points beyond itself. His claim that "the problem inherent in the surface of things, and only in the surface of things, is the heart of things" is his summation of the Socratic pursuit of philosophy. But it is also clearly related to the turn in phenomenology "to the things themselves," begun by Husserl and continued by Heidegger, involving the suspension of given theoretical constructions and the dismantling of "sedimentations" of traditional concepts in practical life as well as theoretical inquiry. In other terms, the phenomenological program is to show the genesis of science out of the prescientific understanding.[9]

Classical political philosophy, as founded by Socrates, did not have to undertake the dismantling of a prior tradition and could investigate the prephilosophic understanding of political phenomena without the aid of historical studies.[10] Strauss underlines that modern students of political philosophy need such studies to uncover what the classical philosophers could grasp directly from experience. But Strauss's phenomenology is not only descriptive; as Socratic it is also dialectical, exposing the fissures and perplexities in the prephilosophic understanding, whereby it follows the Socratic example of seeking to find the clue to the "first things" in the "human things."[11] The spirit of such Socratic inquiry is at the same time aporetic. "Socrates was so far from being committed to a specific cosmology that his knowledge was knowledge of ignorance.... Socrates, then, viewed man in the light of the mysterious character of the whole." The foundation of classical political philosophy is the "understanding of the situation of man which includes ... the quest for cosmology rather than a solution to the cosmological problem."[12] Strauss attempted to show that the metaphysical questions come to light, in their properly aporetic formulation, only through the ascent from the political.[13] Yet his numerous autobiographical comments on his philosophical encounters with Husserl and Heidegger—suggesting the parallel of Socrates's story of his early enthusiasm for Anaxagoras—press one to ask the question: How does Strauss's account of the ascent from the political relate to these roots of his thought?

I start with an indispensable but insufficient formulation. Heidegger and Strauss are linked by the perception each had in his formative years that the Western rationalist tradition had collapsed, an event for which the political catastrophe of their generation, the First World War, gave compelling evidence. More fundamentally, the brilliant arguments of Kierkegaard and Nietzsche had exposed the failure of the civilization of the European Enlightenment.[14] Heidegger and Strauss saw the urgent need to attempt a new beginning through the reconsideration of the origins of the tradition, that is, the most elementary premises on which rationalism is grounded. The possibility of philosophy had to be considered anew in the wake of the self-destructive process that Nietzsche, above all others, had diagnosed and fulfilled.[15] Thus Strauss writes to Hans-Georg Gadamer: "it is necessary to reflect on the situation that demands the new hermeneutics, i.e. on our situation; this reflection will necessarily bring to light a radical crisis, an unprecedented crisis and this is what Heidegger means by the world night."[16] Strauss defends this view of the present age against Gadamer's criticism of Heidegger's account of the "complete forgetfulness of Being" in the present. Similarly he disputes Karl Löwith's charge that Heidegger fails to grasp Nietzsche's true intention, characterizing Heidegger as Nietzsche's genuine successor in thinking through the implications of Nietzsche's account of the present age as nihilistic.[17] All the same, this common ground of Heidegger and Strauss is partly obscured by the appearance, promoted by Strauss himself, that the true issue between the two is the problem of relativism, which Strauss would address by the assertion of absolute norms. As I shall argue, the deeper issue for Strauss is whether Heidegger has remained faithful to his own reopening of the aporia of Being, i.e., the implications of the crisis of philosophy, and whether Socratic skepticism provides (as Strauss argues) the more rigorous and consistent response to the crisis. Although Strauss affirms the superiority of the Socratic way, the novel terms of his rethinking that way are still decisively indebted to Heidegger.

II

For a number of years I have been reading Heidegger with Strauss in mind and Strauss with Heidegger in mind, and the outcome is this study. I am far from considering the thoughts here definitive. I hope to offer some mutual illumination of the two thinkers, but this is exposed to an obvious difficulty: Strauss frequently, if one includes private utterances, declared his intense engagement with Heidegger's thought, but there is no report known to me of any attention paid by Heidegger to Strauss. Thus of the two thinkers only the thought of one of them is significantly formed in response to the thought of the other. The consideration of the relation of Heidegger and Strauss necessarily offers, at least initially, more illumination of Strauss's intentions than of Heidegger's. I believe, however, that the understanding of Heidegger's thought is advanced by viewing it in the light of Strauss's effort to renew "political philosophy." It will not come as much of a surprise to anyone that Heidegger's thought has been provocative for the thinking of another figure, of whatever rank. By contrast, something must be said to justify the claim that Strauss is a figure worth considering comparatively and critically together with Heidegger. I underline that my ultimate goal is not to offer an external comparison of two authors, nor is it to weigh influences. It is to enter into the shared matter of thinking of the two philosophers and to discover what can be learned from their converging while disparate ways of thinking about that matter.

My book is not concerned with the details of intellectual biography. The basic facts of Strauss's studies with Husserl and Heidegger in the early 1920s are well known. After a short exposure to Heidegger's lectures Strauss did not remain in the circle of Heidegger's students, but he maintained lifelong contacts with some who did, and with them he continued to discuss Heidegger's thought.[18] Strauss gives the following account of his attendance at Heidegger's lectures at the University of Freiburg in summer 1922:

> One of the unknown young men in Husserl's entourage was Heidegger. I attended his lecture course from time to time without understanding a word, but sensed that he dealt with something of the utmost importance to man as man. I understood something on one occasion: when he interpreted the beginning of the *Metaphysics*. I had never heard nor seen such a thing—such a thorough and intensive interpretation of a philosophic text. On my way home I visited Rosenzweig and said to him that compared to Heidegger, Max Weber, till then regarded by me as the incarnation of the spirit of science and scholarship, was an orphan child.[19]

As Strauss then explains, it was not simply Heidegger's interpretive powers that impressed him. Both he and Jacob Klein were deeply affected by the intent and the result of Heidegger's interpretation of Greek philosophy.

> Heidegger's work required and included what he called *Destruktion* of the tradition. . . . He intended to uproot Greek philosophy, especially Aristotle, but this presupposed the laying bare of its roots, the laying bare of it as it was in itself and not as it had come to appear in the light of the tradition and of modern philosophy.[20]

The statement might give the impression that Heidegger laid bare the roots of the tradition only for the sake of rejecting them, but in another passage Strauss corrects that interpretation. Noting that "certainly no one questioned the premise of philosophy as radically as Heidegger," Strauss proceeds:

> Klein alone saw why Heidegger is truly important: by uprooting and not simply rejecting the tradition of philosophy, he made it possible for the first time after many centuries—one hesitates to say how many—to see the roots of the tradition as they are and thus perhaps to know, what so many merely believe, that those roots are the only natural and healthy roots. . . . Above all, his intention was to uproot Aristotle: he thus was compelled to disinter the roots, to bring them to light, to look at them with wonder.[21]

One might think that Klein and Strauss understood Heidegger's significance in the following way: he persuaded them of the inadequacy of the traditional accounts of the Greek roots, but his own new readings, while brilliant, were misguided and thus forced them to develop counterreadings that uncover the true roots. It surely is the case that neither Klein nor Strauss was a follower of Heidegger's own philosophy of existence. "Klein was more attracted by the Aristotle brought to light and life by Heidegger than by Heidegger's own philosophy."[22] But the distinction made by this sentence means that Heidegger's reading of Aristotle contained something true and of enduring worth, enabling one "to see the roots of the tradition as they are." Furthermore, Heidegger was able to expose this only through questioning the tradition more radically than anyone else, so that what he exposed was an object of wonder to Heidegger and his listeners. In other words, he made possible a radically untraditional approach to the Greek roots and therewith of the whole tradition of philosophy, one that had intrinsic merit. Through this wonderful disclosure he opened "the possibility of a genuine return to classical philosophy, to the philosophy of Plato and Aristotle, a return with open eyes and in full clarity about the infinite difficulties which it entails."[23] Strauss says this possibility "Heidegger had opened without intending it," for his concern was to go behind Plato and Aristotle to a more primordial thinking on which the thought of these philosophers rested and which at the same time was forgotten and obscured by their thought. Yet in some sense Heidegger's readings of Plato and Aristotle provided the basis for the return to them, for by showing the "infinite difficulties" of the return he paradoxically made the return possible. He showed that the true Plato and Aristotle were unfamiliar and so remote from traditional conceptions of them that one had to relearn completely how to read them. The traditional conceptions had lost all power, and the emergence of strange, unfamiliar conceptions held the promise of grounding a living way of philosophizing.

One can conclude that Strauss saw in Heidegger's thought an insight to which Heidegger's own philosophy proved to be inadequate. It is in this sense that one can read what Strauss says about Heidegger's thought in another work: "It compels us at the same time to realize the need for an unbiased reconsideration of the most elementary premises whose validity is presupposed by philosophy."[24] If one takes this statement the way many readers of Strauss take it, as asserting that Heidegger's "radical historicism" exposes the nihilistic consequences of the modern tradition and so requires a return to ancient philosophy, it gives Heidegger no credit at all for uncovering problems in the roots of the tradition and raising genuine difficulties about the possibility of philosophy, including ancient philosophy.[25] The sentence would then be at odds with the autobiographical passages cited, which establish that Heidegger had shown that a simple return to ancient philosophy from modern philosophy was impossible and that one had to rethink what the Greeks understood by philosophy without presupposing that philosophy in *any* form is possible. The questions that Heidegger raised about the elementary premises of philosophy had to be addressed and could not be dismissed as sophistical. Indeed Strauss does not rule out the possibility that the required "reconsideration" of the premises may leave at least some of Heidegger's questions intact. This result would be compatible with seeing the need for some correction or improvement in Heidegger's thought.

Without a blink of an eye, one can of course counter that Strauss's inquiry about the recovery of classical political philosophy, especially of the Socratics, is wholly distinct from Heidegger's recovery of the question of Being as raised by the early Greeks and then forgotten by the whole tradition that follows. A closer look at Strauss's statements shows there cannot be such an absolute disjunction. In the first place, Strauss avers that the question of Being is central to Plato and Aristotle. "Heidegger agreed with Plato and Aristotle not only as to this—that the question of what is *to be* is the fundamental question; he also agreed with Plato and Aristotle as to this—that the fundamental question must be addressed to that being which *is* in the most emphatic or the most authoritative way."[26] In the passage containing the previously cited statement about the "most elementary premises," Strauss expressly states that the recovery of classical political philosophy (and the problem of natural right) requires the reexamination of the possibility of philosophy as such. Clearly for Plato and Aristotle, the principal classical political philosophers, the possibility of philosophy entails the truth of certain premises about Being. Accordingly Strauss cannot be indifferent to what these philosophers think about such premises. In fact several crucial statements of Strauss assert that the founding of political philosophy by Socrates is inseparable from the discovery of a new way of approaching the questions about Being and the whole. "Contrary to appearances, Socrates' turn to the study of the human things was based, not upon disregard of the divine or natural things, but upon a new approach to the understanding of all things."[27] "In its original form political philosophy broadly understood is the core of philosophy or rather 'the first philosophy.' "[28] "We have learned from Socrates that the political things, or the human things, are the key to the understanding of all things."[29]

This understanding of Socratic philosophy, which Strauss developed over several decades and which emerged fully formed only after the Second World War, is a response to Heidegger's rethinking of the possibility of philosophy, with which it shares the character of being a radically antitraditional account of philosophy and of the philosophic tradition. It is therefore not just a reinstatement of classical philosophy against Heidegger's rejection of it, since Strauss's own radical antitraditionalism has sources in Heidegger's questioning of the tradition. In light of Strauss's claim about the comprehensive philosophic character of the Socratic turn to the human (political) things, one can propose that Strauss's Socratism is an engagement with the fundamental question of Being through the examination of the human way of being as political. As such it belongs in the succession to Heidegger's approach to the question of Being through the analysis of the human way of being in the world, i.e., the exposure of the fundamental structure of that entity (*Dasein*) for whom the question of Being is constitutive.

Certainly it is often maintained with suave assurance that Strauss was basically uninterested in metaphysical matters, that his thought makes no pretense of having comprehensiveness, even that his writings reveal only an unconnected collection of themes and questions garnered from texts that were the object of Strauss's devoted scholarly commentary.[30] A locus classicus for those who want to claim that Strauss turned away from the question of Being to "the primacy of the political," and that he held it was "Heidegger's concern for Being, rather than beings, that led to his indifference to tyranny,"[31] is the conclusion of Strauss's "Restatement on Xenophon's *Hiero*," addressed to Alexandre Kojève. The passage, which clearly refers to Heidegger, reads as follows:

For we [Strauss and Kojève] both apparently turned away from Being to Tyranny because we have seen that those who lack the courage to face the issue of

Tyranny, who therefore *et humiliter serviebant et superbe dominabantur*, were forced to evade the issue of Being as well, precisely because they did nothing but talk of Being.[32]

Far from denying that Strauss is concerned with Being, the statement contains an ironic affirmation that Strauss and Kojève are both concerned with the question of Being and indeed pursue it more adequately than Heidegger, insofar as they do not limit their *speaking and writing* (talk) to Being alone, for such limitation evades the issue of Being. Indeed Strauss affirms "the primacy of the political" as the necessary beginning point for philosophic inquiry, but this is not his final or complete thought. In the same passage, immediately before the concluding sentences, he writes that "on the basis of the classical presupposition, philosophy requires a radical detachment from human concerns: man must not be absolutely at home on the earth, he must be a citizen of the whole." Kojève's account of philosophy, by contrast, calls for enduring attachment to the political ("man must be absolutely at home on earth, he must be a citizen of the earth"). The implied position of Strauss is that adequately addressing the issue of Being requires reflection on the problem of the relation of philosophy to politics (ignored by Heidegger, pursued by Strauss and Kojève) but without losing sight of the ultimate superiority of the theoretical life to the political life, and thus without conceiving philosophy as fulfilled in the realm of practice (contra Kojève). In the end, as one gathers from other sources, Strauss's objection to Heidegger comes close to this criticism of Kojève (suggesting further irony in the passage) insofar as Heidegger's thinking on Being rests on a conflation of such thinking with the historical existence of man as poetic-religious, even if (or because) Heidegger does not for the most part discuss the latter in political terms. The flaw in his philosophy is not the concern with Being but an exclusive concern with Being, which precludes the distinctive features of political life from shining forth. (Again, if concern with Being were a philosophic flaw, then Plato and Aristotle would merit a good scolding from Strauss.) The passage surely points to an intrinsic connection between the manner in which Heidegger pursues his question and his failure to face the problem of tyranny.

III

The present book treats Heidegger and Strauss from the standpoint of philosophical relations between them and takes up politics to the extent it bears on their approaches to philosophy. For some readers it will be disappointing that the book is not more about politics in the narrow sense. I do not delve into the details of Heidegger's involvement in National Socialism or dwell on Strauss's comments on that involvement. Certainly the book takes up the philosophical problem of how Heidegger's philosophy could allow, or rather predispose, Heidegger to engage with National Socialism, and it discusses Strauss's analysis of that problem. It should be observed, though, that Strauss's remarks on Heidegger's philosophy far outweigh in quantity and detail his remarks on Heidegger's political deeds and misdeeds, both in his public writings and in the correspondence. Strauss states that the facts of Heidegger's political engagement "afford too small a basis for the proper understanding of his thought."[33] One can easily construct a facile syllogism: (P1) As political philosopher Strauss is most of all interested in a thinker's political thoughts and actions; (P2) Heidegger's only significant political thoughts and actions relate to his support of National Socialism; (C) What Strauss finds most interesting in Heidegger is the latter's support of National Socialism. Both premises are defective: Strauss understands political philosophy not solely as the theory of politics, or the philosophic treatment of politics, but also as the political treatment of philosophy, which leads the student or interlocutor toward grasping the superiority of the philosophic life among ways of life or the preeminence of philosophic virtue among the meanings of virtue.[34] Its "highest theme" is the tension between the claims of politics and those of philosophy. As to Heidegger's political actions and thoughts, Strauss is ultimately more concerned with the premises, mostly unstated, in Heidegger's philosophic thought about the relation of philosophy to politics than with the overt political choices of Heidegger, although these cannot be separated from those premises. Heidegger's failure to see the problematic relations between philosophy and politics is the heart of Strauss's criticism. It is a subtle point that this criticism applies both to Heidegger's early thought, which is more obviously politically engaged, and to his later thought which has withdrawn from direct political engagement. Insofar as Heidegger's thought is throughout characterized by a fusion of philosophy with the religious-political realm that is "eschatological," it has no "room for political philosophy" in Strauss's sense. Precisely by not reflecting on the relation of philosophy and politics Heidegger's thought is politicized, being shaped by unexamined assumptions about that relation which Heidegger takes over chiefly from the tradition of German Idealism and to some extent from Nietzsche.

Since I am disavowing some common approaches to these thinkers, I shall also mention that my study distances itself from the widespread tendency of writers on Strauss to dwell on clarification, often combined with justification, of his relation to American politics and political science. I believe this was not of ultimate concern to Strauss. He of course engaged in some famous polemics with contemporary American political scientists over the "value-neutrality" of social science, but these debates are peripheral to the core of his thought, or they are only an appendix to his more central critique of Max Weber. About American political thought and events he made very few pronouncements. And it is a related point to say that Strauss's nearly universal reputation as a major "conservative" political thinker is essentially misleading about the nature of his thought. The center of Strauss's reflection is the extraordinary nature of philosophical questioning, whose radicality he contrasted with the moderation required by political action. "The virtue of the philosopher's thought is a certain kind of *mania*, while the virtue of the philosopher's public speech is *sophrosune*."[35] A combination of theoretical traditionalism and political extremism (on the right) is commonly ascribed to Strauss, but it is just the opposite of the truth.[36] In other words, Strauss's thought does not belong to the mainstream Anglo-American conservative tradition for which the burning issue is the moderation or rejection of "rationalism in politics," although Strauss is a strong critic of the transformative and revolutionary approaches to politics that emerged in the modern Enlightenment. He is a critic of the Enlightenment ultimately more for its subordination of philosophy to practice, for obscuring the fundamental unsolved problems under the veil of alleged "progress," than for its possible harmful consequences for political life. As Strauss's critical reading of Burke shows, he regards the post-Burke tradition of conservatism as committing another form of the subordination of philosophy to practice or history. It is important to add that for Strauss theoretical radicality and political moderation are not merely juxtaposed parts of the philosopher's thought but essentially connected. To recognize that philosophical questioning has a radicality inherently at odds with custom and law is to acknowledge a difference in human life that cannot be overcome. The philosopher's political moderation is a manifestation of a prudence that has theoretical grounding. Strauss faults Heidegger for failing to appreciate *this* decisive meaning of difference.

To grasp the peculiar sense of "political philosophy" in Strauss one must examine further why he encouraged the close attention to concrete analysis of political life or, more to the point given our situation, the close study of authors who engage in this analysis. Strauss focused on such study in order to uncover the problems or tensions that are inherent in political life, which he placed under the heading of the "theological-political problem." This expression is frequently and mistakenly identified solely with the dispute between philosophic reason and piety or revelation. However, Strauss, following classic authors, noted the unending debate within political life concerning notions of justice, of law, and of the good. "The meaning of the common good is essentially controversial."[37] Political life is a realm of enduring tensions, one of which is the tension between the authority of divinely sanctioned law and human statesmanship's need for autonomous flexibility in practical judgment, which prefigures the dispute between piety and philosophy.[38] "The ambiguity of the political goal is due to its comprehensive character."[39] Reflection on the ultimate goal of political knowledge or art gives rise to controversies that do not occur about the ultimate goals of other arts (pastoral, military, culinary, etc.). The political, as a kind of whole, discloses the structure of the cosmos of problems considered by philosophy.[40] Strauss's approach to politics as the way into the philosophic problems by no means implies that the political life is the highest life or that reflection on politics constitutes the whole substance of philosophic thought. It is rather that this reflection is the introduction to the problem of the best life, the core question of Socratic philosophy.

As a political being the human is "open to the whole,"[41] or transcends itself toward some completion, albeit ambiguously, as it transcends itself toward the whole of the particular political community and toward the "whole as such," which is variously conceived by all human beings. Strauss asserts that the whole as such is "mysterious," as the ultimate grounds and causes of the whole of things are removed from human understanding. The question of Being must remain, in the decisive respect, a question, on which point Strauss is in basic accord with Heidegger. All of human life is conducted in the light of this mystery and cannot be conceived without reference to it. For Strauss as for Heidegger, the human is that being whose existence is a question for itself. Both thinkers also reflect on the human tendency to conceal or "forget" this questionableness, although only Strauss puts this in political terms: the attachment to symbols, rituals, and doctrines of the "cave," grounded in sacred law, which partially limits and closes off reflection on the whole of problems. The two thinkers agree that philosophy is the intransigent facing of the questionableness of Being, of a sort that few human beings can undertake, much less sustain, in its purity. For both of them Nietzsche is the great exemplar of such philosophic intransigence in recent history.[42]

Both are indebted to Nietzsche, as well, in their conceptions of the history of philosophy (more broadly, of the West) as a decline from lofty beginnings, as a growing oblivion of the Greek way of articulating the fundamental questions, with its unparalleled clarity and openness to the phenomena. There is some kinship, too, in the characterization of the form this oblivion takes in the modern age: for Heidegger it is the dominance of technological thinking, for Strauss the project of mastering nature, which he conceives as a political project embracing a new role for technology. In this regard both thinkers carry forward, with important modifications and criticisms, Nietzsche's attack on the Enlightenment and its utilitarian spirit. The "forgetting of Being" (Being as the disclosedness of beings) is for Heidegger a historical fate, a withdrawal of Being inherent in Being that begins already among the Greeks, most notably in Plato, after the great age of early thinking, and culminates in the occlusion of Being in the "technological world night" in which man is wholly drawn into the control and calculation of beings. This darkness may be the prelude to another beginning.[43] Strauss locates the high point of Greek philosophy in Socrates and his immediate pupils, and his historical scheme of the loss of authentic philosophy after the Socratics is more differentiated than Heidegger's "history of Being." The spirit of Socratic philosophy recovers some vitality in the medieval Islamic and Jewish philosophers, as philosophy emerges from the massive oblivion induced by the eruption of revelation into the world of philosophy. A decisive shift occurs in the founding of modern philosophy by Machiavelli, Bacon, Hobbes, Descartes, and their successors, which is not a historical fate but a conscious human decision to reject the previous tradition and start anew. All the same, it is a crucial aspect of Strauss's dialectical mode of arguing that he at times overstates the philosophic decline inherent in the modern turn. Indeed, Strauss understands the modern founding to be another effort, albeit flawed, to save philosophy from oblivion. More generally, Strauss's sharpening of theoretical antitheses is central to his strategy of provoking awareness of fundamental problems. I shall say more about this later.

IV

This familiar account of history in Strauss rests on an underlying theme concerning a tension intrinsic to the condition of philosophy, present from its beginning, and to which modern philosophy is a novel response. "Philosophy is the attempt to replace opinion by knowledge; but opinion is the element of the city, hence philosophy is subversive, hence the philosopher must write in such a way that he will improve rather than subvert the city."[44] The protective and "exoteric" stratagems of philosophic self-presentation necessarily involve public dilution of the philosopher's radical thinking. In light of the difficulty of attaining definitive results in the quest for knowledge of ultimate matters, the need for such dilution may threaten to corrupt the substance of thinking itself, by exposing philosophy to "the charm of competence" (i.e., of the apodictically demonstrable) or the socially useful. This enduring problem for philosophy was made incalculably more complex by the confrontation of philosophy with revealed religions based on sacred scriptures claiming authoritative insight in ultimate matters.[45] Philosophy was threatened by permanent subservience to theological orthodoxy. The modern philosophers, to recover something of the original natural freedom of philosophic questioning, resorted to the effective means of securing protected freedom by redefining philosophy's goal as universally practical—above all, in practical opposition to theological authority. The gulf between philosophy and the city was bridged by identifying the ends of the philosopher and the nonphilosopher, placing inquiry in the service of the relief of man's estate or "science for the sake of power."[46] Rather paradoxically, the gains for philosophy in greater freedom and for society in diffusion of science and its material benefits (Enlightenment and "progress") were necessarily made at the price of lowering philosophy's sights, as "unqualified attachment to human concerns becomes the source of philosophic understanding."[47]

I can only mention now[48] the suggestion that in Strauss's account the tendency toward a certain forgetting of Socratic philosophy by the later philosophic tradition, arising from philosophy's conflict with the requirements of political life (and especially its pious core), is rooted in what one can describe as metaphysical or cosmic ambiguity. In this regard there is a crucial difference and similarity between Heidegger and Strauss on the sources of "falling away" or forgetting. An initial approach to the difference is to say that Heidegger's account of oblivion is historical, since oblivion is grounded in the self-withdrawal of Being as historical, whereas Strauss finds the sources of oblivion in enduring, transhistorical traits of human nature. But this is misleading insofar as Strauss does not present a doctrine of human nature in the sense of an anthropology that is intelligible apart from the human relation to Being or the whole, and he is in accord with Heidegger on the necessary defects of such anthropology. Rather Strauss seeks to understand the human situation in the light of a fundamental ambiguity that one can describe as metaphysical or cosmological, with the crucial proviso that the metaphysical or cosmological inquiry in question is hypothetical or aporetic. He points to the nature of this inquiry—as both directed toward the whole, not just a part thereof, and also hypothetical—in this pregnant passage of *Natural Right and History*:

The unfinishable character of the quest for adequate articulation of the whole does not entitle one, however, to limit philosophy to the understanding of a part, however important. For the meaning of a part depends on the meaning of the whole. In particular, such interpretation of a part as is based on fundamental experiences alone, without recourse to hypothetical assumptions about the whole, is ultimately not superior to other interpretations of that part which are frankly based on such hypothetical assumptions.[49]

"Interpretation . . . based on fundamental experiences alone" would seem to refer to Heidegger's effort in *Being and Time* to approach the question of Being solely on the basis of the fundamental experience of *Angst* or care (*Sorge*) as the human-existential structure of being-in-the-world that underlies that experience.[50] Strauss knew at this time, as he was becoming aware of Heidegger's later writing, that Heidegger himself became dissatisfied with that approach, and indeed as I show in the second chapter, Strauss acknowledged and investigated an affinity between his own thinking and Heidegger's later path of thinking. A difference, however, remains: Strauss maintained against Heidegger the inevitability of considering hypothetical cosmological principles as illuminating the existence of the human—specifically, the duality of the human as political and transpolitical.[51]

One can approach this issue by reflecting on Strauss's understanding of the problem of nature. Nature (*phusis*) is a Greek discovery, already announced in poets before philosophers, according to which the natural first things are distinguished from the merely humanly made things or conventions (including *muthoi*) and from things known merely through hearsay as contrasted with direct seeing. Nature is "implied in the idea of philosophy," as the idea of an unchanging order discernible by human reason, independent of human willing or making and in principle universally accessible. As such it is an order distinguished from the multiplicity and diversity of human conventions or "caves." After inquiry turns to the question of what is good by nature, the idea of natural right emerges, as the idea of a right that is knowable by reason universally.[52] The search for it entails rejection of the prephilosophic identification of the good with the ancestral. Yet Strauss states that his own inquiry seeks to restore knowledge of "the problem of natural right" or, as he also says, "the idea of natural right." To say natural right is an "idea" is to say it is a "fundamental problem."[53] "Political life in all its forms necessarily points to natural right as an inevitable problem."[54] As Strauss notes, not all philosophers who search for the natural principles endorse the notion of natural right or natural justice. Thus pre-Socratic and Epicurean philosophers distinguish the pleasant as the natural good from the entire realm of the political and moral as conventional. And in Strauss's reading the Socratic answer to the question "What is good by nature?" is contrasted with all political conceptions of justice, i.e., justice understood as serving the ends of the city. Still it is the case that for Socrates the structure of the city reveals something essential about the natural structure of the soul, including its essentially political passion, spiritedness or *thumos*. Both *thumos* and *eros* occupy a place of importance in Socratic philosophic self-understanding but are missing in classical hedonism.[55] But all of this points to nature as a problem rather than as the subject of doctrinaire teaching, and as a problem that is accessible only by starting with political life as a realm of problems centering on the question "What is the best way of life?" Contrary to what is often thought, Strauss does not investigate the prephilosophic "cave" in order to find there sound intuitions or common sense about morality and political practice, on which to base universally evident precepts of the natural law. For him the entire history of thinking about natural right and natural law exposes the fundamental problem of nature. Historicist thought is wrong not in finding nature problematic but in substituting for doctrinaire accounts of nature its own doctrinaire principle of history.[56] There is no question-begging assumption of a natural life-world on Strauss's part, contrary to some prominent critiques.[57]

Accordingly Strauss's criticisms of social science positivism and cultural relativism focus not on skeptical consequences of these positions but on dogmatic ones: these positions render the question of the good life meaningless as a *question*. As to the relation of this critique to Heidegger, the situation is complicated by Heidegger's sharing much common ground with Strauss in the rejection of social science positivism, natural-scientific accounts of the human,[58] and standard cultural relativism on the grounds that they render unintelligible the capacity of the human to raise the question about Being. Yet the question of the good is notably missing from Heidegger's profound account of questioning. Even so, or precisely for this reason, Heidegger's "radical historicism," which through a radical critique of theoretical understanding attains the "highest self-consciousness" of modern philosophy,[59] poses the most severe challenge in all modernity (and perhaps in all philosophy) to the Socratic account of philosophy that Strauss revives.

V

In the chapters that follow I seek to expose and clarify the meaning of "original forgetting" found in these two figures. I argue that the central reflection of each is on the forgetting of radical questioning as an experience inseparable from human openness to the inherently enigmatic whole, and on highly provisional and experimental efforts to recover such questioning. Understood correctly, such forgetting is not something that has happened only in modernity, for it is in the nature of thinking that original insight will be replaced by doctrine and tradition. I argue also that each thinker pursues a primary ambiguity or duality to which a secondary one is attached, wherein an oscillation is set up. For Heidegger the primary duality is that of Being and beings (*Sein* and *Seienden*). Being is that which enables beings to be disclosed, thereby concealing itself in favor of what it discloses yet revealing itself at the same time as that which grounds through withdrawing, i.e., that which is thought-worthy as the "nothing." This sets up the secondary ambiguity. In his later thought Heidegger meditates on a new way of being at home in Being through attentiveness to Being as that which withdraws—being at home in homelessness—and this can be understood as Heidegger's attempt to resolve the tension between radical philosophic questioning and human attachments to people, place, language, poetry, and gods, or to the origins of these. Heidegger is not unaware of the tension between philosophic life and nonphilosophic modes of life, yet he never truly articulates these as human alternatives, since he longs and hopes for a transformation that overcomes their difference. This stance implies that the difference has only a historical character. Yet there is persisting ambiguity evident in Heidegger's later accounts of freedom, in which freedom appears both as radical questioning that transcends the historically given and as receptivity to the call of the historical event of Being as a particular way of dwelling. This ambiguity relates to the complex way Heidegger's rejection of Nietzsche's project of overcoming modernity through an assertion of will is combined with a continuing sympathy for Nietzsche as prophetic figure pointing toward a new founding of human dwelling.[60]

For Strauss the primary duality is that of the city and man, or man's dual way of transcending: toward the political whole and toward the natural whole or "whole as such." That this duality is the source of tensions that are the permanent hinge on which human life turns is the theme of Strauss's writing. He sees the conscious project of overcoming them as the hallmark of modernity, of which Heidegger is the final and consummate thinker. Modern philosophy seeks to fuse itself with practical life and thus to become wholly at home in the world of human affairs, but "the attempt to make man absolutely at home in this world ended in man's becoming absolutely homeless."[61] But Strauss's thought has its secondary ambiguity, pertaining to how the essentially radical essence of philosophy gets realized in its modern form as practical, which in Strauss's view constitutes a break with the premodern account of philosophy as theoretical. How is the "break" compatible with the transhistorical character of philosophy as openness to the "permanent problems"? If the modern revolution constitutes a new kind of philosophy, is not philosophy subject to historical transformation? But if, on the other hand, this revolution is in reality a falling away from genuine philosophy, can one then say that the "quarrel between the ancients and the moderns" is a philosophical one? Furthermore, if genuine (Socratic) philosophy falls or declines into something less than philosophy, how does such a process occur? Strauss offers a powerful account of the practical dangers and perplexities that philosophy always confronts, and his view of the modern approach to philosophy's difficulties, as a well- considered strategy of its founders, offers an illuminating tale of genesis that is absent from Heidegger's *seinsgeschichtlich* scheme of decline as historical fate. But if the modern founders have such clarity about their intent, would it not be the case that they retain the essential freedom of philosophic thought, wherein they do not simply fuse philosophy with practical ends? Strauss suggests that such freedom is still evident in Machiavelli, Rousseau, and Nietzsche and seems equivocal about whether it can be found in other major figures like Hobbes, Spinoza, Locke, Kant, and Hegel. But if one allows that philosophic autonomy exists in the modern era, is there in fact such a drastic falling away from the Socratic beginning of political philosophy, in the decisive respect?

Both Heidegger and Strauss attempt to uncover or renew forms of thinking that lie beyond the modern standpoint. Heidegger would move beyond the modern stance of the will, the Nietzschean type of founding that legislates for humanity a new end or a higher freedom, but in his hope for a new era of "thinking" he retains the modern hope for a fusion of philosophy and practical life. Strauss would disclose the defect of modern philosophy as the creation of "conscious constructs" that limit the vision not only of nonphilosophers but of the philosophers themselves, as "enhancing the status of man and his 'world' by making him oblivious of the whole and eternity."[62] This suggests a view of the modern philosophers as both able and unable to see beyond their self-limiting constructs.[63] In my reading of Strauss, this ambiguity is deliberate, since due consideration of his work shows that he regards modern philosophy as a serious alternative to classical Greek philosophy and that indeed the recovery of Greek philosophy can take place only by means of the confrontation between its premises and the premises of modern philosophy. The latter have become as unknown as those of classical philosophy and are as worthy of archaeological research. The true object of inquiry is not to formulate an ancient doctrine to replace modern ones but to revive awareness of the "fundamental problems" shared by the philosophers. Thus Strauss, writing of the origins of his study of Hobbes, states, "I concluded that the case of the moderns against the ancients must be reopened, without any regard to cherished opinions or convictions, *sine ira et studio*."[64] Strauss does not simply say, "I saw that the return to ancient philosophy was necessary." Furthermore, if Heidegger's thought is "the highest self-consciousness" of modern philosophy, then the confrontation between classical philosophy and Heidegger is indispensable for the recovery of original questioning. As I noted earlier, in Strauss's view such recovery must take the form of the dialectical opposing of theses. In this regard one recalls his oft-quoted remark about the antagonism of revelation and philosophy: "It seems to me that this unresolved conflict is the secret of the vitality of Western civilization."[65] Strauss's readings of the great modern philosophers present them as profoundly aware of this conflict, and thus as sustaining the original questioning of philosophy, although the conventional forms of thought arising out of this modern tradition ("the second cave") have indeed promoted oblivion of such questioning. It cannot be denied, however, that in Strauss's estimation the two recent great figures in whom this conflict is still alive, Nietzsche and Heidegger, fell short in their grasp of its political basis and meaning.

For philosophical-pedagogical purposes Strauss engages at times in one-sided accounts of modern philosophy as "fallen." In this he seems to be a student of Nietzsche insofar as his philosophical writing employs the creation of tensions through deliberate contradiction and exaggeration, or by proposing "simplifying horizons" (satisfying the "will to untruth") from which the philosophical mind must make an effort to free itself and thereby learn the art of thinking.[66] Heidegger also practices a certain version of this art: his accounts of "forgetting of Being" as ever-deepening oblivion are countered by interpretations of Leibniz, Kant, Hegel, Hölderlin, Schelling, and Nietzsche that ascribe to these thinkers levels of insight close to, if not quite equal to, that of the greatest ancient figures. One must distinguish between the prevailing consciousness of modernity and the thoughts that the highest minds of modernity were capable of thinking. For both Strauss and Heidegger philosophizing is incompatible with complacent reliance on historical schemata, even as such schemata must be used to provoke self-awareness that one's "self-evident truths" are essentially questionable.

To sum up this line of argument: only because the modern philosophers still bear traces of the Socratic origin is Strauss able to philosophize in dialogue with them. Modern philosophy has, furthermore, not resulted only in obliviousness to everything beyond the political-practical horizon. Strauss admits this when he tells contemporary readers that in spite of their dwelling within a "cave beneath the cave," they still are open to, and confronted with, the mysterious whole. To mention one important instance of how modern thought sustains an ancient problem (discussed in the final chapter): Strauss suggests that modern ideas of individuality have roots in the ancient poetic and philosophic accounts of tension between the city and the individual. Strauss comments that Hegel is "the profoundest student of Aristophanes in modern times," citing the *Phenomenology of the Mind*: "The individual consciousness having become conscious of itself presents itself as the absolute power." This is a revealing parabasis.[67] Indeed, what is apparently a mere aside points to the neglected crux of the history of Western thought: the peripheral emerges as central. The comic poet Aristophanes, who in histories of philosophy is never treated as a major player (although Hegel's remark on the "triumph of subjectivity" in Aristophanes begins to correct this absence), is according to Strauss the thinker who above all others displays to Plato the poetic alternative to philosophy—as the only genuine alternative to philosophy. This is not because poetic thought comprehends only the unquestioning obedience of piety before the law, but because in its highest form it reflects on the fundamental tension between *eros* and the law in a compelling fashion opposed to philosophy. According to the poetic account, individuals necessarily seek beyond the law a completion that they cannot find, and the authority of sacred law (perhaps as made by poets who in their lawgiving role find satisfaction) must remain the limit for human life, since what lies beyond that limit admits no satisfactory, noncomic and nontragic, definition.[68] This is a stance that Socrates rejects, holding that philosophy transcends the law without comic or tragic failure by uncovering a sustainable way of life based on knowledge of ignorance. The poetic awareness of the problem of the individual's transcending of law (of "the city and man") is the key to the quarrel between the ancients and the moderns, in that the modern philosophers revive the poetic view against the Socratic, with philosophic consciousness of their effort, such that "the quarrel between the ancients and the moderns concerns eventually, and perhaps even from the start, the status of 'individuality.'"[69]

Strauss's treatment of Aristophanes is accordingly his response to Heidegger's turn to the pre-Socratic philosophers, as it shows that the poetic reflection on the problem of the individual and law is the context from which philosophy emerges, in striking affinity with Heidegger's claim that "poetic thinking" must be renewed if we are to grasp how philosophy arose and also how it went astray. But Strauss's poetic thinking, unlike Heidegger's, discloses the structure of the "cave" and its law as political, which is to say, as inherently problematic, as the comic-tragic realm in which philosophy is never wholly at home. While in accord with Heidegger's insight that philosophy cannot be understood except in relation to the world of poetry and gods that precedes it, and that genuine philosophical thought cannot be sustained except by remaining in dialogue with that world, Strauss restates the problem at issue for both poetry and philosophy. Through that restatement Socratic philosophy comes forward as mindful of the poetic-erotic experience that Heidegger claims it forgot, and at the same time as able to offer a coherent alternative to the comic-tragic vision of human life.

VI

I conclude with an observation to prepare for all that follows. For both thinkers the central theme of philosophy is Being or the whole, which is manifest and intelligible only as a question or problem for a being that is part of the whole. Such a being is the human, as the part of the whole that is also open to the whole: "the being that *is* in the most emphatic or the most authoritative way." Thus the human ambiguously transcends toward "its own" (the part that it is) and toward what is beyond its own, toward Being or the whole. This dual manner of transcending conceals itself and forgets itself: the human has openness for the whole beyond itself but only as a relatively self-contained part that must have concern for itself. All questioning must start from, and in some way remain conditioned by, "closed horizons" of thought. Philosophy—the attempt to know the whole—is possible only because such closed horizons are questionable. Strauss sought to advance on Heidegger's formulation of ontological difference or ambiguity by arguing that the human "part" or starting point is inherently political (the "cave" that is both open and closed to the whole), whereby he attempted to show that Socratic thought does justice to the Heideggerian insight and at the same time roots it in permanent necessities of political life. This also clarifies the central place of the gods or revelation in Strauss's reflection, since the divine is the primary indicator of the dyadic character of the human as both of the city and transcending the city: the primary indicator of the tension in the soul between law and *eros*. The human has access to the whole, what is most universal, only by passing through the experience of what is particular and local, the laws of the city with their divine sanctioning. For Strauss the ancient question "What is god?" relates to the wonder that the highest human possibility, the effort to understand the whole, is crucially conditioned in its starting points by a singularity that has questionable grounding in the natural whole, the life of humans in cities under laws. Clearly this reflection is at least thematically linked to Heidegger's thinking about the divine and the gift of the disclosedness of Being. I can only indicate the substance of the affinities and the differences between these ways of thinking by a few words on the structure of this book's discussion:

Part I, "Repetition of Antiquity at the Peak of Modernity," takes up three principal topics: (1) The turnings in Nietzsche and Heidegger to the Greek beginnings of philosophy in efforts to overcome the crisis of European civilization as grounded in its forgetting of primordial questioning. Here it is important to note that for both thinkers the tasks of overcoming and revival have a providential and redemptive character, relating to the concern of the entire German tradition with the justification of evil. (2) Strauss's project of "repetition of antiquity at the peak of modernity" as discussed in letters with students of Heidegger in the period 1930–73 and other writings that disclose how the accounts of original forgetting in Strauss's German predecessors fundamentally frame his thinking. Central to these discussions is the ambiguity of the exposure of modernity's "unradicality," its foundational "certainties," by Nietzsche and Heidegger, since the latter still adhere to some modern (or Christian) notions of progress. (3) An account of Strauss's mature Socratism, his late modern renewal of Socratic political philosophy, which centers on the duality of the human as political and transpolitical and responds to the critiques of Western rationalism in Nietzsche and Heidegger. Strauss's sympathetic stance toward Heidegger's critical reading of Nietzsche and toward the questions Heidegger poses about causality, God, and Being comes to the fore. For both Heidegger and Strauss, philosophy begins with articulating human openness to Being or the whole under a radical suspension of traditional metaphysical premises. At the same time, Strauss seeks to recover, in opposition to Heidegger and with more support from Nietzsche, a classical understanding of philosophy as "cosmic" and transmoral. In this regard Strauss breaks from his German predecessors whose thinking reveals a fusion of religious and philosophic concerns.

Part II, "Exigencies of Freedom and Politics," takes up the political implications of the different versions of overcoming modernity through recovery of antiquity in Heidegger and Strauss. Heidegger's approach to the relation of philosophy to politics and practical life is crucially indebted to accounts of freedom in Kant, Schelling, and Nietzsche, as Heidegger refashions these in an effort to move beyond the oblivion of Being and to arrive at a new beginning. Strauss criticizes Heidegger's view of that relation, as assuming that philosophic freedom can be at one with, and at home with, political life. Central to this criticism is the underlying "eschatological" assumption that persists in Heidegger's later thinking after he "learned the lesson of 1933." In Strauss's conception Heidegger obscures the "tension between philosophy and the *po-lis*, i.e., the highest theme of *political* philosophy." Heidegger's recovery of antiquity and his politics suffer from the forgetting of Socrates's radical questioning of the authority of *nomos*, such that Heidegger's thought on the tragic strife of *phusis* and *techne* does not point to the liberation of the philosophic mind from the mind of the age, the nation, and the *Volk*, or it points to it only tentatively and obscurely.

Part III, "Construction of Modernity," addresses three related topics: Strauss's interpretation of modernity as it underpins his critique of Heidegger, the question of the nature of the break of modernity with antiquity according to Strauss, and suggestions in Strauss that his recovery of antiquity is informed in certain respects by the experiences of modernity and not least by the philosophy of late modernity. Strauss's genealogical criticism of Heidegger's historicism presents it as the most radical form of the modern "historical consciousness," which itself is the outcome of the politicizing of philosophy in early modernity. Mostly forgotten in modernity, in Strauss's view, are not doctrines of teleology and natural law but the duality of the human, the tension between law and *eros*, which entails the permanent "homelessness" of philosophy in human practical affairs. Yet Strauss's account of modernity and its break with antiquity shows that modern philosophy harbors echoes of ancient themes of human duality in its treatments of individuality and poetry. In particular the late modern renewal of the "problem of Socrates" has allowed Strauss to recover the theme of duality in a heterodox way, i.e., without metaphysical premises of the post-Platonic tradition, through reviving the original quarrel of philosophy and poetry.

* 1 *

Repetition of Antiquity at the Peak of Modernity

CHAPTER 1

Primal Truth, Errant Tradition, and Crisis: The Pre-Socratics in Late Modernity

I

The thought on the Greeks in the work of Friedrich Nietzsche and Martin Heidegger has been the inspiration for much original and penetrating philosophic scholarship in the twentieth century. Assuming that Heidegger is the foremost rethinker of Nietzsche's legacy (an assumption that needs to be tested), Nietzsche's writing and Heidegger's teaching and writing began a movement that now includes numbers too great to count. Certainly not all who might be named are philosophically Nietzschean or Heideggerian; they are, however, variously indebted to the new questioning of the tradition. The readings by Nietzsche and Heidegger of the early philosophers have not usually been at the center of this reengagement with the Greeks, despite the fact that for these two thinkers the early philosophers and poets are the source of primordial wisdom from which the modern West must draw for self-renewal. But if one is to understand the roots of some leading recent approaches to the Greeks, including Plato and Aristotle, one must examine these readings. My aim is to consider in broad terms what these thinkers claim to find in the early philosophers and what philosophically motivates their quest. Due to limitations of space, I will not discuss the interpretations of particular ancient figures in detail, and I will also set aside all questions about the scholarly accuracy of their interpretations. To consider the turn to the early philosophers in these two great thinkers is to uncover something fundamental about their philosophies, and thus about philosophy in the most recent period of modernity. Some light will be shed as well, necessarily, on the nature of modernity itself.

I I

Among the notes collected after Nietzsche's death and published under the title *The Will to Power*, there is the following reflection on German philosophy, dated 1885 in the Musarion edition:

> German philosophy as a whole—Leibniz, Kant, Hegel, Schopenhauer, to name the greatest—is the most fundamental form of *romanticism* and homesickness there has ever been: the longing for the best that has ever existed. One is no longer at home anywhere; at last one longs back for that place in which alone one can be at home: the *Greek* world! But it is precisely in that direction that all bridges are broken—except the rainbow-bridges of concepts![1]

Nietzsche surmises that perhaps in a few centuries the real dignity of German philosophy will be recognized for its "gradual reclamation of the soil of antiquity" and for its renewal of the bond with the Greeks, "the hitherto highest type of man." He then concludes:

> Today we are getting close to all those fundamental forms of world-interpretation devised by the Greek spirit through Anaximander, Heraclitus, Parmenides, Empedocles, Democritus, and Anaxagoras—we are growing more Greek by the day; at first, as is only fair, in concepts and evaluations, as Hellenizing ghosts, as it were: but one day, let us hope, also in our bodies! Herein lies (and has always lain) my hope for the German character![2]

Nietzsche here describes German philosophy as a rebellion against modernity, against the Reformation in particular, and as a second Renaissance of antiquity. The recovery Nietzsche seeks is ambiguous, however, for the Greeks are only "the hitherto highest type of man." The hope he places in the German character, whereby he implies he seeks another bridge beyond merely conceptual bridges, is to renew Greekness in mind and body, and thus to rectify a flaw in antiquity, an injustice that antiquity inflicted on itself. This was the wound inflicted on Greek culture by Socrates and his new kind of philosophizing. "The real philosophers of Greece are those before Socrates (—with Socrates something changes)."[3] The early tragic culture of the Greeks succumbed to that wound, but a renewed tragic culture, based on a consciousness of all that had happened since the Greeks, and on a deeper understanding of the sources of mind and body in will, might endure, as incorporating the wound. Nietzsche's German predecessors did not follow this path, as Leibniz, Kant, Hegel, and

Schopenhauer were all avowed admirers of Socrates, and Nietzsche's Hellenism rejects the Hellenism of classical German culture. Yet as efforts to address the soul's homesickness, all German philosophic striving is concerned with the problem of evil. He points to this feature in another note: "The significance of German philosophy (Hegel): to evolve a pantheism through which evil, error and suffering are not felt as arguments against divinity."[4] The note contains this sentence: "I myself have attempted an *aesthetic* justification: how is the ugliness of the world possible?"

The shared project of the German philosophers, including Nietzsche (and Heidegger, as I will argue) could be summed up this way: Burdened with homesickness in modernity, or a sense of loss, they diagnose the ground of that loss and thereby transform the loss, so that it (the illness, wound, or ugliness) is preserved somehow, or justified, in the transformation. And yet, as justified, it is not simply overcome. The renewal of antiquity includes somehow the gulf, the abyss, that separates modernity from antiquity. Nietzsche says that he is the first to justify existence through a critique of morality:[5] "I saw no one who had ventured a critique of moral value feelings."[6] He shows that ugliness, evil, and pain are inseparable from beauty, nobility, and health. Herein he opposes the whole post-Socratic tradition, including Kant and Hegel, who in different ways attempt to "prove the dominion of morality by means of history." But "we no longer believe in morality, as they did, and consequently we have no need to found a philosophy with the aim of justifying morality."[7] Still, there is a sense in which those modern justifications of morality are built upon the undermining of older notions of the nature and supports of morality, such that they opened up an abyss (or exploited an already existing abyss) in freedom, in order to force reason or spirit to discover (or create) a new order in that abyss. In modernity before Kant and Hegel, ideas of freedom with abysmal potentials (such as Rousseau disclosed) emerged, pointing to the need for a synthesis of the ancient and the modern. Nietzsche rejects the classical German Idealist syntheses, so that he does not start with the acceptance of freedom in its modern Enlightenment, democratic meaning, and he does not seek to reconcile it with post-Socratic rational morality. All the same, he offers another synthesis and another justification, in which the most extreme form of modern skepticism is one component and the turn to the early Greeks is another.

Nietzsche rejects the late antiquity of Socrates and Plato—thinkers who employed logic and dialectics as they "took up the cause of virtue and justice."[8] "Since Plato philosophy has been dominated by morality" owing to his portrayal of Socrates, "who was a monomaniac with regard to morality," tyrannizing over the instincts and the senses with his logic, producing the formula "reason =

virtue = happiness," but thereby showing only that "the Socratic disposition is a phenomenon of decadence."[9] "Philosophers are prejudiced against appearance, change, pain, death, the corporeal, the senses, fate and bondage, the aimless."[10] Nietzsche seems to include the early Greeks, but Heraclitus does not wholly fit the charge.[11] With the Socratics, philosophy is put on the path of finding a rational moral teleology of the whole, the search for "morality-in-itself" and the "good-in-itself." The ancient sophistic culture, whose predecessors were Heraclitus and Democritus and whose highest expression is Thucydides, was in accord with "the Greek instincts" in rejecting this quest. It was a "remarkable moment" verging on the first critique of morality.[12] At the core of Nietzsche's appreciation of the Greeks is his revival of non-Socratic moral pessimism: the absence (in the early philosophers and poets) or the rejection (in the sophists and Thucydides) of rational moral teleology. Of course this does not mean that for Nietzsche these thinkers lacked either nobility or reason. To the true nobility and the higher reason he gives the name "Dionysian wisdom."[13]

III

In one of his last writings, *Ecce Homo*, Nietzsche says of his first book, *The Birth of Tragedy from the Spirit of Music*, that it put forth two decisive innovations: the account of the Dionysian phenomenon as a root of Greek art, and the understanding of Socrates as "an instrument of Greek disintegration," the figure who embodies " 'rationality' at any price as a dangerous force that undermines life."[14] The Dionysian is "the ultimate, most joyous, most wantonly extravagant Yes to life," based on the insight that "nothing in existence may be subtracted, nothing is dispensable." To clarify this he quotes his own *Twilight of the Idols*: "Saying Yes to life even in its strangest and hardest problems; the will to life rejoicing over its inexhaustibility even in the sacrifice of the very highest types—that is what I called Dionysian. Not in order to get rid of terror and pity . . . but in order to be oneself the eternal joy of becoming, beyond all terror and pity—that joy that includes even joy in destroying."[15] This points toward the "aesthetic justification" of existence: "I took the will to beauty, to persist in like forms, for a temporary means of preservation and recuperation: fundamentally, however, the eternally-creative appeared to me to be, as the eternal compulsion to destroy, associated with pain."[16] The will is realized not in created form itself (the Apollonian moment of art) but in the act of creating, for which form is but a vehicle. The creative will to life celebrated by the poets is its own *telos*. But in Nietzsche's judgment Socrates and Plato as moral teleologists seek a world in which life will be possible without change, destruction, and pain, and so they necessarily oppose the poets. There exists no truly Dionysian philosopher among the Greeks. "Before me this transposition of the Dionysian into a philosophic pathos did not exist; tragic wisdom was lacking."[17] Among philosophers the thought of Heraclitus comes nearest to it: "The affirmation of passing away and destroying; saying Yes to opposition and war; becoming, along with the radical repudiation of the very concept of being."[18] The doctrine of eternal recurrence as taught by Zarathustra might have been taught already by Heraclitus, but surely in a different mode and for different ends.[19] In a brief passage of *The Birth of Tragedy*, Heraclitus is described as the one philosopher having the aesthetic vision of the whole. Dionysian art "reveals to us the playful construction and destruction of the individual world as the overflow of a primordial delight. Thus the dark Heraclitus compares the world-building force to a playing child that places stones here and there and builds sand hills only to overthrow them again."[20] Heraclitus transposes the Dionysian-poetic vision into philosophic concepts, but does so incompletely. One can surmise that Heraclitus lacks a concept of will to ground the cosmic activity of "world-building." But no ancient thinker could have had that concept, nor the historical consciousness resulting from insight into the will's powers of self-transformation.

Nietzsche remarks that he had to abandon hopes for the recovery of tragic culture by the Germans of his time through the inspiration of Wagner's art, and that he "advanced further down the road of disintegration—where I found new sources of strength for individuals. We have to be destroyers!" In the state of general disintegration "individuals can perfect themselves as never before."[21] The decay of the old values has to be advanced, not held back, so that new values can replace them. Humanity is confronted with the greatest danger, the loss of all ability for higher willing with the collapse of the old values, but this danger affords rare higher human beings the opportunity to create new values and a new humanity. Such human beings do not yet exist: "I wish for a species of man that does not yet exist: for the 'masters of the earth.'"[22] That the human species has such power for willing a new species into being is a thought surely lacking in the Greeks. It has to be added that Nietzsche's prophetic stance and his hopes for such transformation would not be possible without the examples of biblical revelation, which he in general opposes for their moral teachings. In paradoxical fashion, Dionysian wisdom combines affirmation of the world as it is—the rejection of any *telos* beyond the Now—with the hope of radical transformation of man. This apparent contradiction between affirming and transcending is present in the willing of the eternal recurrence, not as theoretical doctrine but as means for the will's self-transformation. "To the paralyzing sense of general disintegration and incompleteness I opposed the *eternal recurrence*."[23] I restate that Nietzsche synthesizes the most extreme form of modern skepticism with the recovery of early Greek wisdom, and that this constitutes in his view not a mere fusing of doctrines but the deepest understanding of the beneficence of evil.

I turn now to the incomplete and unpublished book written soon after *The Birth of Tragedy*, entitled *Philosophy in the Tragic Age of the Greeks*. Two primary concerns of this writing are the individuality of philosophers and the relation of philosophers to their culture. Nietzsche says he is less concerned with the truth of the systems of the philosophers than with their individuality, the "incontrovertible and non-debatable" foundation of their thought in their unique personalities. The inquiry has a higher than merely scholarly aim: to bring to light great human beings whom we must love and honor.[24] But of course we cannot love and honor something unless we can see what is lovable and honorable in it, and the question must be asked whether what is lovable and honorable in the philosophers does not have some relation to the truth or at least nobility of what they sought. Nietzsche speaks of their capacity for wonderment at mundane life, which appears to them as a problem worthy of contemplation. Philosophy is a human possibility that transcends these particular individuals. But Nietzsche himself wonders not only at their wonderment, he wonders also at the Greek culture that was able to produce these great individuals without envy, with admiration for their qualities. Why did Greece have philosophers at the high point of its political and artistic flourishing? Most cultures have no inherent need of philosophy, and the philosopher arises as a mere accident in them. The early Greeks attained somehow a harmony between philosophy and the general culture; this marvel is what Nietzsche puts before the culture of his time, in hopes that it will be emulated. But there is a difficulty in this. Philosophy alone can never initiate a healthy culture, it can only be in accord with an already healthy culture by warding off dangers to its health. In this way early Greek philosophy was in accord with the tragic poetic culture.[25] But this unique harmony must be rooted in something that is uniquely Greek and that neither philosophy nor poetry could create. The theme of the individuality of the early philosophers, who establish various archetypes of philosophy, is mirrored in the individuality of Greek culture as a whole. How can radically unique beings serve as archetypes for others, when even they themselves do not grasp the conditions of their existence? This is a basic problem lurking in this essay.

In any case the great age does not last. The great age is one of the highest reverence for individuals that are whole and complete, which is possible at the early stage of a culture before traditions appear that limit and stifle the powers of individuals. The greatness of the early thought is related to its being the first efforts at philosophic discovery such that each discoverer finds his own way and that way reflects his being and that of no one else. Hence the early thinkers are pure types, and the pure types include Socrates.[26] Interestingly, Nietzsche did not complete the treatise, which ends with Anaxagoras, and Socrates is mentioned only in passing. Starting with Plato, philosophers are mixed types, which means that they rely on traditions of thought from which they select their own approaches, but also that they mix being philosophers with being founders of schools and sects. They are concerned with creating institutions to preserve and protect their activity, a sign that they are not in accord with their world. Philosophers become exiles, conspiring against their fatherlands. The homelessness of philosophy emerges at the very moment when philosophers become preoccupied with the ethical and political. Philosophers begin to seek laws that are different from the customs of their cities. Nietzsche does not mean that the early philosophers are popular thinkers, content to articulate prevailing customs and myths. On the contrary, they are solitary and proud, indifferent to public opinion and oracular in their speech. But admiration for this proud indifference was itself a trait of the culture. To refer to *The Birth of Tragedy*, one might say the early culture was not yet rationally moral and followed an instinct-based custom that revered the great individual.

This bears directly on the relation of philosophy to tragic poetry. It is true that the early philosophers leave mythical thought behind, and they think in concepts rather than images.[27] But they are not simply empirical students of nature and not solely logical in their thinking. They seek the ground and the unity of the whole, which are hidden from ordinary experiences. Extraordinary leaps of intuition are required to make their bold proposals about the ground and unity. This intuition brings them into relation to poetic intuitions about being, and also to the questions that the tragic poets raise about the value of existence, that is, whether individual beings have any right to be at all.[28] Tragic culture, as a whole, shares the belief that greatness exists in individuals, not the species, and is therefore fragile and transient, considered in light of the overpowering whole, which is indifferent to human wishes and human justice. Anaximander's vision is simply pessimistic, but Nietzsche claims that Heraclitus finds a way to affirm the transience. He rejects Anaximander's dualism of a fallen world of individual beings that need punishment for the injustice of simply existing, and of a ground into which they rightly return, by affirming the innocent play of becoming, of creation and destruction, as a contemplated spectacle.[29] Heraclitus is again closely related to the wisdom of the poets, in that he views the world as a work of art and identifies with the artist-god that produces it. As such he is both contemplator and actor, just as "the artist stands contemplatively above and at the same time actively within his work." It might be suggested that Nietzsche here points to a poetic mode of philosophizing that would resolve the problem of individuality and universal archetype. Individuality achieves a kind of universality not through knowledge of timeless essences but through a poetic producing that participates in the creative force behind the whole itself. Heraclitus prefigures Nietzsche's central thought, the justification of existence for and by the great individual through the doctrine of the will to power.

IV

Heidegger's intense engagement with the early Greeks comes after *Being and Time* (1927), in which work, as well as in his studies before 1927 as a whole, they play a minor role. Certainly Aristotle is from the start central to his phenomenological and ontological inquiry, and to a lesser extent Plato. Let us remind ourselves that in *Being and Time* Heidegger seeks to recover the meaning of the question of Being, which he claims has been forgotten.[30] The phenomenological analysis of the average and everyday understanding of Being presupposed by human existence, or by the human way of being in the world, is only a preparation for recovering the question. The human has a special place among the beings in having a unique openness to Being, such that the capacity for questioning about Being belongs to its constitution. As such the human way of existing is the site or place for the disclosure of Being, and can be called Da-Sein, the "there (or here) of Being." Heidegger insists his analysis is concerned not with anthropology but with ontology, and its aim is to show not how the human is there in Being, but how Being is there through the human. He also insists that Being is not a concept, genus, or causal ground but the primordial disclosure of the world, which makes accessible any thinking about beings, including any thinking with and about concepts, genera, and causality. But although Being is the ground of disclosure for any engagement with beings, Being (*das Sein*) itself tends to be concealed, as human attention is focused on the being (*das Seiende*). That which is nearest and most pervasive, Being, is also what is most hidden.

The philosophic and scientific traditions have mostly overlooked Being and promoted its hiddenness, and thus the loosening and dismantling of layers of tradition about Being must be undertaken, the so-called *Destruktion* of tradition. This is not merely a negative undertaking since in a hidden way Being sustains the Western philosophic tradition, and the *Destruktion* will reveal how Being is present even in its absence from explicit reflection. As early as Parmenides, the Greeks already display a tendency to think of Being in terms of worldly entities and to favor entities that are most present at hand, or enduringly present, in their accounts of Being or the world. Greek thinking has a twofold prejudice: With respect to time, it favors the present among the temporal *ecstases*, and with respect to *logos*, it favors assertoric judgments and the logical relations among such judgments. The full scope and power of time and *logos* for the unconcealment of Being, for primordial truth (*aletheia*), was not noticed or developed by the Greeks. The historical inquiry shows how these prejudices unfold from a Greek beginning, which has still some appreciation of Being as disclosure or *aletheia*, into more extreme Being–forgetful forms in the modern subject-object distinction and the mathematical-technical approach to beings. Everywhere in the modern world, beings are the object of calculation and manipulation, and the ground of their disclosure is walled off from awareness. This entails that the human is lost to itself, unaware of its own essence.

It is well known that Heidegger did not complete the planned parts of *Being and Time*, and although his fundamental pursuit remained the same, namely, the recovery of the question of Being, his path toward it changed. This change is related to several obvious external features in Heidegger's later thought: the absence of the formal systematic approach of *Being and Time*, the new emphasis on certain figures (the early Greeks, Nietzsche, Hölderlin), on the themes of poetry, language, and the gods, and also on nihilism and the technological world night. In all of these changes, Heidegger seeks a deeper account of the ground of the disclosure of Being and does so by turning to the history of Being, by which is meant not a historical account of Being, but Being itself as giving or sending a fate or destining (*Geschick*)—a way of disclosure that makes a claim on the human and to which the human must respond. In a relation of mutual dependence, Being appropriates the human, and the human in turn avows its belonging to Being. Being needs the human as the site of its disclosure, such that the human is the guardian and protector of Being, and conversely the human cannot be human without the relation to Being, which gives shelter to the human essence. The most developed account of this historical appropriation (*Ereignis*) by and of Being is found in the recently published *Contributions to Philosophy: From Enowning* of 1936–38.[31] This cannot be my theme directly, although Heidegger's turn to the early Greeks is inseparable from these considerations, and I will necessarily refer to them without the full elaboration they require.

In the history of Being two moments are most decisive: the original opening to Being among the Greeks at the beginning (*Anfang*), in the first questioning about Being, which founds a destiny that carries forward Western history, and the present moment, that of oblivion to the question of Being, or nihilism, which completes the process of forgetting. Nietzsche's thought both fulfills and is a witness to the completion of Western metaphysics in nihilism, and understanding him is essential for pointing beyond the present oblivion to another beginning, a renewal of the opening to Being that also requires the most intense thinking about the first beginning. Heidegger offers some auto-biographical illumination on how he reached this account. Writing soon after the end of the Second World War on his Rectoral Address of 1933, Heidegger notes that in 1932 he found in Ernst Jünger's book *The Worker* "an essential understanding of Nietzsche's metaphysics, insofar as in the horizon of this metaphysics the history and the present of the West is seen and foreseen."[32] Jünger exposed "the universal mastery of the will to power within the planetary scope of history." Heidegger then grasped that what Nietzsche meant by the "death of God" was that this actuality of the will to power follows the collapse of the "effective power in history of the supersensible world, especially the world of the Christian God." Thereupon he saw the need for "a reflection on the overcoming of the metaphysics of the will to power and a dialogue with the Western tradition from its beginning."[33] In this concise account, without evident irony, Heidegger claims that his rallying the university to support the National Socialist regime was for the sake of overcoming the very doctrine, the will to power, that the new regime, usurping Nietzsche's authority, used as a slogan.

Indeed, the Rectoral Address itself contains Heidegger's first published statement on the need for the return to the beginnings within the outlines of the history of Being, as a historical new beginning. He gave seminars entitled *The Beginning of Western Philosophy (Anaximander and Parmenides)* in summer 1932, and on Plato's allegory of the cave and *Theaetetus* in winter 1931–32, that initiate this return. In the address he calls the German people to place themselves "under the power of the beginning of our spiritual-historical existence." He claims that in spite of our great remove from the beginning, "the beginning is itself in no way overcome or indeed annihilated. . . . The beginning *is* still.

It lies not *behind us* as the long since departed, but it stands *before* us. . . . The beginning has entered our future, and stands there as the distant command, bidding us to retrieve its greatness."[34] Only by winning back the greatness of the beginning can "science [*Wissenschaft*] become the inner necessity of our existence." With a reference to Nietzsche's "death of God" Heidegger seals the case that modern man's "lostness among the beings" makes necessary the turn to the beginning. Surely at the time of this address Heidegger was hopeful about the capacity of the new regime to assist in this remarkable metaphysical undertaking, though his hopes were soon dashed. It is notable that there is some parallel to the hopes placed in Wagner by the youthful Nietzsche, which also vanished with more experience. And in each case one has the notion, coming after the disenchantment, that a further advance into the night of nihilism is necessary for the arrival of the new dawn. In the hopeful time of summer 1933 Heidegger restates the claim about the enduring beginning that awaits our response to its challenge, using language that has a central place in his thought thereafter: "The essence of the beginning turns itself about [*kehrt sich um*]; it is no longer the great anticipatory origin, but the incomplete, probing beginning of the future development."[35] The first beginning in the Greeks points us toward a second beginning, and not merely is this pointing a human event, but it occurs within the beginning itself, in its turning about. The turning all the same calls for human response in order to be fulfilled. This is one of many indications that the *Kehre*, the much-debated turning of the later Heidegger's thought, is not just a change or turning in Heidegger's way of thinking.

Although sometime after 1934 Heidegger abandons expectations or hopes of a politically led renewal of the beginnings and calls instead for reflective listening for and awaiting an arrival prepared by our thinking, there is a sense in which his conception remains more hopeful than the mature Nietzsche's. In Nietzsche one finds no claim that the great beginning continues to govern covertly the unfolding of history and no parallel to statements like this one of Heidegger: "The primordial disclosure of Being as a whole, the question concerning beings as such, and the beginning of Western history are the same."[36] Nietzsche exhorts the philosophers of the future to assume extraordinary responsibility, but he admits it is a role that is not prepared by earlier philosophy. Nietzsche through his account of Socrates and Plato shows that philosophy can have dire consequences but not that it has ever alone founded a great culture, much less that it has been the hidden governing force of all Western history, which brings itself and the human toward a second beginning. As his short book on the early philosophers shows, the harmony of those philosophers with their culture (which Nietzsche, one may say, is overstating) was a brief moment in the otherwise precarious relation of philosophic individuals to their culture. The prominence of the philosophic life as a theme in Nietzsche relates to his stress on Socrates, to whom Nietzsche is the profoundly kindred antipode, whereas Heidegger's near total silence on Socrates reflects his neglect of that theme. One could say that Nietzsche's justification of existence for and by great individuals is replaced by Heidegger's justification of the human essence as the erring-revealing site of the truth of Being, a justification for and by Being.

Clearly there is some kinship between Nietzsche's attack on the moral-teleological thinking of the Socratics and Heidegger's account of the Platonic stage of the forgetting of Being. For both Nietzsche and Heidegger, the attempt to ground human ethics and justice in the whole obscures the truth about the whole; hence their justifications of existence are supra-ethical. Heidegger in the early 1930s[37] seeks to uncover the manner in which Plato ambiguously retains a relation to primordial *aletheia* while he also obscures it. In Plato "the coming into presence [*Anwesung*] is no longer, as in the beginning of Western thinking, the emerging of the hidden into unconcealment," since Plato conceives coming into presence as *idea*. The *idea* is not merely "the foreground of unconcealment [*aletheia*] but is rather the ground of its possibility."[38] Subordinated to the *idea*, "truth is no longer the fundamental feature of Being itself but becomes correctness, henceforth the decisive mark of the knowing of beings." Through the highest of *ideas*, the Good, the ground of the existing and appearing of all beings, Plato makes the human and its place among the beings the dominant concern of metaphysics.[39] Yet this turning to humanism is not merely a human event. "Plato's thinking follows a turning in the essence of truth itself [*Wandel des Wesens der Wahrheit*], which turning becomes a turning in the history of metaphysics that in Nietzsche's thinking has begun its unconditioned completion."[40] Nietzsche's thought is the completion of Platonic metaphysics, not its overcoming, since his conception of philosophy as the highest will to power takes the elevation of the human (albeit supra-ethical) to its most extreme point.[41] Even so, Heidegger also writes that the demand for reflection on the Greek beginnings would be "arbitrary and presumptuous" without two figures, Hölderlin and Nietzsche, "who knew the beginnings more primordially than all ages before them, and only for the reason that they experienced for the first time the end of the West, and furthermore: even in their existence and work they *became ends*." This was possible for them only because "they were overpowered by the beginning and were elevated to greatness. Both these moments, reflection on the first beginning and founding an end that is fitting to it and its greatness, belong together in the turning [*Kehre*]."[42] In seeing the end, seeing the beginning in the light of the end, and seeking a new beginning, Nietzsche was unfolding a fate he did not recognize, one leading beyond his self-conception as well as his interpretation of the beginnings. All the same his errors were not mere failures but the inevitable limitations of thinking greatly in the grip of the higher power of Being.

V

In this final section on Heidegger, I want to consider further the way in which experience of the end in the time of the completion of metaphysics is crucial to recovery of the beginning and preparing for another beginning. Heidegger should not be understood as claiming that the beginning was the primordial disclosure of Being whose brilliance is required to illuminate the darkness of modern nihilism. In that case, the beginning would simply belong to the past, as something lost and now to be regained. Rather the beginning is self-concealing essentially and from the start, and its power in the unfolding in Western history lies precisely in self-concealment. Hence the darkness of the forgetting of Being is a darkness belonging to the beginning itself and unfolding as the concealment of Being in Western history. In this way the age of the technological world night can offer an unprecedented illumination of the difference between Being and beings, for those who are able to think profoundly and primordially. Accordingly, in such thinking the Greek beginning receives an illumination that was unavailable to the early thinkers. One could say Heidegger offers a justification of erring as the forgetting of Being that recalls Nietzsche's statement about the significance of German philosophy as the justification of evil, error, and suffering. No predecessor of Heidegger, however, spoke in terms of the truth of Being as the emerging of the hidden into unconcealment. Heidegger restates in such terms the Nietzschean claim that the darkness of nihilism is inherently full of promise. Heidegger often quotes the lines of Hölderlin, "But where danger is, grows / The saving power also."[43] The uncovering of the saving power requires a dual movement of thought, back to the first beginning (which is also the movement of the beginning toward the present) and forward to the other beginning.

Heidegger provides a rich and fascinating account of this structure of thinking in his essay "The Saying of Anaximander," written in 1946.[44] Heidegger dismisses the prevailing understanding of the early Greeks as the precursors of Plato and Aristotle, as rudimentary students of *phusei onta* groping toward the Aristotelian *Physics*, that has dominated since Theophrastus. Nietzsche himself employs superficial traditional categories of Being and Becoming in his readings.[45] The categories modern scholars use in describing the fragment of Anaximander, such as physical, ethical, rational, and philosophical, are absurd, since physics, ethics, rationalism and philosophy did not yet exist.[46] Our disciplinary boundaries and categories must be set aside. We have the problem of interpreting an utterance that is separated from us by an immense gulf, and of transposing our thinking in a modern language into the ancient Greek. Can we make the earliest saying speak to us?[47] Concealed in the chronological remoteness there may be a "historical proximity to the unspoken, an unspoken which will speak out in that which is coming."[48] Perhaps the modern West is journeying into the earth's evening, into an *Abendland* that transcends the European, which may be the place of another dawn. The once (*Einst*) of the first dawn may overtake the once of the latest dawn (the *eschaton*), in the departure of the long-concealed destiny of Being. "As destining, Being is inherently eschatological."[49] If we think out of the eschatology of Being, and ponder the beginning that is approaching, we may be drawn to listen and to have dialogue with the early Greeks. In that dialogue, we can speak of the same Being, though it will be addressed from out of the different.[50] Our success will not be measured in terms of accuracy in the portrayal of "what was really present in the past." The question is whether in the dialogue "that which wishes to come to language . . . comes of its own accord." Being is, in different ways, destined to concern both the Greeks and us. But a fundamental trait of Being is to be more concealed than revealed, at all times. "By revealing itself in the being [*das Seiende*], Being [*das Sein*] withdraws."[51]

Being as withdrawing endows beings with errancy, such that beings necessarily misinterpret the essential. This realm of misinterpretation is history. Errancy is not a human failing, since the self-misunderstanding of humans corresponds to the self-concealing of the illumination (*Lichtung*) of Being. Without errancy the human would have no relation to its destiny. Chronological distance from the Greeks is one thing, but historical distance is something else, and in that regard we are near to them. We are close to Being's primordial refusal, to Being's keeping its truth to itself even as it discloses beings. Being's keeping to itself is the *epochê* of Being, which sense of *epochê* Heidegger distinguishes from Husserl's methodical setting aside of thetic consciousness. Being's *epochê* or holding back of its truth is the grounding of worlds, which are the epochs of errancy. This now for Heidegger is the more fundamental meaning of time: "The epochal essence of Being belongs to the concealed temporal character of Being," in which the ecstatic time of *Dasein* is grounded. Indeed, the epochal essence appropriates (*ereignet*) the ecstatic essence of *Dasein*.[52] Already at the dawn of thinking about Being, the essence of Being as the presencing of beings keeps to itself, and so the difference between Being and the beings themselves, the things that are present, remains concealed. The two are disclosed, the one as ground and the other as grounded, yet the ground comes forward as the highest being, so the difference is extinguished. "The destining of Being begins with the oblivion of Being," although the earliest thought in an unspoken way shows the trace (*Spur*) of the difference, more than does later thought. (Heidegger points above all to the double sense of the genitive in Anaximander's phrase *kata to chreon.*) The difference appears although not named as such.[53] Again, the oblivion is not a deficiency (*Mangel*); it is the event or appropriation (*Ereignis*) of metaphysics, the richest and broadest event in world history. We still stand in the shadow of this event, of this destining, and thus are granted the possibility of being mindful of Being's destining.[54] Later accounts of Being in terms of *idea, energeia, substantia,* and objectivity may deepen the oblivion, but they do not thereby annul the destiny. On the contrary they fulfill it by pointing to the need for reflection on the destiny itself. In that reflection the human becomes the guardian of Being's concealing itself, of its holding back its truth so that errant humans can be historical. The human realizes then the gift of Being that happens in errancy itself. Reflecting on the saving power in danger, thinking becomes questioning, which is the piety of thought.[55]

VI

What cannot be ignored in these late modern readings of the early Greeks? What is compelling about them? I shall raise only a few considerations to be pursued in further reflection. First, the importance of thinking about the history of philosophy itself is made evident in them. Philosophizing addresses certain subjects, but it cannot consist only in addressing them directly, through our own thought and experience. It must include addressing questions to the philosophers themselves, to deepen the grasp of what philosophy itself is; otherwise proceeding on our own will be naïve and narrow. At the heart of philosophy is reflection on the relation of the whole of Being to the ordinary things of experience, a relation that remains elusive and never wholly determined. By simply reflecting, as careful phenomenologists, on our own experiences, we will not come upon all the ways that the relation might be conceived. In sum, entering into the debate about the fundamental relation, the heart of philosophy, seems to depend in a crucial way on the existence of a tradition of thinking. Yet, of course, there were the first philosophers.

This brings me to the second item. Nietzsche and Heidegger remind us that philosophy cannot evade the fundamental questions about the ground and the unity of Being and that the early philosophers may offer deep insight into these questions. What is more, they remind us that traditions have a tendency to conceal their origins, and thus they raise the possibility that the beginning of the tradition may possess thoughts that deserve to stand on their own, and should not be considered only as a "first sailing." The Platonic-Aristotelian account of them as "first sailing" is already placing the first thinkers in a light that is alien to them. On the other hand, Nietzsche and Heidegger note that it is impossible to forget that the early thinkers did begin a tradition, one developing thoughts and concerns not in their sights, such that certain possibilities latent in the early thought may be hidden from or barely grasped by its authors. In this regard the later tradition may in fact provide new disclosures about the beginning.

This brings up the third item. Both thinkers draw attention to tradition itself, as a ground and condition of thinking, and as having positive and negative import for thinking. They are moved to focus on this theme because in their time the very existence of the tradition of philosophy has become problematic. The crisis in the tradition brings attention to its singularity and fragility. Philosophy as directed toward the whole and the universal is still, qua tradition, something singular, having a unique temporal reality. It is mysterious that this activity, philosophy, has a singular beginning in certain times and places and that it unfolds where, when, and how it does, as a tradition. It is also astounding to consider that this tradition might wholly disappear from the earth at some time. Nietzsche and Heidegger think that these mysteries cannot be separated from the wonder of philosophy itself. Heidegger claims that this singularity is the gift and the destiny of the questioning of Being, the gift and destiny that affords dignity to human existence, so that when all other grounds of worth have fallen into nothingness, this alone stands out more purely than ever, as providing human beings with a mission.[56] One may question whether these two thinkers have gained genuine insights into fate and history, and also question whether they have appropriate estimations of the end and dignity of human life. Yet when all this has been properly regarded as questionable, something quite appropriate and essential for philosophy has been gained: some questions worthy of being asked.

CHAPTER 2

"The Unradicality of Modern Philosophy": Thinking in Correspondence

I

The questions that moved the young Heidegger and the young Strauss were surely different, but they have significant affinities. For Heidegger it was the question of Being that has been overlooked by the metaphysical tradition as it has concentrated on the characterization of beings (their "ontical" properties and causal grounds) rather than on Being as the ground of disclosure of beings. The young Heidegger's critical and hermeneutical investigations of the sources of this neglect, which were initially motivated by dissatisfaction with the medieval Scholastic treatment of Aristotle, took him on dual paths: on the one hand uncovering a more authentic reading of Aristotle and the Greek beginnings of the philosophic tradition, and on the other reexamining Christian accounts (the Gospels, Paul, Luther, et al.) of the experience of life emphasizing temporality and the "factic" human encounter with mortality. Both paths were pursued with the aid of Husserl's phenomenological method, but the early concern with "life-experience" as the horizon for the interpretation of Being gave Heidegger's phenomenology a more practical orientation than Husserl's. Indeed in its early stage a defense of religious experience against the rational claims of philosophy seemed to be its core, although the atheistic bearing of Heidegger's inquiry in *Being and Time* (1927) was unmistakable. As Strauss saw and appreciated, Heidegger's thought after the 1920s grew into a more Greek, less biblical, effort to rethink the central question of philosophy.[1]

The problem of revelation engaged Strauss at the start as well. He was a committed Zionist in the 1920s but troubled by the attempts to fuse Jewish orthodoxy with rationalism in the Jewish Enlightenment and in its romantic-nationalist successor, Zionism. Strauss became convinced that the modern rationalist critique of biblical orthodoxy, as espoused by its greatest exponent, Spinoza, rested on a merely asserted and unproven superiority of reason to revealed truth. His early studies of Friedrich Heinrich Jacobi, Moses Mendelssohn, Lessing, and Spinoza, focusing on the problematic foundations of the Enlightenment, related to a widespread criticism of rationalism that found expression in "new thinking" about the sources of religious tradition (Karl Barth, Franz Rosenzweig).[2] But Strauss's dialectical manner of thought remained open to rationalist claims, as indicated by his sympathy for Lessing, whose exposure of false compromises in modern rationalist theology provided Strauss with a model for posing questions in terms of stark alternatives.[3]

In the 1965 American preface to his first book, *Spinoza's Critique of Religion* (completed in 1928), Strauss speaks of a "change of orientation" in his thought following the publication of this work. Strauss states that he saw the danger in a critique of rationalism that could justify any orthodoxy or induce a romantic longing without content. This and "other observations and experiences confirmed the suspicion that it would be unwise to say farewell to reason." Strauss began "to wonder whether the self-destruction of reason was not the inevitable outcome of modern rationalism as distinguished from pre-modern rationalism," and thus he reconsidered the premise on which his Spinoza study was based: "the premise, sanctioned by powerful prejudice, that a return to pre-modern philosophy is impossible."[4] In the deepening of his critique of modern rationalism, Strauss exposed the modern criticism of revelation in terms of "prejudice" (*Vorurteil*); in such criticism, reason is implicated in a fusion (*Verquickung*) with revelation through its very attempt to free itself from the power of its opponent.[5] The modern efforts to replace prejudice with a new rational doctrine produced new forms of prejudice and gave rise to repeated efforts to establish a final doctrine achieving definitive "progress" over all past doctrines. The modern engagement in a massive transforming of opinion (the battle against prejudice) had to be distinguished from the premodern striving of philosophic individuals to free themselves from opinion. Strauss saw in the new approach to opinion as prejudice the core of the argument between ancient and modern philosophy, whereby the changed political stance of philosophy became the key to understanding the entire tradition. After 1930, Strauss's correspondence discloses how this conception of the tradition enabled him to place the radical critiques of tradition in Nietzsche and Heidegger within the broad movement of modern philosophy. In other words, Strauss's own radical reflection on the tradition had the effect of diminishing the apparent radicality of the two thinkers who above all others had led the revolt against rationalism.

In the period 1930–37 Strauss studied the major figures of medieval Islamic and Jewish philosophy for their accounts of the relation of philosophy to revelation, wherein the latter is understood in terms of law, and teachings on providence and divine law are considered part of political science. The medieval philosophers thus maintain the Platonic view of piety as belonging to the realm of opinion or the "cave," a view they convey by means of "esoteric" writing outwardly respectful of the divine law.[6] This approach enabled them to attain a genuine freedom of spirit, whereas the attack on prejudice entangled the modern philosophers in the project, both destructive and creative, of forming a new "second cave." The world-transforming appearance of revealed religions grounded in authoritative texts complicated the ascent from opinion, adding a "historical difficulty" to the "natural difficulties" of the ascent. But the medieval Islamic and Jewish philosophers found means for addressing the new difficulty that preserved intellectual independence. Strauss, following their example, sought to renew the premodern view of the natural situation of the philosopher as confronting the unalterable reality of the theological-political order, such that the enduring alternative to philosophic freedom of mind is the "law" in the sense of the comprehensive nexus of religious, moral, and political authority. Reflection on law is the necessary starting point for the philosopher insofar as the philosopher understands himself as gaining freedom from its authority even as he must at the same time attempt to justify his life before that authority. Strauss saw the problem of law and philosophy as thus essential to the grounding of the possibility of philosophy, and reflection on it as central to philosophic self-knowledge. In the preface to the German edition of his Hobbes study Strauss noted that "the theological-political problem has remained *the* theme of all my investigations."[7]

Although Strauss was silent on Heidegger in his writings throughout the 1930s, that thinker was a forceful presence in his thought, as Strauss's correspondence shows. As Strauss made his discovery of premodern rationalism and moved toward affirming the possibility of its rebirth, he saw that Heidegger's criticism of the rationalism of the entire tradition had to be weighed in the balance, as his account of the defects of modern rationalism had undeniable power. How might Heidegger's interpretation of ancient philosophy affect the recovery of the premodern account of the theoretical life's claim to supremacy, which Strauss saw as grounded on its raising of the Socratic question "What is the best life?" Strauss's letters are extremely helpful for exposing the complexity of his thinking on this issue.

I preface my comments on the letters with the observation that Strauss's dialectical approach to questions must be kept in mind when evaluating positions
he adopts or appears to adopt in the course of his inquiry, some of which he
stresses in his public presentations of his thought. His criticism of Heidegger is
accordingly far better known—as publicly more prominent—than his avowed
kinship with Heidegger, which is compatible with that criticism although understated relative to it. From the early 1930s onward he is, with varying emphasis, clear about that kinship in letters. For example, writing to Jacob Klein
about Hans Jonas in 1934, Strauss remarks "that [Jonas] also strives, if perhaps
not as clearly, in the same direction as we do beyond or behind Heidegger."[8]
This "direction," as both inspired by Heidegger and yet deviating from him,
pertains to the critique of modernity, as Strauss states in a letter to Gerhard
Krüger of 1932, wherein he writes of "the unradicality of modern philosophy"
as consisting in its belief that "it can presuppose the fundamental questions as
already answered, and that it therefore can 'progress.'"[9] Dogmatism, not skepticism, is the hallmark of modern thinking, and it is evident in two forms of
failure: "the neglect [*Versäumnis*] of ontology, which Heidegger has uncovered,
and the neglect of the Socratic question, which Nietzsche denounced." The
same letter contains a criticism of Heidegger: "Modern philosophy from its
beginning and including Heidegger understood itself as progress and as pro-
gressing," a stance based on its "struggle against the tradition since the seventeenth century," which has as its "genuine meaning the restoration of the Greek
freedom of philosophizing; it was genuinely a Renaissance movement." In all
of its "foundations" of philosophic and historical thought, modern philosophy
has one striving: "the reclaiming of an original natural basis" for philosophy.
The root of this dual evaluation of Heidegger can be found in Strauss's relation to the critical and destructive thought of Nietzsche and Heidegger, who
both argue that modernity has come to an end even as they remain entangled in
modernity. "To me modern philosophy appears to have come to its *end*, to lead
to the point at which Socrates *begins*. Modern philosophy thus shows itself to
be a violent 'destruction of tradition,' and not 'progress.'"[10] Completing this
destructive process, Nietzsche and Heidegger make possible a postmodern
rebirth of Socratism without reaching it themselves.

What prevents these thinkers from achieving full release from the modern
dogma of progress? It is the same factor in Western thought that results in the
modern foundations and their new account of nature: Christianity. "Of modern philosophy this holds: without biblical belief one did not and does not

enter it, and with biblical belief one cannot stay in it. . . . Modern philosophy is possible only so long as biblical belief is not shaken from the ground up, as it has been since and through Nietzsche. In Nietzsche, too, there is a Christian heritage." The evidence of this heritage is Nietzsche's "probity" (*Redlichkeit*) of conscience, a secularized version of Christian virtue, which in Nietzsche's own judgment is "necessary for so long, and is indeed possible only as long, as there is a Christianity that must be fought."[11] Nietzsche was ultimately in pursuit of an ideal of natural philosophy, with which Strauss is in principle in accord. In this regard Nietzsche comes closer to the postmodern renewal of Socratism than Heidegger, whose renewal of the ontological question, in itself profound and necessary, is more bound up with Christian categories. "In Heidegger's *Dasein*-interpretation, a truly adequate atheistic interpretation of the Bible can, for the first time, be possible."[12] Heidegger's thought belongs in the long line of modern critics of religion, far outstripping in depth such predecessors as Feuerbach, and his thought marks the victory of the Enlightenment even as it would overcome the Enlightenment. Heidegger endorses the progressivist claim of Christianity on which the modern Enlightenment builds as it attacks Christianity, namely, its discovery of a new depth unknown to antiquity, thereby making possible an appreciation of the "historicity" of man.[13] Heidegger claims that "the philosophy that becomes for the first time possible after the destruction of Christianity preserves the 'true' in Christianity; this philosophy is therefore deeper and more radical than ancient philosophy."[14]

With such statements Strauss makes clear that his critique of the Enlightenment attack on religion is not a defense of religious orthodoxy but an effort to gain genuine freedom from it. Yet this is a freedom that does not rest on willing alone; it can be acquired only through theoretical analysis. For this purpose Strauss thinks one must question the principle of "historicity" in the light of a nondoctrinaire, Socratically inspired quest for nature. Strauss confesses to Krüger: "Our difference has its ground in this, that I cannot believe, that I must search for a possibility where I can *live* without belief. There are two possibilities of this kind: the ancient, i.e., the Socratic-Platonic, and the modern, that is, the Enlightenment," of which the chief figures are Hobbes and Kant. "It must be asked: Who is right, the ancients or the moderns? The *querelle des anciens et des modernes* must be repeated."[15] Yet one would think that the question has been answered if modernity has come to an end in a self-destructive process—unless self-destructive thinking could be somehow philosophically superior. And indeed Nietzsche and Heidegger provide powerful evidence of modernity's philosophical vitality in a final, paradoxical form. Given their dependence on revelation, Strauss's question implies that he can consider the possible truth of Christianity's claim to uncover a depth unknown to antiquity. This cannot surprise very much, in light of Christian Rome's indebtedness to Jerusalem. The problem of Christianity and modernity pertains to the way in which Athens and Jerusalem have combined in them.[16] By saying he is open to renewing the quarrel of the ancient and the moderns, Strauss is open to considering the opposing claims of "pure" philosophy and of the fusion of philosophy and revelation. It may be the case that Nietzsche and Heidegger achieved the deepest versions of the fusion. Yet Strauss declares that he cannot believe, and if that is so, can any version of the fusion be philosophically plausible for him?

In letters to Krüger, Strauss applies the phrase "the second cave," meaning the "cave beneath the original cave," not only to recent modernity or even modernity as a whole, but also to Christianity.[17] "The problem of the 'second cave' is the problem of historicism [*Historismus*]. The 'substantial and historical core' of historicism is, *as you say correctly*, 'the factual rule of Christ over post-antique humanity.' What results from this for one who does *not* believe, who thus denies the justice, that is, the divine justice, of this rule?"[18] He remarks that the Heideggerian conclusion (that post-Christian philosophy is deeper than ancient) "is perhaps correct—it must in any case be proven to be correct. But this is possible only through a *direct* confrontation of modern with ancient philosophy." This is the legitimation for Strauss's setting up a direct confrontation of Hobbes with Plato, through which Strauss confronts the "starting question [*Ausgangsfrage*] of the moderns and the Greeks" and "analyzes their presuppositions." In other words, modernity as derivative from Christianity may rest on a depth that is accessible to a nonbeliever, but it must pass the test of philosophic scrutiny. Also at issue, Strauss says, is the fact of the "second cave": "My thesis concerning the 'second cave'—which without *proof* is a pure aperçu—could be false." Thus are the modern philosophers in fact limited in their thinking by a set of presuppositions they have not examined?

The claim of superiority made by modern philosophy, that of progress over antiquity indebted to Christianity, is questionable but not self-evidently false. The crisis of modernity does not constitute a self-refutation, and the radical questioning of Nietzsche and Heidegger may expose a new depth of thought that is owing to revelation but whose authority or truth-claim does not rest on belief. Strauss considers two related questions: Why did the modern philosophers, in seeking to free themselves from tradition for a truly natural philosophizing, not return to the Socratic way of philosophizing? Why did the most radical thinkers of the modern era, Nietzsche and Heidegger, not reach the renewal of antiquity to which their thought points? The first two months of 1933 offered crucial insight. Strauss states that his studies of Spinoza and Hobbes have shed light on what Nietzsche and Heidegger have undertaken. "I believe, in the end, that I understand the genuine aporia of Nietzsche."[19] Nietzsche discovered "the good [*das Gute*] whose opposite is the bad [*das Schlechte*], in a countermove to good-evil [*Gut-Böse*], that is, the moral conception. This discovery was a *re*discovery of the *original* ideal of humanity," which was denied and forgotten through "the common work of Socrates-Plato and Christianity." Yet Nietzsche failed to overthrow the powers he struggled against, his difficulty lying in his opposing knowing (*Wissen*) to manly valor (*Tapferkeit*) and the corresponding character of his philosophizing as "philosophizing with the hammer." By this means Nietzsche could never overcome the spirit (*Geist*) that overthrew valor, as it "always falls behind his back. Therefore one must ask: whether one must stay with the *antithesis* valor-knowing."

Strauss's acquaintance with Plato's *Laws* had shown him that this antithesis is not required. Indeed from Plato he had learned he could "pose *Nietzsche*'s questions, thus *our* questions, in a simpler, clearer, and more original way." Certain observations about medieval philosophy had led him to see that an experiment (*Versuch*) with Plato was advisable.[20] Strauss also says that his Hobbes interpretation was crucial to his correction of Nietzsche. In a double paradox, Nietzsche's manly spirit of philosophizing has a hidden kinship with Hobbes's fearful spirit, and Nietzsche's deepest intent is better fulfilled by Plato, his antipode, than by Nietzsche himself. Put another way, Nietzsche's discovery of the transmoral meaning of philosophy was, without his realizing it, a rediscovery of the Platonic view, and his attack on Platonism-Christianity rested on modern, Hobbesian assumptions indebted to Christian morality.

III

In correspondence with Karl Löwith, who wrote important works on both Nietzsche and Heidegger, Strauss's reflections on the two thinkers and their relation grow in subtlety and penetration. Writing of Nietzsche, Strauss confides that between the ages of twenty-two and thirty "I believed literally every word I understood in him" and says of Löwith's formula for Nietzsche's work ("the repetition of antiquity at the peak of modernity") that it "speaks to my soul."[21] He gives now an account of Nietzsche's project as having two phases: a polemical introduction attacking the tradition from the stance of "probity," followed by recovery of the ancient ideal. What should have been mere introduction, the polemic, dominates Nietzsche's thought and ties him to modernity. Thus Nietzsche presents the ancient doctrine of the eternal recurrence as an object to be willed for the future, and in stressing the will he remains trapped in modern assumptions.[22] Strauss, however, notes a parallel between Nietzsche's two-phase project and his own, since he must begin with an overcoming of the present time. "We are natural beings who live and think under unnatural conditions—we must reflect on our natural essence in order to transcend in thought the unnatural conditions." This natural reflection, which is "neither progress nor a resignedly accepted fate," is "an unavoidable means for overcoming modernity. One can overcome modernity not with modern means, but rather, only insofar as we are natural beings with natural understanding."[23] But then a doubt is introduced about whether this naturalness is available to Strauss and his contemporaries. "The means of thinking by the natural understanding are lost to us," and they cannot be recovered by our own efforts. "We attempt to learn them from the ancients." Strauss adds a sharp sally at Heidegger, in whose historicity "nature is brought *fully* to disappearance." But one confronts the difficulty that the "second cave" is not self-evidently false, and since that is so, the putative naturalness transcending it is also not self-evident. It would seem to be an act of faith, or at least a bold experimental hypothesis, to suppose that by studying the ancients one will recover the naturalness that has been lost.

The obstacle facing modern men who would try to recover ancient nature was overcome by Swift and Lessing, "the greatest exponents of the ancient side of the *querelle*," who saw that modern philosophy shares something essential with Christianity (Strauss mentions Machiavelli). Indeed they "knew that the genuine theme of the quarrel is antiquity and Christianity." Somehow these exceptional figures maintained their natural understanding and had "no doubt that the ancient, that is, the genuine philosophy, is an *eternal* possibility."[24] Strauss briefly refers to "the sentimental nineteenth century" and so provides an echo of an earlier letter to Krüger:

> Do you recall the first page of Schiller's "Naive and Sentimental Poetry"? The naive human *is* nature—for the sentimental human, naturalness is only a *demand*. We moderns are necessarily "sentimental." That means however: that we must in a "sentimental" manner—thus in recollection, historically—investigate what the Greeks "naively" investigated; more precisely: we must through "recollection" bring ourselves into the dimension in which we, understanding the Greeks, can investigate "naively" with them.[25]

Strauss goes on to say that the "achievement" of modern historical understanding is not "a more radical dimension, such as a more radical cure of human illness or at least a more radical diagnosis, but the *modern* medicine for a *modern* illness." Asserting that he holds just as strongly as Krüger "the impossibility of 'naive' philosophy in our world," he says that what separates him from Krüger is the fact that he, Strauss, "does not in this impossibility see progress in *any* sense." Similarly Strauss writes elsewhere: "We need a propaedeutic the Greeks did not need, precisely that of book learning." "The historical consciousness is linked to a certain historical situation. Today we have to be historians because we do not have the means at our disposal to answer the real questions properly: 'second cave.'"[26] One more statement on Christianity as the second cave is particularly revealing. To Krüger Strauss writes that the need for historical studies "is an external fact to philosophy" that arises from "the nonsensical interweaving of a *nomos* tradition with a philosophical tradition, that is, biblical revelation with Greek philosophy, a tradition of obedience with a 'tradition' of questioning, and the consequent struggle in modernity against the revelation tradition," which has maneuvered modern men into a second cave so that today they "no longer have the *means* for natural philosophizing."[27]

Taking these statements together, one is faced with a certain ambiguity in the meaning and status of the "second cave." One side of the ambiguity is a very radical thesis. The second cave is not only the historical tradition created by Christianity and modern philosophy, which makes it difficult for contemporary men—the late modern inheritors of a well-developed tradition—to begin to philosophize in a natural way. More fundamentally the second cave is the ("nonsensical") Christian tradition of the fusion of revelation and philosophy, which prevented the founders of modern philosophy from attaining the natural philosophizing they sought, conditioning their thought in a way that limited their vision, drawing them into a conflict in which they imitated the fusing of philosophy and *nomos* in Christianity in a bid to overthrow it. The modern philosophers were historically conditioned and unable to criticize the fundamental presupposition of their thinking. Already conditioned by Christianity to conceive philosophy as devoted to practical conquest of the world by doctrine, they were satisfied to regard their practical victory over Christianity as a definitive answer to the fundamental questions. They lacked the radicality of genuine philosophy, which questions its most basic presuppositions. One wonders whether the term "philosophy" is then fitting for their thinking. Yet Strauss affirms that as philosophers they undertook the "reclaiming of an original natural basis" of philosophizing—an affirmation hard to reconcile with the radical thesis of modern philosophy's unradicality and conditionedness.

The radical thesis is also hard to reconcile with Strauss's modest assertions about his own inquiry, to the effect that the philosophic inferiority of modern philosophy is not self-evident, that to renew the quarrel of the ancients and the moderns is to consider the parties with equal seriousness, to look for proof of philosophic failure and not to assume it. But to characterize modern philosophy as incapable of self-examination concerning its basic dependence on Christianity is already to place it in a position of philosophic inferiority. By means of one stroke Strauss purports to undermine the foundation of all modernity and thus make progress beyond it.

This stance seems to be the essence of the modern philosophic attitude he opposes! (It recalls the description of modern philosophy as reclaiming nature through a polemical attack on earlier tradition as well as Strauss's avowal that he shares with Nietzsche a structure of philosophizing with a polemical first phase.) But Strauss also says that the natural reflection he undertakes is not a form of progress—of building on foundational certitudes. This would have to mean, consistently, that there is no foundational certainty about the failure or collapse of modern philosophy. The ambiguity can be restated in terms of the need for historical studies. More modestly this would mean that only through historical study can we rediscover the forgotten questions animating the whole tradition of philosophy, embracing the distinction between ancient and modern. Strauss speaks this way when he says that by confronting Hobbes and Plato he exposes their presuppositions and analyzes them, uncovering the arguments between them. The attempt to recover these arguments is an experiment, a probing of the possibility of the rejected way of ancient philosophy without presuming that one has adequately understood either way, ancient or modern. On the other hand the need for historical study can mean, less modestly, that one starts from the insight or assumption of the "unnaturalness" of the whole tradition after pagan antiquity and endeavors with the necessary help of books to free oneself from the blighted condition that includes both Christianity and modern philosophy. For it is somehow evident to us "natural beings" that only the ancients pursued the natural mode of philosophizing. Strauss speaks of how Nietzsche awoke him to the possibility of a transmoral ideal of natural philosophizing, but also of how Nietzsche with his "probity" remains indebted to Christianity. This duality in Nietzsche seems to be crucial to the ambiguity in Strauss. For insofar as Nietzsche, the rediscoverer of ancient natural philosophizing, also remains in the thrall of biblical revelation, he shows that the modern fusion is both terribly flawed (through his critique of it) and remarkably powerful (through his exemplifying it).

Indeed it can strike one that there is something almost hasty and ill considered in Strauss's expression "nonsensical interweaving" of traditions. Of course he would not say that the great thinkers who continue that interweaving, Nietzsche not the least of them, are thinking mere nonsense. For that matter, when he discovers Plato's exoteric practice of legislating and teaching new forms of piety, he discloses a certain form of that interweaving. Insofar as Plato created a new form of *nomos* decisively shaped by philosophy, did he introduce something "nonsensical"? The difference, one can surmise Strauss would claim, is that Plato's thought is not itself in any way governed by the pious doctrines of virtue and the soul that he invents, whereas both Christian and modern thinkers are, by his account, blinded to the genuine freedom of philosophizing through the determining place revelation has in their self-understanding. The Enlightenment as a practical engagement against revelation, and the subordinate role given to theoretical reason with respect to the practical, are adduced as definite evidence of the unfreedom of the modern philosopher's thought. Yet is the evidence so clear? Could not the modern philosopher's primary self-presentation as a practical benefactor be an exoteric means through which the philosopher finds his way to "original natural freedom"?

Another way to approach Strauss's thought is to return to an earlier point: the supremacy of the sacred text, of the book, in the traditions of revelation that Strauss treats as antithetical to philosophic "nature." "The fact that a tradition based on revelation has come into the world of philosophy has increased the *natural* difficulties of philosophy by adding the historical difficulty."[28] The natural difficulties of philosophy are presented poetically in the Platonic image of the cave. The historical difficulty can be illustrated by saying: "There is *now* yet another cave *beneath* the cave." "The turn from admitted ignorance to book learning is not natural."[29] Sacred writings—books—changed *nomos* so powerfully that philosophers had to begin, in their pursuit of the natural starting points, with the authority of the book, thereby losing sight of the true natural starting points. Yet some philosophers living in a world governed by the book, notably Muslim and Jewish medieval philosophers, discovered again the natural way, which involves the reinterpretation of revelation in terms of politics: the sacred law is political. But the modern philosophers replaced the books of revelation with the powerful rhetoric of new books—the polemical and politically revolutionary writings of Enlightenment. Paradoxically, postmodern philosophers must turn to the book—to historical studies—to discredit the authority of books and to uncover the Greek natural way of philosophizing in

terms of the political and its law. And Strauss's manner of pursuing the philosophical questions is through a close reading of books that has often been
called "Talmudic," with its search for the intricate hidden structure of the argument. Is this a philosophizing that can see its way toward, or transform itself
into, a freedom from the book?

I V

After the Second World War, Strauss took up the reading of Heidegger with
renewed interest. This was indeed in spite of Heidegger's well-known sympathies for the National Socialist regime. But Heidegger's philosophical work
during the entire Nazi era had been unknown to the outside world (in fact he
published very little in this period) until writings began to emerge in the late
1940s. Strauss turned back to Heidegger while investigating the problem of
history and also reading Wilhelm Dilthey and Ernst Troeltsch. These reflections resulted in the lectures, and later the book, *Natural Right and History*.
In a letter to Jacob Klein Strauss writes: "much has become clear to me which
I actually no longer knew—above all, Heidegger, whose *deinotes* really far surpasses everything done in our time."[30] He notes that "it seems to me that the
problem of causality lies at the ground of this whole matter, which Heidegger
indicates through the relation to *ex nihilo nihil fit*, but conceals through the
'mood-based'-metaphysical interpretation of the *nihil.*"[31] The matter (*Ange-
legenheit*) in question is evidently that of history. Noting that the basis of this
causal problem is "Kant, or the unsolved Humean problem," Strauss says
that "the insight into the absurdity of Heidegger's solution does not help in
the decisive respect." This statement, rather than being a simple dismissal of
Heidegger, implies that Heidegger has exposed a genuine problem to which
his approach (interpreting the absence of metaphysical insight into the causal
ground of Being in terms of *Dasein*'s mood of anxiety) provides no solution.
For Strauss it remains the case that the lack of a proof of *ex nihilo nihil fit* is
a stumbling block for rationalist metaphysics, and in this sense he is a post-
Kantian thinker for whom the "whole is mysterious." Therewith the engagement in Nietzsche and Heidegger with revelation—at the limit of rational argument and explanation—remains for Strauss a philosophic stance worthy of
respect. The issue for him, one can surmise, is whether one can acknowledge
this limit of rationalism while not taking the turn toward biblical thinking in
an "interweaving" of philosophy and revelation that results in the historical
understanding of human thought.

After this date Strauss's correspondence and his published statements on Heidegger of the period 1950–73 disclose two phases of Strauss's thinking on Heidegger, shaped by two major publications: the collection of essays called *Holzwege* of 1950 and the lectures on Nietzsche delivered in 1936–41 and published as *Nietzsche* in 1961.[32] These writings made Strauss aware of a new direction in Heidegger's thought, which turned from the analysis in *Being and Time* of the temporal horizon of human existence (*Dasein*) as the access to the question of Being, toward Being itself as disclosing itself to the human in a relation of mutual dependence that grounds history through dispensations or "fates" that determine the human way of interpreting Being. Löwith in a letter to Strauss stressed the Hegelian aspect of this change: " 'Being' is certainly a super-Hegelian 'absolute' and at the same time it absorbs the historicity of *Dasein* and renders it metaphysical. It is an 'overcoming' of historicism (in the usual sense) and at the same time the most radical historicism (in the Straussian sense)."[33] Löwith here refers to Strauss's extension of the term "historicism" beyond its prevalent designation of nineteenth-century historical thought (the historical school, Troeltsch, Dilthey, etc.), which claimed in various ways to achieve a science of history, to apply as well to Nietzsche and Heidegger, for whom history (and therewith all human thought) has an inexplicable ground. Löwith adds that "Heidegger's effort is a religious one."

In reply Strauss writes that Heidegger is religious only in the sense that all moderns are. Yet Heidegger's sharp turning from Kierkegaard to Nietzsche after *Being and Time*, which Strauss says "strongly speaks to me," shows "where Heidegger wants to go."[34] In this letter Strauss acknowledges the power of Heidegger's critique of the tradition, although a doubt is expressed, and then essentially dismissed, about whether Heidegger is a philosopher. "I don't know whether a true philosopher must have a good will, but in the end it comes down to the quality of his arguments." Heidegger has "definitely refuted all that was and is in our century." The central issue for Strauss is "whether he is right in his critique of Plato." This concerns "whether the subordination of the question of Being to the question of the highest being is legitimate or, as Heidegger maintains, illegitimate." Strauss concludes with noting that "the darkest point" in Heidegger's thought is his assertion that "there are beings without Being," that is, "Being, not beings, exists only insofar as *Dasein* exists." This assertion is also mentioned in *Natural Right and History* as an apparent objection to Heidegger, who is there unnamed.[35]

Somewhat later Strauss credits an article of Löwith with "helping to strengthen a newly awakened sympathy for Heidegger; for *the* Heidegger who is true to himself insofar as he makes no concessions to belief."³⁶ All the same on the question of belief Strauss finds Heidegger "flat and insufficient" compared with the "now completely Christianized and forgotten Nietzsche." Yet he sees both as striving in the direction beyond modernity (with its enduring Christian origins). "In Heidegger's thought modernity comes to an end, and his thinking is thus important to us for that reason and only that reason, because we ourselves cannot be free of modernity when we do not understand it."³⁷ For this aim it is especially important to be clear about the later Heidegger's thought, which, however, maintains the primary motivation of *Being and Time* and does not question its fundamental historicist premise. A critical note is again sounded about Heidegger's "absurd" claim that "there are beings—and not Being (*Sein*)—when there is no *Dasein*." The recurrence of this issue shows that it weighs heavily on Strauss; he seems to brush Heidegger's view aside, and yet it comes back to perplex him. In any case Strauss credits Heidegger, in making the movement from *Existenz* in *Being and Time* to *Sein* in the later writings, with achieving a "remarkable maturity" that leaves behind the "German youth-movement aura" of the earlier work.

Löwith's account of the *Nietzsche* lectures, nearly ten years later, elicits from Strauss his strongest expressions of admiration. "I myself feel now more strongly than ever the attraction exercised by Heidegger."³⁸ At this point there is a remarkable change of tone and stance toward Heidegger's perplexing thought. Strauss speaks, against Löwith and on Heidegger's behalf, on "*Sein* needing man."

> I believe that Heidegger's view is supported by the difficulties to which the alternative is exposed: the self-sufficient God as *ens perfectissimum*, which necessarily leads to the radical degradation and devaluation of man. Differently stated, if Heidegger were wrong, man would be an accident, there would be no essential harmony between thinking and being, the hopeless difficulty of Kant's thing-in-itself would arise.

If Being needs man, the implication is that without man there will be beings but not Being, or at least that Being cannot be fully Being without man. (This is not to say that man and Being are identical.) The thought Strauss earlier called absurd he now finds well supported. It is admittedly speculative to go further and suggest that Strauss, in accordance with this change, would now side with Heidegger's criticism of Platonism, although Strauss more sharply than Heidegger distinguishes between Plato and Platonism. In his own radical readings of Platonic dialogues, Strauss maintains that the idea of the Good is not Plato's final word and that the genuine Platonic account of the ideas is indicated in the deliberately abortive and playful presentations of descent from the Good or the One (the completion of dialectic in the move from higher ideas to lower through division or *diairesis* of kinds), which fail to achieve knowledge of determinate kinds. Only philosophy as love of wisdom, and not wisdom, is available to humans since the problem of the organization and structure of the realm of ideas must remain unsolved.[39] While noting some convergence between Strauss and Heidegger, one also has to observe the difference between them, which relates to Strauss's uncovering of exoteric devices—and therewith his taking seriously the comic elements—in the Platonic art of writing dialogues, an approach to reading Plato not taken by Heidegger.[40]

The remaining exchanges with Löwith on Heidegger focus chiefly on Löwith's charge that Heidegger has misread Nietzsche's intent and on Strauss's defense of Heidegger. Strauss says he is reading the *Nietzsche* volumes, which have just appeared, while preparing a seminar on *Beyond Good and Evil*, and remarks that in spite of Heidegger's questionable reading of what Nietzsche intended, "one may of course raise the question whether Nietzsche achieved what he intended and whether the difficulty which obstructed his return to 'nature' does not justify Heidegger's own philosophic attempt and therewith also Heidegger's interpretation of Nietzsche. . . . What makes difficult Nietzsche's return to *phusis* is of course 'history,' and it is history which is the starting point and the theme of Heidegger."[41] One can relate this point to Strauss's observation in the 1930s that Nietzsche's recovery of antiquity is obstructed by his modern account of freedom. Heidegger, while deeply indebted to Nietzsche, "is naturally concerned with avoiding the pitfalls into which Nietzsche fell." Heidegger learned from Nietzsche and only from him that "There is no Without," or "there can be no 'objectivity' in the last analysis. From this point of view 'nature' is no longer possible except as postulated in the critical moment." Accordingly Nietzsche's doctrine of eternal return is "nature qua being through being postulated." Strauss concludes that when one concentrates on Nietzsche's radical historicism "there is no possibility known to me superior to Heidegger's philosophic doctrine of which his interpretation of Nietzsche forms an integral part."

This claim of Heidegger's superiority could be read as referring only to Heidegger as the best Nietzsche interpreter or as the most consequential thinker on the basis of Nietzschean premises. Yet Strauss credits Heidegger, as has been shown, with insights on causality, God, and the relation of Being to man. These indications of agreement come close to suggesting that Strauss holds a version of the view that "There is no Without." Indeed Löwith seems rather alarmed by what he calls Strauss's "concession" to Heidegger, and he wonders whether Strauss finds something resonant in Heidegger's "history of Being," which Löwith finds to be only a "hypothetical construction."[42] Strauss replies, "I do not make 'concessions' to Heidegger," which surely does not rule out agreement with Heidegger, since agreement is not concession.[43] Reminding Löwith of the contradiction between eternal return and freedom, he asks if Löwith did not himself assert that "the repetition of antiquity at the peak of modernity (as distinguished from unqualified return to the principles of antiquity) constitutes an insoluble difficulty? In other words you have to make a choice: Are the classical principles simply sound or is the modern criticism of these principles not partly justified?" Speaking of Heidegger's history of Being (*Seinsgeschichte*), Strauss writes, "I do not understand the *Seinsgeschichte*, but many things he presents under this heading are intelligible to me, and some of them are in my opinion profound insights. Especially he has cleared up the relation between science, art, and will to power." But a further remark makes clear that Heidegger is not a definitive interpreter of classical philosophy and that his criticisms of Plato miss the mark. "On the other hand I believe that what he says about the apriori in Plato and particularly on the idea of the good is simply wrong." Although there is a rejoinder to Heidegger on Plato, it is unclear whether or to what extent it addresses the "insoluble difficulty" of "the repetition of antiquity."

The penultimate letter to Löwith resumes the discussion of Heidegger.[44] Strauss complains that the account of nature that Löwith maintains against Heidegger's historicism has no place for "the question of the *pos bioteon*," the question of how one should live. Opposing both Löwith and Heidegger, Strauss asserts that the primary human concern is *kata phusin zen*, the concern with living rightly, living naturally. From this one can arrive at the answer of happiness as consisting in *theoria*, a way of life that is engaged with the world as a whole. But the question of the life according to nature is a question, the natural is not self-evident, and Heidegger is on surer ground than Löwith in this respect. Strauss does not endorse Heidegger's view that " 'nature' is only a specific *interpretation* of states of affairs that can be more fittingly designated by something like his 'fourfold' [*Geviert*]," but he asks, "Do the Japanese have a word for 'nature'? The biblical Jews have none. The Hebrew word for 'nature' is a translation of [ancient Greek] *charakter*." In another context Strauss makes the related point that Heidegger correctly grasps that the words for "thinking" in Western languages may offer only a limited basis for approaching what thinking is.[45] In other words, "nature" is a problem, one with which we in the West necessarily begin. The only position that can be superior to

Heidegger's is one that nondogmatically examines our most basic premises, and even in this regard Heidegger surpasses all his contemporaries. In any event, it is notable that in these exchanges with Löwith Strauss does not revert to his language of the "second cave" and seems not inclined to speak of the modern starting point as an unnatural condition for "natural beings." Also absent is the earlier charge that Heidegger's thought makes the unreflective assumption of "progress" over the Greeks on the basis of its appropriation of Christian categories. The later Heidegger cannot be set aside so easily.

In his final letter to Löwith, Strauss makes this comment on Heidegger: "For some time it has struck me that to my knowledge there is not a single place in Heidegger's writings where the name of Jesus appears, not even 'Christus' (unless it happens in a Hölderlin interpretation that I do not know). That is indeed very remarkable."[46] Although Heidegger's thought is not in its later form specifically Christian, the question remains for Strauss (as other sources show)[47] whether Heidegger does not continue to develop an "interweaving" of philosophy and revelation in relation to his fundamental historicist premise.

V

These thoughts of later letters are usefully juxtaposed with a lecture given at St. John's College in 1970, "The Problem of Socrates," which contains one of Strauss's most extended public statements on Heidegger.[48] For present purposes I focus on only certain remarks, and to begin with, the notable comment "in all important respects Heidegger does not make things obscurer than they are," which takes direct issue with Georg Lukács and others who claim that Heidegger renders Being unintelligible. "Lukács only harmed himself by not learning from Heidegger," whose "understanding of the contemporary world is more comprehensive and more profound than Marx's."[49] These comments immediately follow a paragraph in which Strauss remarks that Heidegger's claim that the origin of man is a mystery is a "sensible result" of an argument, which Strauss summarizes: "(1) *Sein* [Being] cannot be explained by *Seiendes* [being or entity]—cf. causality cannot be explained causally—(2) Man is *the* being constituted by *Sein*—indissolubly linked with it > man participates in the inexplicability of *Sein*."[50] In this context Strauss again refers to the problem of causality in Kant, "Kant found 'nowhere even an attempt of a proof' of *ex nihilo nihil fit*," and notes that Kant's transcendental legitimation of this principle as necessary for rendering possible any possible experience points to the primacy of practical reason. Then "in the same spirit" he quotes Heidegger in German: *"Die Freiheit ist der Ursprung des Satzes vom Grunde* (Freedom is the origin of the principle of sufficient reason)." One has to take Strauss as agreeing with Kant and Heidegger that there is no purely theoretical grounding of the principle of intelligible causality, i.e., the principle that Being is grounded only in causes available to human understanding. The origin of Being, therewith of man as open to Being, is a mystery. But there is no endorsement of Kant's resolution, which is grounded in morality or practical reason, or of Heidegger's interpretation of freedom as the ground of the principle.[51] On the other hand the positions of Kant and Heidegger suggest that the absence of a theoretical proof poses a problem for morality or practical reason: morality, but perhaps not philosophy in the "purest," Socratic sense, demands such proof or something that takes the place of such proof on a prephilosophic plane. The positions of Kant and Heidegger point to the interweaving of philosophy and moral or religious concerns in their thought—to the "primacy of the practical" characteristic of modern philosophy.[52]

The lecture begins with "the problem of Socrates" as renewed by Nietzsche, who saw in Socrates the optimistic rationalist who held that "thinking can not only fully *understand* being but can even *correct* it; *life* can be *guided* by science."[53] For Nietzsche the crisis of the entire rationalist tradition, with the exposure of the groundlessness of its ultimate fruit, "the belief in universal enlightenment and therewith in the earthly happiness of all within a universal society," has made necessary the questioning of its origin. Nietzsche sees in Socrates "the single turning point and vortex of so-called world history," and on the basis of insight into the essential limitations of science Nietzsche declares, "the time of Socratic man has gone." Strauss brings forward Xenophon, not Plato, as a corrective to Nietzsche. Xenophon hints at but conceals Socrates's radicality. He minimizes the difference between Socrates and the gentleman for whom "nothing is more characteristic than respect for the law." It was the heart of Socrates's theoretical activity to call into question the authority of the law, to expose its human origin, "for laws depend on the regime." Yet Xenophon's Socrates never raises the question *ti esti nomos* (What is law?).[54] In other words, Strauss suggests that Xenophon saw, but did not expose, something missed by the later tradition, after Plato and including Nietzsche and Heidegger, namely Socrates's radical freedom from every sort of moralism and thereby from optimistic rationalism. Thus Xenophon's silence (he "points to the core of Socrates' life or thought but does not present it sufficiently or at all") seems to speak eloquently of a radicality never fully described or presented in any of the other portrayals of Socrates, whether by friend or foe.

That the philosophies of Nietzsche and Heidegger remain restricted to the horizon of history is directly related, in Strauss's judgment, to their failure to grasp this true radicality. Strauss adduces a metaphysical consideration at this point. Heidegger rightly stresses the mystery of the human origin, but for Strauss, in contrast with Heidegger, "it seems that one cannot avoid the question of what is responsible for the emergence of man and of *Sein*, or of what brings them out of nothing." Granting that *Sein* "is the ground of all beings and especially of man" and that this "ground of grounds is coeval with man and therefore also not eternal or sempiternal," there remains this consideration: "*Sein* cannot be the *complete* ground of man." *Sein* is the essence of man, the *what* of man, but not of the emergence of man, the *that* of man.[55] To remain open to the question of the ground of the *that* is to remain open to a possible ground beyond Being, and therefore beyond history and time. This is not to say that an answer to this question is available to human reason. In other words, Strauss agrees with Heidegger that Being, as the ground of the openness to beings, is coeval with man and history. But something crucial to the human is not coeval with its history, namely, its coming into being, its prehistory. The need to bear in mind the question of the prehistorical origin seems connected to Strauss's appreciation of Socratic philosophy as open to questions that transcend altogether the moral and the political realm, while being aware of the difficulties such questions cause for practical human life. In this way Socratic questioning exposes a duality in the human—as both belonging to the moral and political realm and transcending it. A philosophy that would overcome that duality by limiting reflection to the historical disclosures of Being is avowedly or unavowedly governed by political concerns, and this, in Strauss's estimation, has been true of modern philosophy from its inception.

CHAPTER 3

On Caves and Histories:
Strauss's Post-Nietzschean Socratism

I

In a public lecture delivered in Syracuse, New York, in 1940, Leo Strauss gives an account of the roots of his inquiries in the German situation of philosophy after the First World War.[1] It is a bold statement in that Strauss acknowledges that his greatest philosophic debt is to Nietzsche and Heidegger, two thinkers in different ways associated with the current German regime with which Strauss's recently adopted homeland was gradually sliding into war. The significance Strauss accords to Nietzsche in the lecture can be summarized briefly. Nietzsche called into question more powerfully than any other figure the modern beliefs in the scientific solubility of human problems and in the progressive view of civilization as a meaningful process culminating in human perfection. His critique of modern civilization was made in the name of classical antiquity. While maintaining that all truth is historical, Nietzsche saw the problem in regarding the historicist premise as an objective theoretical premise, and accordingly he called for a historical consciousness whose sole basis is the promotion of life. Nietzsche carried forward a German tradition of criticism of science-based civilization—a tradition that began with Rousseau's criticism of civilization on behalf of original nature, and that became in Kant and his heirs an idealistic critique on behalf of freedom. Whereas Hegel and others had appealed to history—the realm of rational freedom or Spirit, realized uniquely in the modern West—as the ground of human dignity and elevation above mere nature, Nietzsche made history problematic in light of his own account of nature or "life" (or "existence" as it became known in the existential movement), thereby questioning the prevailing assumption of the superiority of the modern West to all other civilizations. Through this critique Nietzsche's philosophy "was the most powerful single factor in German post-war philosophy."[2]

The opening paragraphs of the lecture are remarkable for their assessment of the German philosophic tradition and perhaps even more for the way in which Strauss situates his thought in relation to it. He begins with the statement that "both the intellectual glory and the political misery of Germans may be traced back to one and the same cause: German civilization is considerably *younger* than the civilization of the West." The Germans on the one hand have had less experience of being citizens—*free* citizens—than their Western neighbors. On the other, their philosophic tradition has developed a criticism of civilization—of the very *idea* of civilization, but especially of the modern form. Strauss implies that this criticism, like the political inexperience, is made possible by the youthfulness of German civilization. He notes that this criticism is disastrous in the political field "but necessary in the philosophical, in the theoretical field." These remarks reveal how experience of the situation of Germany granted Strauss insight into the conflicting requirements of politics and philosophy: political success and philosophic depth do not combine easily. But furthermore they show that Strauss sees himself in some sense as carrying forward the German critique, especially Nietzsche's version of it, as philosophically necessary. For the "process of civilization means an increasing going away from the *natural* condition of man, and increasing *forgetting* of that situation," and perhaps one needs an "acute recollection" of that situation if one is to understand "the *natural*, the basic problems of philosophy." Strauss refers to Nietzsche's description of German thought as a longing for the past and for origins, and most of all for building a bridge leading back from the modern world to the world of Greece. Implicitly Strauss allies himself with this tendency in two ways. He is in accord with this tradition insofar as it has seen a theoretical problem in the ideas of progress and science-based civilization central to the Western Enlightenment, and thus on a practical plane he cannot deny having profound misgivings about the modern democratic natural right tradition, which his adopted country is dedicated to defending. At the same time Strauss regards the practical attempts, i.e., German attempts, to reverse the modern development as having politically disastrous consequences, and he makes clear that such consequences cannot be separated from a theoretical critique of the German tradition. Strauss might be said to concur with Nietzsche's dictum on the Germans if its meaning is restricted to philosophy and excludes a political sense: "They belong to the day before yesterday and the day after tomorrow—*as yet they have no today.*"³ Does philosophy ever have a "today" politically? As Strauss sees in his own case the fate of genuine philosophy at all times is homelessness.

Strauss notes that Nietzsche changed the intellectual climate of Europe as Rousseau had about 120 years before, and that "the work of Nietzsche is as ambiguous as that of Rousseau." In spite of Nietzsche's enormous impact on politics, "if I understand him correctly, his deepest concern was with philosophy, not politics."⁴ Nietzsche's claim is that genuine philosophy is the concern of "natural men . . . men who do not need the shelter of the cave, of any cave." He decried an artificial protection against the *elementary* problems not only in the premodern tradition (of providence) but likewise in the modern tradition. It was against "history," against the belief that "history" can decide any question, that progress can ever make superfluous the discussion of the primary questions, against the belief that history, that indeed any human things, are the elementary subject of philosophy, that he reasserted hypothetically the doctrine of eternal return. Through this assertion he sought to "drive home that the elementary, the natural subject of philosophy still is, and always will be, as it had been for the Greeks: the *kosmos*, the world."⁵ In the midst of this paragraph Strauss inserts parenthetically and in quotes "philosophy and the State are incompatible," whereby he raises a primary theme of Nietzsche inseparable from the stress on the cosmic core of philosophy, and at the same time he points to the true meaning of his own concentration on "political philosophy." The passage thus makes evident that Nietzsche led Strauss toward his reflection on the tension between philosophy and politics, or on the necessary duality in human ends, before Strauss took up examining it in the premodern authors.

For Strauss, modernity's effort to reconcile philosophy and politics, in which the critique of orthodoxy and revelation (the Enlightenment's replacement of "political theology" by rational theology and "culture")⁶ was the crucial negative instrument, and whose high point is Hegel's system, had been problematic from the standpoint of his early questions about the possibility for the renewal of Judaism under modern conditions.⁷ It became clear to Strauss that the modern philosophic critique of revelation rested not on an adequate refutation, grounded in a comprehensive account of nature as whole, but on the assertion of a human construct—the new political order of natural rights and of humanly constructed culture—intended to replace any consideration of the superhuman whole. Accordingly the will-based modern construction rests as much as revelation on an act of faith and can claim no theoretical superiority. The actualization of wisdom seemed to be realized in the new political order, through the creation of conditions supportive of the freedom to pursue philosophy. As founder of this political-philosophical reconciliation, Hobbes (or Machiavelli before Hobbes, as Strauss would claim later) had given political philosophy an unprecedented importance, whereby it achieves political results far exceeding the political expectations of the classics.[8] But philosophy achieves the resolution of its tension with politics at the price of abandoning its genuine object, the reflection on the superhuman (and supramoral) whole. The autobiographical lecture indicates that Strauss turned from concentrating on the consequences of modern thought for Jewish questions and, in more Nietzschean (and ultimately classical) spirit, focused on its consequences for philosophy. The lecture makes clear that Strauss's prime concern was not with politics as such.[9]

One could say that Nietzsche exposed an apparently tragic and insuperable problem: that the moral-political order that guarantees security and freedom to the highest human activity, the contemplation of the eternal and cosmic whole, also diminishes the goals and character of that activity, turning the philosophic life into a human-all-too-human dedication to the progress and welfare of mankind. This again is what Nietzsche rejected in modern philosophy, modern scholarship, and the educational system of the modern state: their self-imposed subservience to history and the "needs of the age." Although Nietzsche exposed the problem of the modern historical consciousness and took the first steps toward transcending it, Strauss found that Nietzsche did not investigate the sources of that consciousness and understand how it had become necessary.[10] The genetic account of the historical consciousness—an account that did not assume the truth of historicism, one seeking the adequate overcoming of "history" that Nietzsche had not achieved—became a central part of Strauss's philosophical endeavor. In the 1940 lecture, Strauss mentions that he saw the first stirring of the historical consciousness in the seventeenth-century foundations of modernity[11] and he refers to Descartes's methodical break with "natural knowledge" as a primary source.[12] Strauss concluded it was necessary to clarify this origin with "the eyes of pre-modern philosophy," and Socrates offered the classic example of the philosopher who starts from the natural view of the world, the world as known prior to the scientific modification of it. But precisely on that point there was an immense theoretical obstacle, one posed by Nietzsche himself.

Nietzsche forcefully argued that Socrates is the thinker who initiates the flight from the elementary problems into the protection offered by an "optimistic" account of the power of reason to overcome the evils inherent in Being. Nietzsche asks: Did not Socrates turn philosophy away from the contemplation of the suprahuman and supramoral cosmos, the magnificent theme of his predecessors, and subordinate philosophy to moral and political concerns, shoring up this turn with arguments and myths about providential supports for the life of virtue? In later writings Strauss continues to credit Nietzsche with reviving the "problem of Socrates" and compelling admirers of the classical alternatives to modernity to return to the sources of our knowledge of Socrates for a careful reconsideration. Strauss noted the kinship between the Aristophanic and the Nietzschean critiques of Socrates, as both concern not only the young Socrates's reckless disregard of pious and noble tradition but his failure to be an "erotic" thinker.[13] The outcome of Strauss's investigation of the Platonic and Xenophonic defenses of Socrates is not only to underscore the practical prudence and moderation of the mature Socrates but (since philosophic thought is inherently "manic") to disclose Socrates's awareness of the tension between erotic philosophizing and the requirements of political life.

The lecture's remarks on the origins of Strauss's critical genealogy of historicism in confrontation with Nietzsche show that it was animated not so much by the need to refute the relativism of values as by a desire to carry forward, beyond Nietzsche's own historicism, the attack of Nietzsche on the modern unification of philosophy and history, which claimed to be the definitive solution to the human problems. The true issue is not skepticism but the dogmatism of alleged progress. Strauss was thus led to reconsider the classical reflection on the contrast between the "cave" of political life and the natural good of philosophy—not for the advantage of politics but for that of philosophy. All the same this renewed study was "both necessary and tentative or experimental," since not only Nietzsche but all of modern philosophy spoke against the possibility of a return to classical philosophy in its original form.[14] Strauss wondered whether the original Socrates did not philosophize in a way that is as "natural" and open to the problems, without the intellectual protection of the cave, as Nietzsche's own example of genuine philosophizing. In his pursuit of this possibility, Strauss was assisted by other developments in the German situation besides Nietzsche, as the prestige of modern science (and hence modern philosophy) was under broad siege. Max Weber's defense of the vocation of science revealed science in the modern sense as unable to justify the choice of itself as way of life or to offer any wisdom. Edmund Husserl's phenomenology exposed the inadequate starting point of all modern philosophic and scientific explanation and called for a return to "things themselves" by careful description of the prescientific understanding of the world.[15] Husserl proposed a new form of "rigorous science," but the prevailing mood was to turn away from science in any form to other grounds of authority, above all revelation (Karl Barth and Franz Rosenzweig as leading versions of the "new thinking" in theology) and the absolute obligation to the state (Carl Schmitt). But most important for the philosophic critique of modern rationalism, as offering a new opening to premodern philosophy, was the thought of Husserl's young student: Martin Heidegger.

Strauss remarks that Heidegger's teaching, which he heard in Freiburg in summer 1922, "made perhaps the most profound impression which the younger generation experienced in Germany" in the postwar period, for under his guidance "people came to see that Aristotle and Plato had *not* been understood."[16] Modern philosophy came into being through a refutation of the Aristotelian philosophy, but Heidegger showed that the founders of modern philosophy had refuted only the Aristotelians of their time without understanding Aristotle himself. And a thinker "cannot have been *refuted* if he has not been *understood*." Heidegger's interpretation of Aristotle, "an achievement with which I cannot compare any other intellectual phenomenon" of the period, demonstrated the decisive role of interpretation in the recovery of lost philosophical questions. For Strauss a consequence of Heidegger's "destruction" of the tradition was the insight that "*la querelle des anciens et des modernes* must be renewed" and staged with greater fairness and greater knowledge than in the original quarrel of the seventeenth and eighteenth centuries.[17]

II

It must be noted that this brief yet highly revealing remark on Heidegger's significance with respect to classical philosophy was not Strauss's last such statement. Indeed in the later years of his life Strauss was expansive on the subject,[18] following a long period of reserve in public pronouncements, during which, however, there are numerous comments and references, often without naming Heidegger. Strauss wrote one of his most pregnant utterances on Heidegger in a prologue to a lecture in 1959 which was not delivered. Here he remarks that "no one has questioned the premise of philosophy as radically as Heidegger" and that "by uprooting and not simply rejecting the tradition of philosophy, [Heidegger] made it possible for the first time after many centuries ... to see the roots of the tradition as they are."[19] Some eleven years later a public account of Heidegger's importance, again linking his thought to classical philosophy, ends with this comment: "What distinguishes present-day philosophy in its highest form, in its Heideggerian form, from classical philosophy is its historical character; it presupposes the so-called historical consciousness."[20] The statement implies the closeness of Heidegger's thought to classical philosophy (one cannot imagine any sentence that would begin "What distinguishes logical positivism from classical philosophy . . .") but also points expressly to what separates Heidegger's thought from Strauss's approach to classical philosophy through political philosophy: "I was confirmed in my concentration on the tension between philosophy and the *polis*, i.e. on the highest theme of *political* philosophy, by this consideration." In compressed fashion, Strauss suggests that classical political philosophy as reflection on the "tension" provides the means to understand the genesis of the historical consciousness, since that consciousness results from modern philosophy's effort, in a break with classical thought, to resolve the tension. Thus one must understand the historical consciousness as arising from the break with the ancient account of philosophy as essentially suprapolitical, or as transcending the cave in thought. "Politics and political philosophy is the matrix of the historical consciousness." Heidegger did not uncover the roots of the historical consciousness, simply presupposing the validity thereof, whereas Strauss saw the grounds of that consciousness in questionable modern attempts to resolve the central problem of political philosophy as expounded by Socrates.[21]

Yet in other respects Strauss avows a close kinship between classical thought and Heidegger. Thus he notes in one passage from lectures of 1954–55 (where Heidegger is not mentioned) that historicism is "the serious antagonist of political philosophy" because of its superiority to positivism on the following: (1) It abandons the distinction between facts and values, since all understanding involves evaluation; (2) It denies the authoritative character of modern science, as only one form of human orientation in the world; (3) It refuses to regard the historical process as progressive and reasonable; (4) It denies that the evolutionist thesis makes intelligible the emergence of the human from the nonhuman.[22] This restates essentially what Strauss in the 1940 lecture described as the fundamental questioning of modern premises by German thought in the early decades of the century, especially by Heidegger, which questioning offered a problematic and incomplete liberation from modern philosophy. While such passages confirm the view that a primary impulse to turn to classical philosophy came from Heidegger, it is also the case that Strauss was just as struck by alien elements in Heidegger's pre-1933 thinking, beyond the persistence of historicism. (Strauss's alienation was of course confirmed and strengthened by Heidegger's endorsement of Nazism.)[23] The elements in question Strauss characterized as Heidegger's effort in *Being and Time* (1927) to provide an atheistic interpretation of biblical experience or to give an account of human existence in Christian categories, together with the lack of any ethics in his thinking.[24]

A renewed and deeper engagement with Heidegger occurred in the 1950s as Strauss acquired the publications of the later thought, whose character and direction were largely unknown to the world as it developed during the dark period 1933–45 when Heidegger published little.[25] Evidence of Strauss's appreciation of the so-called "turn" in Heidegger's thought[26] is found in a 1956 lecture giving a detailed account of Heidegger's self-criticism.[27] Strauss notes that Heidegger pursued a deeper critique of the philosophic tradition as he sought to overcome the persisting elements of modern subjectivity in his earlier "existentialist" phase, culminating in *Being and Time*. No longer does Heidegger emphasize authentic resoluteness of will as the ground of projected ideals of existence—the response of the early Heidegger to the loss of all absolute grounds of authority, including the failure of scientific rationalism to authorize itself. Heidegger's later thinking surely has continuity with the earlier as engagement with the question of Being, but it relates to the earlier thought in the way that Hegel's philosophy (on Hegel's own estimation) relates to Kant's, as the deeper fulfillment of Kant's intention. A return to something like metaphysics is necessary, although "the return to metaphysics is impossible. But what is needed is some repetition of what metaphysics intended on an entirely different plane." Thus Heidegger develops a higher reflection on historicity as grounded in Being that surpasses (or comprehends without simply negating) the existential account of the temporality of human being-there (*Dasein*) as the horizon for interpreting Being.[28] Strauss too, it must be noted, undertakes a return to classical thought without a return to metaphysics as the tradition conceives it, and also in his way seeks to recover "what metaphysics intended," wherewith he would transcend modernity. Strauss also observes that Heidegger had uncovered fundamental flaws in Nietzsche's attempt to overcome modernity through his account of Being as will to power. Accordingly it was necessary to examine Heidegger's claim to have achieved the standpoint of an overcoming that is no longer, as is Nietzsche's thought, hobbled by internal contradiction.[29]

There are many indications that Strauss considered it essential to test his own approach against this later direction of Heidegger (as in the statement cited above, "I was confirmed . . .") and that a true transcending of modernity required coming to terms with his thinking.[30] We have seen a number of such statements in the correspondence, but they also occur in public utterances. Not merely did Heidegger question rationalism; he showed that all rationalism is genuinely questionable.[31] Heidegger's later thinking in particular raised the issue of whether he had revealed a true limitation in Platonic philosophy.[32] Heidegger uncovered a possibility of thinking about Being that was not merely humanistic, while revealing that the human is "needed" by Being,[33] a way of thinking for which Strauss disclosed a certain sympathy. It seems that Heidegger pointed to inescapable difficulties for any attempt to understand the Good as a highest being or cause in the metaphysical sense, and yet his thinking is to be faulted for abandoning the question of the Good altogether.[34] At the heart of Strauss's reconsideration of Socratic philosophy is the inquiry into whether the question of the Good can be accorded due centrality in philosophy, while acknowledging the metaphysical or cosmological problem uncovered by Heidegger.[35] Can the question of the Good be regarded as the opening to Being or the whole without implying a merely "humanistic" or anthropocentric account of the whole?[36] Strauss turned to the sources of Socratic philosophy to explore the possibility that such a way of thought is the core of the Socratic dialectic. In what follows I outline fundamental tenets of this Socratism as they appear chiefly in writings from the 1950s and early 1960s.

III

Strauss states that "contrary to appearances, Socrates' turn to the study of the human things was based, not upon disregard of the divine or natural things, but upon a new approach to the understanding of all things."[37] "In its original form political philosophy broadly understood is the core of philosophy or rather 'the first philosophy.'"[38] "We have learned from Socrates that the political things, or the human things, are the key to the understanding of all things."[39] How can one justify giving the study of politics this privileged place in philosophy? Let us consider how Strauss characterizes the "new approach to the understanding all things." Socrates identified the science of the whole with the understanding of what each of the beings is, that is, he understood being such that "to be" is "to be a part," an intelligibly distinct or noetically heterogeneous part of the whole. The intelligible parts are the classes or kinds of things that first become known through their manifest shape or form and that cease to be intelligible if reduced to allegedly more primary elements, as was done by Socrates's philosophic predecessors. The surface of things, or what is "first for us," is the guide to the articulation of the whole. This new approach to the study of the whole favored the study of the human things.[40] The whole as such, however, is "beyond being," and the roots of the whole from which it arises may not be accessible to human thought. Therefore the knowledge of parts is itself not perfect knowledge. "There is no knowledge of the whole but only knowledge of parts, hence only partial knowledge of parts, hence no unqualified transcending, even by the wisest man as such, of the sphere of opinion."[41] Thus Socratic philosophy is "knowledge that one does not know; that is to say, it is knowledge of what one does not know, or awareness of the fundamental problems and, therewith, of the fundamental alternatives regarding their solution that are coeval with human thought."[42] Such formulations do not make immediately evident, however, why the concentration on intelligible parts and the avowal of the elusiveness of the whole should lead to (or be the same as) the view that the political things, among all of the parts of the whole, are "the key to the understanding of all things."

One must turn to more formulations on Socratic philosophy. "Knowledge of ignorance is not ignorance. It is knowledge of the elusive character of the truth, of the whole." In light of the mysteriousness of the whole, philosophy articulates the more familiar "situation of man as man," which does not entail leaving the question of the whole behind, since to articulate the human situation "means to articulate man's openness to the whole."[43] To articulate the human situation as including "the quest for cosmology rather than a solution to the cosmological problem" was "the foundation of classical political philosophy." The crucial term is "openness to the whole," which is the basis for the quest for cosmology. To articulate that openness is to acquire knowledge of "the fundamental and permanent problems," which according to Strauss are "the unchangeable ideas." Human openness to the whole is inherently problematic, and articulating the problems inherent in that openness is the same as articulating the structure of the human soul. Among all the parts of the whole, the human soul has a unique place. "The human soul is the only part of the whole which is open to the whole and therefore more akin to the whole than anything else."[44] Owing to this kinship "the true knowledge of the souls, and hence of the soul, is the core of cosmology."[45] But again one must underscore the problematic character of this knowledge: the true knowledge of the soul is knowledge of the problems inherent in human openness—problems that must be confronted by the quest for cosmology. There is no access to the whole or the cosmos that can bypass or ignore those problems. One could say the problems belong to the possibility of the access to the whole (they do not merely obscure it, much less prevent it). But where do the problems inherent in human openness have their most familiar forms, where are they most manifest or "writ large"? Socrates's answer, according to Strauss: in the political realm.

One can regard this interpretation of the Socratic turn as Strauss's way of taking the phenomenological turn to "things themselves" and to the "natural understanding" of which the scientific understanding is only a modification, but Strauss notes that Heidegger's version of phenomenology had the advantage over Husserl's of emphasizing the human practical engagement with things. "The natural world, the world we live in and act, is not the object or product of the theoretical attitude; it is a world not of mere objects at which we detachedly look but of 'things' or 'affairs' which we handle."[46] The reference is to Heidegger's analysis of human being-in-the-world as the concern with *pragmata*, which is undertaken not for its own sake but to disclose the temporal horizon for the interpretation of Being. The analysis is only preparatory to recovering the meaning of the ancient question "What is Being?" Similarly, Strauss understands the Socratic turn to the speeches and opinions that guide the analysis of the political things as conducted not in order to arrive at norms and dicta (or natural laws) based on commonsense beliefs, but to articulate the human openness to the whole. This is the Socratic path to the question of Being, a superior path to those followed in the phenomenological movement. The political-moral "surface" of life contains the fundamental problems, which do not adequately emerge if one focuses on such notions as concern with *pragmata*, the life-world, or "embodied experience." Only when the problems inherent in moral-political life are allowed to unfold can one then uncover the starting points of philosophy. As Strauss puts it, the renewal of Socratic philosophy considers what is first for us for the sake of an "unbiased reconsideration of the most elementary premises whose validity is presupposed by philosophy."[47] At the same time, the uncovering of the problems calls for a historical and "destructive" aspect, as we have seen, since the philosophic tradition has overlaid the surface of primary questions with a tradition of other concepts: historical inquiries are necessary to ascend from the "cave beneath the cave."

To take the account a step further, the Socratic inquiry (which in Strauss's renewal has to be assisted by historical investigations) turns to prephilosophic opinions about such things as the good, the just, and the noble that form the core of moral-political life, which itself is always a realm of debate and controversy. The examination of such opinions, guided by the philosopher's quest for knowledge of the whole, leads to uncovering contradictions and obscurities in these opinions. This in turn leads to the thought that the conflicting opinions exist merely through being humanly held or that they are conventional, and then to the question of whether there may be some thoughts on such matters that are not merely humanly held or humanly made and that are "by nature." The questions arise about "what is by nature" right, noble, and good, and a dialectical ascent is attempted from established law to nature. But thereby the authoritative opinions of the city, and preeminently the pious opinions about divinely grounded law, are put in doubt.[48]

Strauss's claim that this Socratic attempt is aporetic or "knowledge of ignorance" may occasion a misunderstanding, for this does not mean that the effort makes no progress in articulating the opinions and in arriving at cogent distinctions between fundamental notions (between the noble and the good, between merely moral virtue and philosophic virtue, etc.), and even in establishing a certain natural order or hierarchy of notions. But Socrates uncovers such distinctions ultimately to illuminate what is hidden, or presupposed, behind what is revealed. All prephilosophic opinions are implicitly opinions about the whole, about what is primary within it and what structures or governs it. "All knowledge, however limited or 'scientific' presupposes a horizon, a comprehensive view within which knowledge is possible," or "all understanding presupposes a fundamental awareness of the whole," which Plato describes metaphorically as "a vision of the ideas, a vision of the articulated whole."[49] Knowledge of aporia or of ignorance arises in the attempt to uncover the intelligible composition and unity of the articulated opinions or "parts"—in attempting to move from the natures of parts to nature as whole. Indeed there could be no uncovering of a problem of the whole—the knowledge of the problem that is "knowledge of ignorance"—without making progress in the articulation of parts. This again is to say that the "fundamental problems" are essential to the access to the whole and do not merely obscure or obstruct it.

The problematic effort of dialectical ascent puts the philosopher at odds with the traditional laws and customs of the city, as noted. The ongoing questioning about ultimate matters not only results in suspension of belief in the traditional laws but also denies the philosopher the leisure needed for participation in the activities of citizenship. Even so, it is misleading to describe the philosophic life in terms of a "resolve to think freely" and to contrast that freedom to "obedience to the laws."[50] This describes the philosopher's quest in moral terms, as confrontation with the law and morality, without providing a motive for such confrontation. It abstracts from the content of philosophy, as knowledge of fundamental problems. Similarly the philosopher's effort is not exhausted in attempts to "justify" his activity with respect to the claims of the laws. "To articulate the problem of cosmology means to answer the question of what philosophy is or what a philosopher is."[51] Even so, it is crucial to Strauss's account of the Socratic approach that the tension between philosophic inquiry and authoritative custom is at the heart of the articulation of human openness to the whole. The tension occasions not only a practical problem of prudence but a theoretical problem. The reflection on this tension is at stake when Strauss claims that for Socrates the human things are "the clue to the whole."[52] In terms of the Socratic turn to the noetically heterogeneous parts, the Socratic philosopher grasps that "the political things are a class by themselves, that there is an essential difference between political things and things which are not political." What is of most concern is the *difference*: "There is an essential difference between the common good and the private or sectional good."

It is above all to reflect on that difference that Socrates examines the common opinions about the just, the noble, the good, and so on. To say "Socrates is the first philosopher to do justice to the claim of the political" is to say that he is the first to see the full import of the nonreducible difference between the political and the nonpolitical; it "means he also realized the limitations of that claim. Hence he distinguished between two ways of life, the political life, and one which transcends the political life and which is the highest."[53] This "difference" proves to be the crucial articulation of parts that provides the "clue to the whole." One is easily tempted to say that the articulation is only a matter of exposing the nullity of the claims of politics and morality, of discrediting the authoritative laws and beliefs so as to show that the true whole is correctly grasped by the philosopher as simply transpolitical and transmoral. Strauss's own language at times could suggest this, as in the praise of Nietzsche's attempt to recover the "natural" way of philosophy in the 1940 lecture. But this would be to overlook the subtle point Strauss makes about the access to the whole as an access through problems. It cannot be the case that the political-moral realm is grounded in mere illusion if there is an essential difference between the political and the nonpolitical, or a natural articulation of two competing claims on human life.

In doing justice to the claims of the political, Socrates notes its practical priority as the most "urgent." The political realm, because it addresses the most urgent human concerns, may have its true dignity as the condition for what is higher, the life of inquiry. But as such it is not in itself simply cut off from what is higher. "The political things and their corollaries are the form in which the highest principles first come to sight." Indeed through the political things the whole itself comes to sight "since they are the link between what is highest and what is lowest, or since man is a microcosm."[54] That the political realm is not simply the "other" of the nonpolitical, and that it transcends itself by pointing beyond itself to the "difference" while not overcoming its own limitations, is what I take Strauss to mean by the "theological-political problem," which he never expressly defines.[55] The problem is not simply the tension between philosophy and the political but the tension within the political itself, which is a tension within the human soul, making philosophy possible. Philosophy makes that tension explicit and thematic and thereby in a certain way achieves a coherent life that is not bound to the political and its internal rifts. The political is indeed paradoxical, insofar as it is essentially different from what transcends it and yet points beyond itself toward it. But that is the paradoxical quality of the human soul, which is both a part of the whole and yet open to the whole beyond itself and akin to it. The study of politics is the study that most reveals the nature of the soul; at the same time, it allows one to see how the soul is the adumbration of the whole. The togetherness of the inherently urgent or compelled and the inherently free or pleasant in this "part" of the whole raises a perplexity about the whole itself. "The whole is not one, nor homogeneous, but heterogeneous." This peculiar class, the political things, with its difference from other classes, being internally differentiated, linking the high and the low, is the clue to cosmic difference.[56] And thus "the most important truth is the obvious truth, the truth of the surface." The common view that noble things are not reducible simply to the pleasant is a clue to the character of the whole. But it can be such a clue only by way of philosophic reflection on the relation of the two as a problem. To describe Socrates as the "founder of political science" is to say he is the founder of the study of politics as offering philosophic access to the character of Being.

IV

Strauss characterizes this situation by employing the Platonic image of the cave. By his own account it is a problematic image involving a deliberate overstatement, in keeping with an abstractive feature of the *Republic* as whole, namely, its suppression of *eros*. The image shows this in two ways, by denying that the cave dwellers have any desire for what lies beyond the shadows they see, and by denying that philosophic souls who escape the cave have any *eros* for the political communities they leave behind. Both cave dwellers and philosophers must be compelled if they are to leave their congenial place and move toward the other place.[57] But such dramatic exaggerations in Plato have the effect of bringing forward truth. Strauss expresses it this way: "The city is both closed to the whole and open to the whole." Political life is "life in the cave which is partly closed off by a wall from life in the light of the sun. The city is the only whole within the whole or the only part of the whole whose essence can be wholly known."[58]

Political life is not just a part but a whole, albeit one that seems to its residents more whole and complete than it is. Its way of seeming to be complete to itself is, one could say, its essence. Yet it may be an exaggeration on Strauss's part, ironically reflecting the nature of political life, to say that this "essence can be wholly known." The abstraction inherent in the character of political life is here reflected in the philosophic description of its character. But the purpose of such abstractions is to bring out their own limitations. "The city is completely intelligible because its limits can be made perfectly manifest."[59] Certainly what can be made perfectly manifest is the tendency of human life to seek a kind of closure and shelter within the limits of laws and customs, although this effort is always precarious, never wholly successful. Strauss's account of the argument of the *Republic* is that it makes manifest the limits of political life by offering a "city in speech" that shows how human life would appear if "perfect justice" were achieved. In such a city human life is deformed not only by the suppression of private life for the guardian class but by the artificial subordination of the philosophic life to the needs of the city. The natural desires, or *eros*, of both the guardians and the philosophers are suppressed. Socrates with the help of his interlocutors constructs this ideal city not seriously for practical actualization but for philosophic instruction as to the nature of the soul and of politics. By maximizing or absolutizing the claims of politics so as to produce a comic and grotesque result, Socrates uncovers a fundamental tension between those claims and the soul's full range of possibilities.

Yet Strauss sees more than this in the Platonic account of how the city is both closed and open to the whole. Since political life, whose core is justice as defined by the law, forms a kind of whole whose limits can be experienced as limits, humans are capable of the questioning of law (the limits), which allows for the transcending of law. The whole or Being as problem or question can come into human view only because humans occupy a part of it that has an imperfect and ordinarily deceptive completeness. Political life's way of offering images of wholeness that allure and detain the soul without truly satisfying it is the condition for the discovery of philosophy as the pursuit that truly satisfies. In this way politics is the "link" between high and low. Human beings are not fitted directly to encounter and grasp Being or the whole as such. Political life in the form of laws, customs, rituals, duties, and attachments offers various experiences of something whole, and a sense of shelter from the mystery of human existence, with its unknown origins and unknown destiny. It then provides a ground for some human beings to look for the "true whole," although it has to be said that political life offers the metaphor or image of "the whole" guiding the philosophic quest, and the appropriateness of the language and idea of "the whole" itself may be questionable. One can restate this by saying that there could be no opening to the question of "What is?" or of Being without the difference (or limit) inherent in politics.[60] The fact that humans have a way in law-governed communities of "forgetting" the whole to which they are naturally open—a way that is relatively solid or "substantial" compared with the disorder of lawless forms of life—is indispensable for facing and sustaining the openness. Politics provides the foundation—as that which lies under or supports—for the possibility of transcending politics. This has a certain kinship with Heidegger's account of how Being is disclosed only through "ontological difference," and how the "forgetting" of Being is inseparable from standing in its disclosure. But for Strauss what Heidegger sees only in terms of the fall into "ontic" thinking, the concern with metaphysics as causal-substantial, is better illuminated by relating forgetfulness and difference to the political nature of the human. Attention to the "surface" of political life, for which Heidegger has little or no regard, shows an intrinsic connection between reflecting on the difference that conditions theoretical transcending, and "common sense" moderate practical approaches to the basic texture of political life, the warp and woof of law and desire.

Strauss characterizes the theme of difference in one more way: in terms of the two roots of morality. He asks, "how can there be a unity of man?"[61] Morality has "two really different roots," namely, the "moral requirements of society on the one hand and the moral requirements of the life of the mind on the other," which two roots, while radically different, still agree "to a considerable extent." What was said of the cave can be said of man as such: The unity of man consists in the fact that he is that part of the whole which is open to the whole, or, in Platonic language, that part of the whole which has seen the ideas of all things. Man's concern with his openness to the whole is the life of the mind. The dualism of being a part while being open to the whole, and therefore in a sense being the whole itself, is man.

Starting from the notion of the individual human being, the difference now appears as that between two modes of transcending by the individual toward two wholes, "society and the whole simply." Nobility consists in "dedicating oneself to something greater than oneself," and thus nobility can take the form of dedication to the common good of political life or dedication to the pursuit of knowledge of the whole. But this duality of modes of transcending is a great perplexity and cause of wonder.

This wonder seems to be related to Socrates's experience of disappointment as he sought in his early days as a student of nature to find a teleological account of the whole, especially through the guidance of Anaxagoras. What he sought was a causal knowledge of how the whole and each part of the whole are for the best, such that all parts are in harmony.[62] But the kinds of causality available in the study of nature were two: genesis through material parts that could account for individual beings but not for universal properties, and noetic mathematical ideas that could account for universals but not for individual beings. No kind of cause was available to link these, until Socrates noted in a "second sailing" a certain togetherness of them in human speeches about beauty, goodness, and justice. The human concern with the just is a kind of cause in which universal notions are applied to individual cases, as when Socrates affirms the condemnation of the city of Athens by choosing to remain in prison when he has the chance to escape. Yet the judgment of the city itself was unjust, contrary to the natural good of philosophy. Accordingly the same action might be regarded as both just and unjust, as one looks to either the common good of the city or the private good of the philosophic life. The nature of justice is inherently controversial. Therefore the problem of the unity of the causes reappears in the sphere of human moral and political judgment, where, however, there is a certain unity within duality or agreement "to a considerable extent," making human life possible. Socrates fastens intransigently on the wonder of that unity within duality, so as to espy whatever oblique clues it may offer about the nature of the whole.

But the aporia in first principles cannot be resolved. Strauss has another prominent statement on fundamental dualism, which needs to be related to the duality of man's two modes of transcending. "The knowledge which we have is characterized by a fundamental dualism which has never been overcome," the pole of mathematical homogeneity in arithmetic and productive arts and crafts, and the pole of heterogeneity, especially in knowledge of heterogeneous ends. The statesman has a knowledge of ends to make human life complete or whole, "but this knowledge—the political art in the highest sense—is not knowledge of *the* whole."[63] Two kinds of knowledge must be combined, the heterogeneous and the homogeneous, "and this combination is not at our disposal." The two poles seem to parallel the two wholes to which human life is open, the transpolitical and the political. Socratic philosophy realized the true whole cannot be found through a simple transcending of the city and that the problem of the true whole is the same as the problem of the unity of man. That problem cannot come into view unless one starts with man as political. Strauss presents this as the fundamental cosmological problem in Platonic thought, and he refers to it again, apparently, when he refers to "the difficulty with which every teleological physics is beset."[64] Philosophy is possible with this persisting aporia, for as knowledge of ignorance it does not require a "specific cosmology."

Yet it could be said that Strauss goes beyond the Platonic presentation of Socratic philosophy by the bluntness with which he presents the human situation as a cave-dwelling that opens onto a mysterious whole. By asserting that the human belongs to both realms—thereby already thrusting the reader toward the mouth of the cave—and that the ascent from the cave issues not in the pure light of the sun or knowledge of the causes but only in "fundamental problems," Strauss creates the doubt that the human is wholly at home anywhere. It is a doubt that can be resolved only through taking up the Socratic life of knowing one's ignorance. The classical account of this life Strauss presents unadorned, without the consoling piety of the supersensible realm. Strauss's writing is in this respect decidedly "late modern" writing. Coming after centuries of philosophic tradition, the political cave is for most readers no longer a secure, habitable place in the age of global technology—and Strauss ventures to say this to his readers who have undergone the instruction in Enlightenment and then passed beyond that instruction. The cave no longer has providential supports of any sort—whether from premodern belief in higher powers or from modern confidence in human mastery and scientific progress. Strauss addresses a post-Nietzschean world, as does Heidegger. What arises in this situation is a new clarity. The hope that history would render the human political habitation completely livable has collapsed, allowing a renewal of the classical reflection, in its original form, on unbridgeable dualism: the city and man. But philosophy's self-awareness of homelessness proves to be its own justification, for "the very uncertainty of all solutions, the very ignorance regarding the most important things, makes quest for knowledge the most important thing, and therefore also a life devoted to it the right way of life."[65]

* 2 *

Exigencies of Freedom and Politics

CHAPTER 4

Freedom from the Good: Heidegger's Idealist Grounding of Politics

I. INTRODUCTION

Commentators on Heidegger often note three phases in his thinking as it relates to politics: (1) the analysis of human existence or *Dasein*, culminating in *Being and Time* of 1927 and ending in 1933, which is apolitical or at least has only implicit and rather vague political implications; (2) the explicit political engagement with the National Socialist revolution from 1933 to around 1936, in which Heidegger sees the chance to link his philosophical efforts for spiritual renewal of the West to the dominant political forces in Germany; (3) the withdrawal in the middle to late 1930s from an active political approach to the overcoming of Western nihilistic technology, with the adoption of a stance of awaiting the next dispensation of Being in the arrival of new gods, as heralded by Hölderlin, the poet of the German nation who speaks for Germany's spiritual leadership of the West.

But it has also been claimed that the authentic comportment toward existence described in *Being and Time* entails, in its account of the resolute affirmation of fate, a radical decisionism that is continuous with Heidegger's political engagement of 1933, even if specific features of National Socialism, such as its biological racism, are not indicated by, or even compatible with, Heidegger's existential analysis.[1] Indeed one might discern an underlying continuity to all three phases. Herman Philipse, in his recently published *Heidegger's Philosophy of Being*, has put forth the interesting hypothesis that the project running through Heidegger's work is theological: *Being and Time* pursues a "Pascalian strategy" of characterizing human existence as miserably fallen so as to provoke rejection of the spiritually devastated rationalism of Western civilization and therewith a search for redemption, whose features are essentially Christian;[2]

Heidegger then in the years just following *Being and Time* (1929–32) attempts to find what Philipse calls the "metaphysical grace" for which the analysis of *Dasein* was preparation, an effort that ends in failure; Heidegger takes refuge in Nazism, a desperate action that Philipse describes as religious conversion; that too ends in disaster, and Heidegger's later thought consists in developing what Philipse terms "postmonotheist theology" to save the West.[3] Philipse argues that in Heidegger's later theological or eschatological scheme, Nazism still plays a positive role insofar as it furthers the completion of the technological age through its absolute assertion of the will to power. Since moral criticism of any agent in the fulfillment of the West's historical destiny is beside the point, Heidegger's disavowal of Nazism could never be more than equivocal at best.[4]

Philipse's formulation has helpful features, but it overlooks some explicit statements of the later Heidegger that strikingly show that the political reality of the National Socialist movement held for him, even from the standpoint of utter defeat and personal disgrace in 1945, a promise that he believed that he and others in positions of authority in the early 1930s failed to fulfill. These assertions shed important light on Heidegger's political thinking; they indicate that Heidegger perhaps never learned the "lesson" that *all* political engagement on behalf of his philosophic vision is inherently mistaken.[5] They point to a conception of politics that, paradoxical as it may seem, might be called "idealist." I want to show that this conception of politics, which surely in the years of Heidegger's service to the revolutionary regime contains no hint of a basis in traditional revelation, is well grounded in Heidegger's thought of the period 1929–32. It is philosophically a kind of idealism that drastically rejects theological or "metaphysical" grace, or any turn to an infinite (superhuman) reality.[6] And it is an idealism in crucial ways descended from the great tradition of German Idealism, by Heidegger's own avowals. It also contains, I argue, an internal paradox that illuminates the so-called "turn" (*die Kehre*) in Heidegger's thinking and that can be viewed as the hidden link between the Kantian idealism of Heidegger's 1929 Davos disputation with Ernst Cassirer and the post-Kantian idealism of later writings. Philipse's continuity hypothesis must undergo revision through more attention to this philosophical stratum in Heidegger.

II. HISTORY AS METAPHYSICS

Heidegger penned a remarkable document in 1945, "The Rectorate 1933/34: Facts and Thoughts," which he gave to his son Hermann with the instruction to publish it at "a specified time," and which appeared with the Rectoral Address of 1933, "The Self-Assertion of the German University," in 1983, seven years after Heidegger's death.[7] It is a self-serving and in verifiable ways mendacious document, to be sure.[8] Yet it is not simply dismissive of the National Socialist movement; indeed Heidegger offers what is perhaps his most articulate justification for participating in the revolution of 1933. "I saw at the time in the movement that had come to power, the possibility of an inner gathering and renewal of the people [*das Volk*] and a way for it to find its historical Western destiny. I believed that the self-renewing university could be called on to work as the standard for the inner gathering of the people."[9] In hindsight he does not say that this perception of the movement was a mere delusion, although he does grant that "mediocre and incompetent" persons in the movement stood in the way of achieving higher goals. Instead Heidegger poses a remarkable "what if" question—a sort of question he acknowledges to be risky. "But the question may be put: what would have happened and what could have been prevented if in 1933 all the competent forces [*vermögende Kräfte*] had aroused themselves and slowly, in secret persistence, purified and moderated the movement that came into power?"[10]

Heidegger never anywhere suggests that another regime or movement, actual or possible, had the possibility for such direction from the "competent forces." Certainly no Western democratic regime could be directed in this way. Thus the Heidegger of 1945 had not broken with the Heidegger of 1933 as to the philosophical rightness of his placing his prestige and talent behind the National Socialist revolution, as rector of the University of Freiburg. His error was only in underestimating the difficulties he would face in his efforts to shape the regime toward higher ends.[11] Behind Heidegger's affirmation of the philosophical rightness of his move is a conception of the relation of philosophy to practical life that persists in his thought from early to late.

Scholarship on Heidegger has lacked the proper terms for describing this relation. It is seldom noted that the hope of shaping the direction of political life through the university, and the project of subordinating political life to higher philosophical or cultural aims, are both well established in the tradition of German Idealist thought.[12] Even when this is noted, the deeper philosophical premises behind this account of the relations of university, politics, and philosophy are not uncovered. This failure is not unrelated to the fact that contemporary scholarship takes for granted the truth of many or most of these premises, in some form. Most basically, this account assumes that philosophy is, or can be, the dominant force in human affairs and that human history is most fundamentally the history of philosophy. Accordingly the principles of ordinary actors in political and social life express, more or less directly, principles arrived at philosophically. This must mean that politics, morality, and religion ultimately are derived from philosophical thought; the ordinary moral actor is thus in possession of a metaphysical principle of morals, as Kant says. The spheres of politics, morality, and religion do not maintain any degree of autonomy from philosophy; but conversely, philosophy does not maintain any degree of autonomy from practical life. Philosophy comes to mean wholly transforming practical life; or rather, it becomes that transformation itself, the historical spirit effecting such transformation. This is not to deny that certain individuals—philosophers, poets, and statesmen—can have central historical roles as the leading spokesmen of that spirit.

Heidegger's version of this idealism is supported by another assumption bearing an unmistakable Kantian stamp: the core of existence for all human beings is a kind of freedom, a capacity for transcending concerns variously described as empirical, heteronymous, anthropological, or ontic. As Heidegger puts it, the core of human existence is the understanding of Being; the transcendence that makes all human thought and action possible is philosophical transcendence. As thus capable of transcending mere beings (*Seienden*) toward the whole of Being (*Sein*), the human essence has the ability to look past the vulgar concerns with comfort, security, and happiness, to face resolutely the totality of existence, which is limited only by death. As becomes evident in the Davos disputation, Heidegger is fully aware of the idealist and more specifically Kantian origins of this account of freedom. It is not possible to argue here how this idealist notion emerged in the eighteenth century in response to the perception that modern scientific naturalism failed to provide an adequate account of the unity and the ends of human knowledge.[13] It would also be very helpful in this context to show that Heidegger, in his effort to provide the foundation of metaphysics in the analysis of *Dasein*, saw himself as addressing in the early twentieth century a situation much like that Kant faced: the dominance of mathematico-empiricist philosophies that overthrew the authority of metaphysics as the ground of the unity of the sciences and as the reflection on the highest human *telos*.[14]

Heidegger is much aware of his debt to the German Idealist tradition, and this debt has also been widely discussed in the scholarship. What has not been seen is the full scope of what that debt means. When Heidegger asserts that Kant is the first philosopher since Plato and Aristotle to take a further step in metaphysics,[15] the place of freedom in Kant's metaphysical thought is present to Heidegger as central to that advance. But with the Kantian account of freedom comes a particular conception of the relation of metaphysics to practical life. I will argue that a version of this conception always underlies Heidegger's thinking—at times quite plainly, at others more covertly. Heidegger's version certainly no longer supports Kant's Enlightenment-universalist idea of human dignity, but instead after 1932 it undergirds a romantic exaltation of particular people or folk (the Greeks, the Germans) who have a universal mission of a philosophical nature.[16] My concern is with showing how Heidegger grounds his *völkisch* thinking in idealist premises. I begin with the Kantianism of the Davos disputation and then return to later utterances in which the *völkisch* element is pronounced.

III. THE REVISION OF KANT

The theme of freedom is a crucial link between the writings before and after 1933; a central factor in Heidegger's thinking on freedom is his study of Kant, which is especially intense in the late 1920s and early 1930s.[17] For the significance of Kant to Heidegger one of the most important documents is the spring 1929 disputation with Ernst Cassirer in Davos, Switzerland.[18] Heidegger was at the time writing *Kant and the Problem of Metaphysics*; this interprets the *Critique of Pure Reason* as providing the foundations of ontology in the productive imagination, which provides temporal intuitions as "schemata" for the categories of the understanding.[19] Heidegger saw in Kant's argument an anticipation of his own account of the temporal openness of human existence as the condition for understanding Being.[20] In the dispute with Cassirer, Heidegger defends his interpretation against the Neo-Kantian view of Kant as providing a theory of the natural sciences. Cassirer for his part asserts that he is not a Neo-Kantian as Heidegger defines Neo-Kantian, and that for two reasons: (1) he inquires into the productive imagination for understanding the symbolic as the basis for a general theory of culture; (2) he sees that the central problem for Kant is ethical: How is freedom possible? In this latter inquiry Kant takes a remarkable step into the supersensible, the *mundus intelligibilis*, wherein he discloses a universal moral law that establishes the reality of freedom. At this point Cassirer challenges Heidegger to make sense of this aspect of Kant on his interpretation. If Heidegger treats Kant as a philosopher of finitude, for whom all knowledge is relative to human *Dasein*, then what place can Kant have for the move into the infinity of the supersensible and the eternal truths of the ethical?

Heidegger's reply is impressive and in part convincing. He notes that in the *Critique* Kant is concerned not with "regional ontologies" of the physical (nature) or the psychic (freedom or culture) but with *metaphysica generalis*, the basis for any ontological inquiry. Heidegger then denies that the move into ethics is for Kant a move into the infinite; ethical imperatives can hold only for finite beings; the moral is identical with autonomous or self-supporting reason and is not derivable from a higher eternal ground; it is the transcending of the creatural that can be carried out only by a finite creature. But now Heidegger calls ethics itself into question, by claiming it is an error to stress the normative function of the moral law. Through self-legislation *Dasein* constitutes itself, thus disclosing the ontological significance of the law. Human existence does partake of a certain infinity, the free "self-giving" or *exhibitio originaria* whereby the transcendental imagination projects Being as a whole. Only a finite creature can have an ontology; God as eternal being has no temporal projection of Being. Thus Heidegger links the moral law to a finite being's understanding of Being as "thrown project": *Dasein*'s projective effort to illuminate Being, which remains fundamentally opaque and mysterious, as simply given to *Dasein* and not created by it.

Then more radically Heidegger asserts: the truth of Being exists only if a finite human being, such as *Dasein*, exists. Eternity has meaning only within such a being's "inner transcendence of time"; there is no eternal "beyond" finite being. He then pronounces the task of his *Destruktion* of the philosophical tradition: his whole critique of that tradition is that only on the basis of time as the gathering together of past, present, and future is anything like substance, *ousia*, idea, and the eternal law intelligible; since antiquity the problem of Being has been interpreted in terms of time, which was always addressed to the subject matter in an unintelligible way. Kant made the first step toward uncovering this presupposition, and to this end he raised the question "What is man?" therewith initiating the metaphysics of *Dasein*. Heidegger says that as with Kant, his raising of the question "What is man?" is not anthropological but metaphysical: it discloses *Dasein*'s temporality as the condition for metaphysics. And as with Kant, his analysis emphasizes the finitude of *Dasein*. Accordingly such anthropological themes as anxiety and living toward death are adduced only for illuminating the structure of human temporality.

Heidegger poses at this point the delicate question of the relation of his philosophy to "worldview," a question that clearly relates to that of the moral significance of freedom. Is Heidegger's analysis of *Dasein* pre-ethical, perhaps ethically neutral? He handles this question with ambiguous, not to say obfuscating, formulations. Philosophy does not have the task of providing a worldview, although worldview is the presupposition of philosophizing. This presupposition is not, however, a doctrine, but solely the philosopher's effort to disclose in the act of philosophizing the highest freedom of human existence. He shows freedom not as an object of theory but as the act of setting free. This at the same time discloses metaphysics as a human happening, as historical. The philosopher pushes human freedom to its limit and forces man to confront at the limit of existence the Nothingness that is inseparable from Being. This exposure of *Dasein* as free is for Heidegger the *terminus a quo* of philosophy, and the entire problematic of his thought. He has not formulated the *terminus ad quem*, which is the first concern of Cassirer, namely, a philosophy of culture. But can Heidegger deny that his renewal of the question of Being is motivated by a view of the worth and end of human existence?

He proceeds to say that the philosophic exposing of the nothingness of human *Dasein* is "not an occasion for pessimism or melancholy." Rather one must grasp that an authentic existence needs opposition and that philosophy must "throw man back into the hardness of his fate, away from the lazy aspect of a man who exploits the work of the spirit." Thus genuine philosophy must be destructive, a radical "bursting open" (*Sprengung*) of tradition, as in the case of Kant, who in attempting to lay the foundation of metaphysics was pressed toward finding that foundation in the abyss (*Abgrund*). The foundation of philosophizing never ceases to be questionable; the *terminus a quo* and the *terminus ad quem* to this extent coincide. The form of life that affirms the inescapable questionability of the starting point is the highest form of existence. Yet man finds himself thrown into Being in a historical, even accidental way. Echoing Aristotle's remark on the nature of the theoretical life, Heidegger says that man is allowed only a few rare glimpses, at the pinnacle of his possibility, of the totality of existence. Otherwise his life is overwhelmed by the beings (*Seienden*) in terms of which he tends to view himself: as something "ontic," an empirically given object, not as the "eccentric" being open to beings as a whole and himself at the same time. Human life ordinarily is either dispersed among beings or withdrawn into itself: the hardest thing is to see that the self is inseparable from Being, openness to which makes possible openness to self.

As an aside, Heidegger remarks that interpreting Kant's problematic in this way precludes viewing it in an "isolated ethical" sense. The radicality of questioning precludes assuming an ethical end or justification for that questioning. Moreover, it seems for Heidegger to preclude an orientation of radical questioning toward the ethical or political questions, as the subject matter for a thinking that tries to answer the question "What is man?" Here Heidegger strikingly separates himself not only from Kant but from the entire tradition of philosophy since Socrates. Still one discerns a certain indebtedness to Kant, who is the first philosopher to propose that the inquiry into the moral, or the good, can be divorced from the nature of man, and in particular, the human

natural concern with happiness. Heidegger advances further in this direction
by divorcing freedom from the good entirely.

IV. THE IDEALISM OF THE *VOLK*

In the memoir of 1945 Heidegger offers a sketch of the philosophic prehistory to his assumption of the rectorate. He mentions first his 1929 Freiburg
inaugural address, "What Is Metaphysics?" whose concern, he notes, was to
uncover the essential ground of the scattered multiplicity of academic disciplines in a concept of truth.[21] It thus took the first step toward a philosophic
reform of the university on the basis of the questioning of *Being and Time*,
which sought the ground of the possibility of metaphysics in the analysis of
human existence as temporal. Heidegger then mentions a seminar and lecture
on Plato, and a lecture on the essence of truth, from the period of 1930–32.[22]
The Plato seminar and lecture are centrally on the cave image of the *Republic*.
One can surmise that Heidegger mentions them because they expound the
basis for an anti-Platonic *paideia*, in which liberation from the cave advances
toward the truth not as *idea* but as the unconcealment (*Unverborgenheit*) of
beings that was uncovered by the pre-Socratic philosophers. Plato's doctrine
ambiguously presupposes and conceals that original ground of thinking, with
fateful consequences for the West. Heidegger claims that these lectures were
censored by the Nazi authorities.[23]

The crucial moment in this prehistory of the rectorate is Heidegger's account of "how he saw the historical situation at that time."[24] In 1930 and 1932
Ernst Jünger published the essay "Total Mobilization" and the book *The
Worker*; Heidegger notes that he discussed these in a small circle with his as-
sistant Brock, and in these discussions Heidegger "tried to show that in these
writings an essential understanding of Nietzsche's metaphysics was expressed,
insofar as in the horizon of this metaphysics the history and the present of the
West were seen and foreseen." The circle reflected on what was coming (*das
Kommende*), and later events, Heidegger adds, confirmed what Jünger fore-
told, namely, the universal domination by the will to power as the planetary
destiny. Nietzsche declared the advent of this reality with his pronouncement
that "God is dead," which expresses not just ordinary atheism but the conviction that within the history of humanity the supersensible world, especially
Christianity, has lost its moving power (*wirkende Kraft*). Heidegger quoted
this line of Nietzsche in the Rectoral Address of 1933.[25] The event of God's
death, Heidegger now states, alone makes intelligible the two world wars. In
sum, Heidegger claims that in the period 1930–33 he became aware of nihil-

ism as planetary destiny, an awareness that forced on him a radicalizing of the problem of the search for the ground of the sciences and the renewal of the university.

It made clear to him the need to reflect on the overcoming of the metaphysics of the will to power through a conversation with the Western tradition that returns to its origin.[26] This remark refers to Heidegger's efforts in the same period to go behind Plato, in whom he saw the roots of the metaphysics of the will to power, to the origin of the West in pre-Socratic thinking about Being. And he now asks rhetorically whether the urgency of the problem did not warrant, for the sake of this reflection on the part of the Germans (*bei uns Deutschen*), awakening and leading into the field (*ins Feld zu führen*) those places that are considered the seat of the pursuit of knowledge and learning—the German university. "With the assumption of the rectorate I dared to make the experiment to save, purify and secure the positive (in the National Socialist movement)."[27]

What did Heidegger see as positive in this movement? He asserts that in the Rectoral Address his attempt was to see beyond the "deficiencies and crudities" of the movement, toward its potential "to bring, one day, a gathering of the Western-historical essence of the German."[28] His failures as administrator, he observes, should not distract from the essential: that we stand in the midst of the consummation of nihilism and the death of God, and every "time-space is closed off from the divine." At the same time "the overcoming of nihilism is announced in German thinking and singing," although the Germans do not perceive this and instead measure themselves by the standards of the prevailing nihilism. Thus they "misunderstand the essence of a historical self-assertion." Heidegger's thought can be reconstructed as follows: only the Germans are capable of leading the West out of nihilism because only they have the capacity to recover the forgotten beginning of the West; if the Germans are to fulfill this mission, they must be led by the spiritual leaders in the universities; the latter must have the support of political authority; only a movement that is both antidemocratic and intent on asserting German superiority among the nations has the requisite authority; such a movement came to power in 1933. Heidegger states that less possibility exists in the present moment of 1945 than existed in 1933 "of opening blinded eyes to a vision of the essential."[29]

Whereas Heidegger carefully grounds his 1933 assertion of the world-historical destiny of the Germans in earlier reflections, it is striking that the writings before 1933 lack stress on Germanness. Section 74 of *Being and Time* briefly connects the resolute affirming of destiny to the history of a people (*Volk*) as the destiny to be affirmed.[30] Yet that work's analysis of human existence as preparation for raising the question of Being does not give a special role to the Germans in fulfilling that analysis. It seems to characterize the human situation in universal and even timeless fashion. According to Heidegger's own account of how his eyes were opened, it was Jünger who portrayed the darkness of the present in such terms as to make evident the need for a radical overcoming of the nihilistic age, through a historical recovery of the origins of the West. Such overcoming, since it was to be realized in the world as a whole and not only in exceptional philosophic individuals, would have to be carried out by a people or folk, the modern successors to the Greeks. In no other way, it appeared to Heidegger in 1933, could the original question of Being be raised again.

This national or *völkisch* grounding of philosophy is found in statements such as this one in the Rectoral Address: "For the Greeks science [*Wissen-schaft*] is not a 'cultural value' [*'Kulturgut'*] but the innermost determining center of the whole popular-national existence [*volklich-staatlichen Dasein*]."[31] For related thoughts one can turn to the lectures of 1935, *Introduction to Metaphysics*, which Heidegger published as a book in 1953.[32] Heidegger writes that philosophy cannot be immediately effective in practical life, or expect resonance quickly, even though it may be in accord with "the inner history of a people."[33] He speaks of the depth of the connection between *Volk* and philosophy in the following: "Philosophy opens up the paths and perspectives for the knowing that establishes measure and rank, in which and out of which a people [*Volk*] grasps its existence [*Dasein*] in the historical-spiritual world, and brings to completion the knowing that inspires, threatens, and necessitates all questioning and judging."[34] Philosophy fulfills the destiny of a people, not by lightening human burdens, as in securing the foundations of a culture, but through inducing struggle and hardship, since these are the condition for greatness.[35] In Heidegger's account the Germans have already been granted the gift of struggle testing them for greatness, by a historical fate that places them in a pincers between Russia and America.[36] These powers embody the technological nihilism of modernity: "The same dreary technological frenzy, the same unrestricted organization of the average man."[37] In this situation the Germans, who are the "metaphysical folk," must decide to move themselves and the history of the West into the primal realm of the powers of Being, or suffer the spiritual annihilation of Europe. The Germans alone can overcome the modern misinterpretation of spirit (*Geist*) as cleverness, technical skill, and cultural value, by raising anew the question of Being.[38]

But how can a folk accomplish this; what does it mean to say that a folk thinks metaphysically? Heidegger in another set of lectures quotes approvingly the line of Hegel that "a cultivated people without a metaphysics is like a richly decorated temple without a Holy of Holies."[39] Yet Heidegger asserts that only a few actually philosophize. "Which few? The creative transformers, the converters." They arouse the folk to gather its forces, teaching it that its destiny is to further philosophical questioning and thereby to assert spiritual leadership in the world. But as in other contexts, Heidegger indicates here a paradoxical character to this effect of the few with respect to the many: the teaching of the thinkers works slowly through imperceptible pathways and detours, until at last their thought is no longer original philosophizing, but "sinks down into the self-evidence of daily existence." It therefore must always be the task of the thinkers to unsettle the comfortable state of metaphysical certainty that eventually arises out of their own thought, and to expose the people once again to the hard truths of their spiritual destiny.

I conclude this discussion with a general observation: the writings of Heidegger that discuss political matters directly show that these are of interest to him only insofar as they can be brought to bear on the renewal of the question of Being. Heidegger's political engagements show that the furthering of that renewal takes precedence over any considerations of the good, the moral, and the just, as these have been understood in the philosophic tradition as having some universal articulation, reflecting ends (happiness, perfection, virtue) inherent in human nature or reason.[40] Indeed for Heidegger the meaning of the renewed question entails a reinterpretation of such concerns as modes of fallenness, to the extent that they tend to be placed ahead of the primary human historical concern of "gathering forces" for the renewing of the question. Such a fall occurs when discussions of National Socialism stress its moral evil rather than inquire about its role in the history of Being's disclosure. It is wrong to think of Heidegger's failure to comment on the moral evil of Nazism as merely a personal failure, unrelated to his thought. Nor can one say that Heidegger simply did not get around to discussing moral good and evil, because his concentration was on the preliminary task of uncovering the ground in Being for such discussion. The turn to Being is understood by Heidegger as entailing a complete reevaluation of the meaning and place of "morality" in human affairs, such as very few people are prepared to undertake or accept—as Heidegger himself discovered.

V. IDEALISM WITHOUT FREEDOM

Heidegger in 1929 and after is forced to confront a certain paradox, not unrelated to one in Kant. On the assumption that human beings possess universally a radical kind of freedom, in an openness to Being that transcends all given beings, how is it that human beings are universally "fallen" into the forgetting of Being? And how has the present age emerged as one of an especially deep forgetfulness? How can freedom be gained and lost, if it has no empirical or ontic basis? Heidegger saw that his move from analysis of *Dasein*'s temporality to Being (*Sein*) itself, by passing through the "destructive" history of the ontology of time, which he planned as the second half of *Being and Time*, could not provide him with the answer to that question. The freedom for openness to Being has been occluded by technological domination of the world; this has its roots not in an ordinary "fallenness" of *Dasein* into beings, but in the planetary-historical fate in which Being withdraws into oblivion. Accordingly Heidegger introduced a new formulation about freedom: man is possessed by freedom, not freedom by man.[41] In the last analysis freedom for openness to Being is a gift of Being, granted to certain peoples in certain epochs.[42] It was such a gift that, in Heidegger's view, Germany and therewith the West were granted in 1933, with the ascent to power of Hitler and his revolution—a gift that was misunderstood and improperly used by the Germans. At the same time, Heidegger's noting the universal fallenness or *Seinsvergessenheit* of the epoch implies a greater gulf between the philosopher and his milieu than was implied in the analysis of *Being and Time*. Even as the philosopher would ground his insight more deeply in the folk's potential for openness to Being, he necessarily separates himself more sharply from its historical actuality. This peculiar combination of identification and distance is possible only on the basis of a transmutation of the folk into the "ideal" such as occurs in Heidegger's thought.

In sum, the radicality of freedom that has no ground in human nature can appear, or disappear, only at the whim of history, or fate, which demands the proper attunement of mankind for its reception. Indeed the promise of such freedom will appear most forcefully in those moments when ordinary reality, with its ontic or merely "natural" concerns, is most threatened with destruction. In this way nihilism, as the complete immersion in beings, can destroy itself when its negative force is turned against the beings, thus compelling human life to be free for openness to Being. The scourge of the earth is its savior: "Where danger is, there grows salvation." Since, however, the promise of the 1933 revolution was not fulfilled, and in 1945 the darkness of the American-Soviet imperium descended over the world, mankind must await, indefinitely and indeterminately, in the long convalescence (*Verwindung*) of the technological world night, for the saving of mankind by other, more efficacious deities than those that appeared in 1933.

Heidegger has a profound grasp of the radicality of philosophical questioning comparable with that of the greatest figures in the tradition.[43] But his divorce of questioning from any natural-teleological basis, for which the German Idealist concepts of freedom helped set the stage, has a paradoxical consequence. Such questioning is unable to see clearly the political-moral phenomena that must nourish it; a questioning that cannot see these phenomena cannot gain true distance on them, and so risks becoming their slave. The paradox is not mitigated if the servitude is not unwitting but voluntary, as in the case of Heidegger.

CHAPTER 5

Heidegger on Nietzsche and the Higher Freedom

I

In his 1946 essay "The Saying of Anaximander," Martin Heidegger writes: "To hunt after dependencies and influences between thinkers is a misunderstanding of thinking. Every thinker is dependent, namely on the address of Being [*vom Zuspruch des Seins*]. The extent of this dependency determines the freedom from distracting influences. The broader the dependency, the more capacious is the freedom of thinking, and therefore more powerful the danger that it will wander past what was once thought, only perhaps to think the same [*das Selbe*]."[1] In referring to the dependency of the thinker on history—and for Heidegger "history" is the history of Being, of course—Heidegger speaks of a realm of freedom that is also a realm of danger. For Heidegger, genuine freedom exists only in the response to an address, or challenge, from somewhere beyond the individual's will. The address can be overpowering, even to the point of obliterating insight into crucial differences. Indeed this result is inherent in the address of Being, in that Being must suffer oblivion that is "by no means the result of forgetfulness of thinking, but belongs to that essence of Being which it itself conceals." Insofar as Being (*Sein*) tends to be hidden by the very beings (*Seienden*) that it makes available, and this self-hiding belongs even to the most essential thinking, Heidegger surely does not exempt his own thinking from the dangers of distortion and failure. Danger belongs to the freedom of thinking. Heidegger also avows the power exerted by certain earlier thinkers within his own thinking, and Nietzsche is not least among these. In being addressed by Being with or through Nietzsche, Heidegger is exposed to the danger of uncovering only "the same" in Nietzsche and missing what was "once thought."

In a 1936 comment on Hegel's relation to Schelling, Heidegger writes: "The greatest thinkers can fundamentally never understand each other, precisely because they desire the same [*dasselbe*] in the shape of their own greatness. If they desired what is different, then mutual understanding, that is, indulging another [*das Gewähren lassen*] would not be so difficult."[2] The greatest thinkers are addressed by the greatest question, the question of Being, in which their thought is taken up in a radical dependence on the matter to be thought. This is very unlike ordinary thinking, in which the thinker maintains a safe distance between himself and the object of his thought. The philosopher can lose sight of the individual standpoint from which he thinks the greatest questions, and also lose sight of the standpoint from which another thinker approaches them, as well. If there is some inevitable misunderstanding of Nietzsche from Heidegger's side, it takes place through the freedom of the thinker, a freedom that is based on radical dependence. Nietzsche and Heidegger, the thinkers, share the gift and the danger of this radical freedom. Is it possible that they share the question of freedom itself, of the freedom of thinking? If the freedom of thinking claims and addresses both thinkers, perhaps they share in that thinking similar questions about dependency and freedom, and about freedom and danger. Perhaps this configuration belongs to the same, *das Selbe*, that they think.

Again the 1936 Schelling lectures offer illumination: "The treatise of Schelling [on the essence of human freedom] has nothing to do with the question of freedom of the will, which in the end is posed perversely, and therefore is no question. For here freedom means not an attribute of the human, but the opposite: the human is above all the property [*Eigentum*] of freedom. Freedom is the encompassing and pervasive essence in which the human is embedded, and first becomes human. This is to say, the essence of the human is freedom."[3] Here Heidegger speaks for himself and not only for Schelling, it can be said. Of course it is risky to take the language of Heidegger's reading of another philosopher and to regard it as adequate to Heidegger's own thinking. But what is undoubtedly Heidegger's own language (if it can be said that language ever unquestionably belongs to the speaker) is from the essay "On the Essence of Truth," first published in 1943. "The essence of truth is freedom," Heidegger writes. "Resistance to this statement loses itself in prejudices, which in their most stubborn form declare that freedom is an attribute of the human. The essence of freedom needs and endures no further inquiry."[4] And further, "Freedom for the disclosure of the open [*Offenbaren eines Offen*] allows each of the beings to be what it is. Freedom reveals itself as the letting-be of the beings."[5] Freedom therefore is not something over which the human has power. "The human 'possesses' freedom not as an attribute, but rather the opposite is above all the case: freedom, the existing disclosing *Da-Sein*, possesses the human, and this in such an original way that only freedom provides to a given form of the human a relation to beings as a whole that first grounds and makes out history."[6] Insofar as freedom grounds the historical existence of the human in which beings are disclosed, freedom as the essence of truth is inseparable from the truth of Being.

II

Where in Nietzsche could Heidegger find traces of this thought on freedom? Is not the language of freedom the language of German Idealism, which Heidegger appropriates from Kant, Schelling, and Hegel to uncover what is unthought in it with respect to the relation of freedom to truth? Yet surely Nietzsche, too, has an account of freedom, in which he also distinguishes the true meaning of freedom from freedom of the will, while stressing his opposition to the "intelligible world" of Kantian freedom. Indeed in the lectures of 1951–52, *What Is Called Thinking?* Heidegger gives a central place to Nietzsche's thought on freedom in his presentation of the problematic of what thinking is. At the beginning of lecture 6, Heidegger states: "With greater clarity than any man before him Nietzsche saw the necessity of a change in the realm of essential thinking." He was "the first man to recognize clearly, and the only man so far to think through metaphysically and in all its implications, the moment when man is about to assume dominion of the earth as a whole."[7] Heidegger says that Nietzsche saw that the man of today is faced with hitherto unknown decisions. The assumption of dominion over the earth poses the question of worldwide government. Has the man of today given thought to the conditions for such government? Is modern man prepared to manage the powers of technology and ready to address the unfamiliar decisions of world rule? "Nietzsche's answer to these questions is *No*." Heidegger continues: "There is the danger that the thought of man today will fall short of the decisions that are coming, decisions of whose specific historical shape we can know nothing."[8]

Let us pause for a moment. Heidegger's language lets us see that the historical moment, or Being in its present historical disclosure, calls for attentive listening and receptive thinking, but also for decision. And herein lies a danger, since the needed decision may be neglected, or the wrong decision may be taken. Here within the response to the historical we have a glimpse of freedom, the freedom to decide and act in response to the disclosure of Being. Nietzsche was the first to see clearly the challenge of the historical moment, and the danger of failure it poses, and thus he was the first to grasp clearly the demands made by freedom in this moment. Heidegger proceeds to find authority in Nietzsche's writing for this view of the present. But first he notes that the Second World War "decided nothing," that is, it contributed nothing to deciding "man's essential fate on this earth."[9] European culture has not yet risen to the challenge that Nietzsche addressed to it. The weakness was manifest in the crucial decade following World War I, when Europe was unable to come to terms with what was looming on the horizon. But Nietzsche foresaw this weakness in the summer of 1888, in his diagnosis of the modern situation entitled "Critique of Modernity," an aphorism of *Twilight of the Idols*. Heidegger quotes a substantial part of the aphorism, and I here reproduce that portion:

Our institutions are good for nothing anymore; on this point all agree. However, it is not their fault but *ours*. Now that we have mislaid all the instincts from which institutions grow, we lose institutions altogether because *we* are no longer good for them. Democracy has always been the form of decline of organizing power: in *Human, All Too Human* I, 349 (1878) I already characterized modern democracy, together with its mongrel forms such as the "German Reich," as the *form of decline of the state*. If there are to be institutions there must be a kind of will, instinct, imperative, antiliberal to the point of malice: the will to tradition, to authority, to responsibility for centuries to come, to the *solidarity* of chains of generations forward and backward ad infinitum. When that will is present, something like the *Imperium Romanum* is founded: or something like Russia, the *only* power today that has endurance in its bones, that can wait, that still can have promise—Russia the counterconcept to that miserable European particularism and nervousness which has entered a critical condition with the formation of the German Reich. . . . The whole West no longer possesses those instincts out of which institutions grow, out of which a *future* grows; nothing else, perhaps, goes so much against the grain of its "modern spirit." Men live for the day, men live very fast—men live very irresponsibly: precisely this is called "freedom." The thing that *makes* an institution an institution is despised, hated, rejected: men fear they are in danger of a new slavery the moment the word "authority" is even mentioned.[10]

Heidegger follows the quotation with five observations: (1) Nietzsche in these remarks not only comments on current politics but indicates that human nature is not yet "fully developed and secured," and is thus unprepared for the great decisions ahead; (2) The human is not yet secured because, on the basis of Western thinking, it lacks unity and is divided into separate and clashing elements, the rational and the animal. "This rupture prevents man from possessing unity of nature and thus *being free* for what we normally call the real"; (3) Nietzsche's doctrine of the superman (*Übermensch*) is the account of how we must go beyond man as he is, into a complete determination of man, a determination that leaves behind our "boundless, purely quantitative, nonstop progress": (4) The supermen will appear in small numbers, after a new "rank order has been carried out" that rejects the doctrine that all men are equal; (5) Hölderlin's words on Christ as brother of Hercules and Dionysus announce "a still unspoken gathering of the whole of Western fate," from which the West "can go forth to meet the coming decisions—to become, perhaps and in a wholly other mode, a land of dawn, the Orient."[11]

Central to Nietzsche's analysis and Heidegger's sympathetic reading of it is the critique of the democratic account of freedom, as a mere freedom from, not a freedom for—a freedom that flies from the great responsibility of building an enduring civilization, a task that calls for the rejection of equality and for the revering of rank and authority. Freedom in the higher sense is the acceptance of a historical task and the readiness to make difficult decisions for it. But this requires that the dispersed elements of human nature be drawn together in a new unity, overcoming traditional distinctions of body and spirit, faith and reason. This new ordering of life cannot rely on common conceptions and demands a way of thinking remote from that found in "the public figures who in the course of current history emerge in the limelight."[12]

Heidegger does not comment on the aphorism of Nietzsche just preceding the "critique of modernity," but it bears very much on the questions at stake and has the heading "My conception of freedom."[13] I will quote a few lines. "The value of a thing sometimes lies not in what one obtains with it, but in what one pays for it, what it costs us." Liberal institutions are valuable only as long as we are fighting for them; then they promote freedom. War is a training in freedom. "For what is freedom? That one has the will to self-responsibility. . . . How is freedom measured, in individuals and in nations? By the resistance that has to be overcome, by the effort it costs to stay *aloft*." Great danger is what makes nations and individuals great. "First principle: one must need strength, otherwise one will never have it." Closely related is another aphorism entitled "Freedom as I *do not* mean it . . ."[14] The modern ideas of freedom—"the claim to independence, to free development, to *laisser aller*"—are symptoms of decadence, of degeneration of instinct. "Today the only way of making the individual possible would be by *pruning* him: possible, that is to say *complete*."

It is not hard to find the spiritual affinity between these remarks and Heidegger's thoughts on the essence of freedom as the affirmation of historical dependence, or fate, and the call to higher decisions, the exposure to danger, that such freedom brings. Freedom is not the arbitrary exercise of individual will but the gathering of forces into a true unity—a higher completion of the human that overcomes age-old distinctions and divisions. But freedom in this sense entails the transcending of the human as it has been known. It is the surpassing of metaphysical thinking, the forgetfulness of Being, which is not a movement toward a determinate goal, since we face decisions "of whose specific historical shape we can know nothing." "What is most thought-provoking in our thought-provoking time is that we are still not thinking." The "still not," Heidegger notes, does not mean that we are not thinking at all, and it does not mean that we can simply put behind us, at will, a certain failure in thinking. It implies that we are already on the way to a thinking that eludes the forms of representation to which Western man is accustomed. The prospect cannot, therefore, be described in terms of palpable outcomes—pessimistically or optimistically—such as representational thought expects and demands. "The thought-provoking thing turns away from us, in fact has long since turned away from man." The withdrawing of the thought-provoking, of Being, is what properly gives food for thought. In this way it develops its nearness, and whoever is drawn into this withdrawing is drawn "into the enigmatic and therefore mutable nearness of its appeal."[15] "And what is most thought-provoking—especially when it is man's highest concern—may well be also what is most dangerous. Or do we imagine that a man could even in small ways encounter the essence of truth, the essence of beauty, the essence of grace—without danger?"[16] Nietzsche saw our time as the time of the growing wasteland and of the approaching reign of the nihilism of the "last man." The response to this possible event cannot be an appeal to "common sense," the fruit of Enlightenment thinking about human improvement. The response involves a higher freedom, the freedom of the opening to a thinking beyond the representational. And it is to such thinking that Nietzsche's highest thoughts—the will to power, the superman, and the eternal recurrence of the same—point us.

But Nietzsche is only a pointer. His "thinking gives voice and language to what now *is*—but in a language in which the two-thousand-year-old thinking of Western metaphysics speaks, a language that we all speak, that Europe speaks."[17] Nietzsche begins a profound analysis of the account of reason, of *ratio*, as culminating in the last man's forming of ideas to reckon with things. "Nietzsche calls it blinking, without relating blinking explicitly to the nature of representing or idea-forming, without inquiring into the essential sphere, and above all the essential origin, of representational ideas."[18] Nietzsche still thinks in metaphysical terms of a deliverance from nihilistic thinking, the thinking that is the revenge against time. In particular, he thinks in the terms of the metaphysics of the modern era, which determines the Being of beings as will. Once again Heidegger calls on the authority of Schelling: "In the final and highest instance, there is no being other than willing. Willing is primal being, and to it alone belong all predicates: being unconditioned, eternity, independence of time, self-affirmation. All philosophy strives only to find this highest expression."[19] Heidegger remarks that Nietzsche thinks the same thing as Schelling when he defines the primal nature of Being as will to power. Schelling and Nietzsche share the distinction of being thinkers who, while still thinking metaphysically, all the same point toward postmetaphysical thinking—and this is for both a thinking centrally about freedom. It is the freedom that appropriates man, that is not a property of man. What these philosophers still did not see or say is that such freedom appropriates man not as will but as the opening of Being in history, the opening that is more primordial than willing and the representational thinking grounded in willing. But both thinkers had the sense of a fundamental crisis in Western life, the sense that man is faced with unprecedented catastrophe. Heidegger takes up this theme. The opening to Being as historical is inseparable from danger and destruction—it calls for the destruction that occurs through and then ultimately to the representational thinking grounded in willing. The summons of fate is the exposure to death, to the nothingness of the "sound common sense" of modern life. "Nietzsche sees clearly that in the history of Western man something is coming to an end; what until now and long since has remained uncompleted, Nietzsche sees the necessity to carry to a completion."[20]

III

Nihilism, or the oblivion of Being, must be carried toward and through the end point, in order to arrive at another beginning. That Heidegger held something akin to this view as early as 1929, while commenting on Kant, and before his close engagement with Nietzsche, can be gathered from his disputation with Cassirer at Davos. Once again the language of the argument is the language of freedom. "Freedom is not an object of theoretical apprehending" but "the setting free," or the "self-freeing of freedom in man." "The setting free of the *Dasein* in man must be the sole and central thing that philosophy as philosophizing can perform."[21] Such freedom is evident in Kant's "radical bursting open" of the traditional concept of ontology, through which he found himself pressed toward the grounding of ontology in an abyss (*Abgrund*). Thus Kant grasped that "the freeing of the inner transcendence of *Dasein* is the fundamental character of philosophy itself," a "becoming free for the finitude of *Dasein*. . . . Just to come into the thrownness of *Dasein* is to come into the conflict that lies within the essence of freedom."[22] Philosophy has the task of "throwing man back into the hardness of his fate," so as to make manifest to him "the nothingness of his *Dasein*." "This nothingness is the occasion not for pessimism . . . but for understanding that authentic activity takes place only where there is opposition."[23] In this period of fruitful appropriation of Kant, Heidegger seeks to show that "the question of the possibility of metaphysics demands a metaphysics of *Dasein*," which moves beyond anthropological thinking about man. Therefore Heidegger still speaks the language of metaphysics. Freedom and the setting free of *Dasein* are bound up with the conception of the transcendental horizon of the thrown project, with its obvious Kantian roots.

According to Heidegger's 1945 thoughts expressed in "The Rectorate 1933/34," Nietzsche's thought as mediated by Ernst Jünger had a decisive role in changing this orientation. Heidegger (participating in the early 1930s in a Jünger reading circle) found that Jünger clarified the historical situation of the West on the basis of an "essential understanding of the metaphysics of Nietzsche" within whose horizon the "history and the present of the West were seen and foreseen."[24] "What Ernst Jünger thinks in the thoughts of the dominion and shape of the worker, and what he sees in light of this thought, is the universal dominion of the will to power, viewed within planetary history. . . . From this reality of the will to power I then saw already what *is*. The reality of the will to power lets itself be announced, as Nietzsche means it, in the sentence 'God is dead.'" Heidegger then asks: "Did this not offer sufficient ground and essential urgency to think ahead in original reflection toward the overcoming of the metaphysics of the will to power, that is, to begin a conversation with Western thought by a return to its beginning?"[25] In light of the planetary situation of nihilism, there can be no freeing of the inner transcendence of *Dasein* without first an uprooting of the metaphysics that dominates the present, which in turn requires a recovery of the entire history of Being in the West. Nietzsche is at once guide and obstacle to such recovery and uprooting. But Nietzsche saw the necessity for the true thinkers to assume responsibility for the destiny of Western man, which means, in the first place, to carry the metaphysics of the will to its radical completion.

There is clearly no radical break in Heidegger's thought, no specific date at which a turn begins, and *die Kehre* has too many aspects to be subsumable under a formula. But one could speak of a shift in the meaning of freedom as central to the development of Heidegger's thought in the 1930s, insofar as freedom, in the highest sense, assumes the task of the appropriation of history for the overcoming of nihilism. This is at the heart of the turn to *Seinsgeschichte* and to the effort to recover the historical opening of Being in Parmenides and Heraclitus at the start of Western thinking. In the early 1930s Heidegger sees this task as falling not just to himself and thinkers who shared his way but to the German people as a whole. The fate of philosophy is directly linked to the fate of particular peoples. As Heidegger writes in the Rectoral Address, "For the Greeks science [*Wissenschaft*] is not a 'cultural value' but the innermost determining center of the whole popular-national *Dasein*."[26] The 1935 lectures *Introduction to Metaphysics* continue this theme: "Philosophy opens up the paths and perspectives for the knowing that establishes measure and rank, in which and out of which a *Volk* grasps its *Dasein* in the historical-spiritual world, and brings to completion the knowing that inspires, threatens, and necessitates all questioning and judging."[27] Philosophy both discloses the essence of a people and fulfills its destiny. Surely with the emphasis on Western metaphysics as destiny Heidegger at this time moves closer to Schelling and Hegel, as well as Nietzsche. It is Hegel who writes, "a cultivated people without a metaphysics is like a richly decorated temple without a Holy of Holies," a maxim that Heidegger quotes in his lectures on Parmenides.[28] In the mid-1930s, even after the disenchantment of the rectoral year, Heidegger has hopes that the renewal of the West will arise out of Europe and particularly out of *das Land in der Mitte*. But in 1945 Heidegger writes that less possibility exists "now" than before the war "of opening blinded eyes to a vision of the essential."[29] And we have read the endorsement in *What Is Called Thinking?* of Nietzsche's judgment on the "miserable particularism" of Europe. After 1945 Heidegger does not entertain hopes of the renewal of Europe through political movements or political actions of any kind.

I V

I wish to dwell for a while on the account of historical destiny in *Introduction to Metaphysics* for the light it sheds on the higher freedom as Heidegger conceives it in the 1930s, and the place of Nietzsche's thought in that conception. One has to bear in mind that this writing belongs to the era of Heidegger's engagement, albeit wavering, in contemporary politics. The Germans, being singled out for a philosophical destiny, are as such exposed to great hardship. Philosophy fulfills the destiny of a people not by lightening burdens, or by securing the ground of culture, but through the knowing embrace of struggles that bring forth qualities of greatness.[30] The Germans have been granted the gift of struggle by being placed in a pincers between America and Russia. These powers embody the technological nihilism of modernity and its extreme egalitarian ethos: "The same dreary technological frenzy, the same unrestricted organization of the average man."[31] Heidegger echoes Nietzsche's aperçu on the spiritually flattening preoccupation with speed and efficiency. "Time is nothing but speed, instantaneity, and simultaneity; time as history has vanished from the *Dasein* of all peoples." This is a time of decision, above all for the Germans who, as *das metaphysische Volk*, have the calling to overcome the modern manifestation of spirit (*Geist*) as cleverness, technical skill, and cultural value.[32] "The people will acquire a fate from its vocation only when it creates in itself a resonance . . . and grasps its tradition creatively." This, then, is the highest freedom, whereby a people moves itself and the history of the West into the originary realm of the powers of Being. Such freedom is the response to Being, in raising anew the question "How does it stand with Being?" The question is raised "*not* in order to compose an ontology in the traditional style," but rather "the point is to restore the historical *Dasein* of human beings."[33]

But the notion of a metaphysical people contains an inherent problem, and it poses a special danger to the philosopher who speaks for the metaphysical spirit. Those who actually philosophize are few. Which few? They are "the creative transformers, the converters." They arouse the people to gather its forces, to assert its spiritual leadership. All the same, philosophic thought works mostly in indirect ways, on imperceptible pathways and detours, and in the end, the thought that gets wide currency is no longer philosophy but thought that has sunk down into the self-evidence of daily existence.[34] The summons to move thought beyond representational thinking, beyond the formulaic, becomes itself the accepted rule of life and another form of sound common sense. Therefore the genuinely creative thinker must be the destroyer not only of accustomed ways but of his own ways, once they harden into the familiar. The thinker who attempts to make a new beginning finds his thought unable to hold the beginning as original and sees it pass before his eyes into an established way. There can be no definitive surpassing of merely representational thinking; genuine thinking is perpetual war, *polemos*. The originating thinkers of the tradition, Sophocles, Parmenides, and Heraclitus, were fully aware of this paradox. In the exegesis of the first choral ode of *Antigone*, the account of man as the most uncanny (*das Unheimlichste, to deinataton*) of beings, Heidegger writes that "those who rise high in historical Being as creators, as doers," are necessarily "violence doers" who become "*apolis*, without city and site, lonesome, uncanny, with no way out amidst beings as a whole, and at the same time without ordinance and limit, without structure and fittingness [*Fug*], because they *as* creators must first ground all of this in each case."[35] Their difficulty belongs to the structure of Being itself, since the overwhelming power of Being as *dike* must be disclosed through the gathering force of human *techne*, with the *polis* as the site of this encounter. The gathering of *techne* and *logos*, which brings Being into disclosure, also must conceal what it gathers. "The uncanniest (the human being) is what it is because from the ground up it deals with and conceives the familiar only in order to break out of it and let what overwhelms it break in." Heidegger observes that this authentic poetic-philosophic thinking of the early Greeks is fundamentally at odds with later thinking in terms of "moral appraisal."[36]

V

In *Introduction to Metaphysics* Heidegger avows his debt to Nietzsche's interpretation of the Greeks. "Nietzsche did reconceive the great age of the inception of Greek *Dasein* in its entirety in a way that is surpassed only by Hölderlin."[37] Specifically, in the account of *Dasein* as the self-transcending of the familiar toward Being as the overpowering, and the struggle of *techne* with *dike*, one sees a kinship with Nietzsche's encounter between Apollonian limits and the overwhelming force of the Dionysian. Heidegger already points to this connection in the 1929–30 lectures, *The Fundamental Concepts of Metaphysics*, where he notes that Nietzsche offers the deepest account of our contemporary situation through his analysis of the Greek world and especially in certain passages from *The Will to Power*.

> I was fundamentally concerned with nothing other than surmising why precisely the Greek Apollonian had to grow out of a Dionysian understanding: the Dionysian Greek needed to become Apollonian: that is, to shatter his will for the immense, for the multiple, the uncertain, the horrifying, upon a will for measure, for simplicity, for classification in rules and concepts. . . . Beauty is not bestowed on the Greek, just as little as logic, or as naturalness of morals,—it is captured, willed, fought for—it is his *conquest*.[38]

Let us restate this in Heidegger's terms. The Dionysian, overpowering force of Being cannot be disclosed, brought into the open, without gathering into limits, which is the work of *logos* and *techne*. The freedom in human *Dasein* of the letting-be of beings is the freedom of a violent, dangerous act, which ventures into the groundless and unfathomable, for it acts on behalf of the overpowering force even as it gives it measure and form. The higher destiny of the Greeks is to confront the power of Being and to preserve that power in the great works of poetry and philosophy, and also in the state, the temples, and the gods, which express not simple repose but the striving to disclose the force of *phusis*, the emerging of Being into presence, without reducing it to the familiar, the calculable, and the common.

The noble form of freedom in both thinkers is avowedly paradoxical. The higher power, the Dionysian or *phusis*, appropriates the human, and the human is thus moved toward a new completion, a transformation in a higher unity, a new gathering of forces. At the same time, every determination, every gathering is inherently partial, mutable, tentative. *Logos*, even or especially as great poetry and philosophy, cannot uncover an authoritative law for humanity as a whole. Indeed the establishment of stable, permanent laws runs contrary to the ground of human excellence, which lies in being tested by struggle and conflict. Philosophy, indeed, is the highest awareness of the provisionality of all articulations of Being. Heidegger thus writes of philosophic interpretation:

> There is no universal schema that could be applied mechanically to the interpretation of writings of thinkers, or even to a single work of a single thinker. A dialogue of Plato, for example the *Phaedrus*, the conversation on the beautiful, can be interpreted in totally different spheres and respects, according to totally different implications and problematics. This multiplicity of possible interpretations does not discredit the strictness of thought content.... Rather, multiplicity of meanings is the element in which all thought must move in order to be strict thought.[39]

Furthermore, the purest thinker, who remains drawn into that which withdraws, is like Socrates a thinker who does not commit thinking to writing. "For anyone who begins to write out of thoughtfulness must inevitably be like those people who run to seek refuge from any draft too strong for them. An as yet hidden history still keeps the secret why all great Western thinkers after Socrates, with all their greatness, had to be such fugitives."[40]

Can this highest philosophic freedom, this resistance to simplification and reduction, this rigorous openness to the elusive complexity of the whole of Being—can this be the completion of humanity for which the thinker after Nietzsche is hoping and waiting? Is it conceivable as a general condition for humanity? Is it thinkable that philosophy or some other postphilosophical thinking would ever overcome the human tendencies to rely on the familiar stabilities of the calculable, the easily recognized, and the average—on unreflective *nomoi*? If the highest truths cannot even be faithfully preserved in writing, how can the highest freedom be realized in the human world as a whole—in a "new beginning"? In both Nietzsche and Heidegger the involvement of philosophy in legislative projects is ambiguous and tentative—or it becomes so for Heidegger after the 1930s. The new dispensation of the sway of *phusis* eludes the control of the human philosopher-legislator or philosopher-poet, who finds that his meditation on the higher freedom takes him down solitary paths far from the prevailing *nomoi*, to say nothing of the centers of political authority. This does not affect, however, the persisting tone of expectation or call for extraordinary changes in the political world whose means of actualization are left unexplained. Heidegger rejects the Greek classical account of the philosophic life as radically detached from hopes and expectations concerning the fate of the *nomos*, beyond the prudential regard for nontyrannical rule as providing necessary conditions for that life. Such conceiving of philosophy is not sufficiently tragic.

I close with passages that reveal Nietzsche's awareness of the paradox of his own project. Again they are taken from *Twilight of the Idols*. Nietzsche announces his "great liberation," in which "the innocence of becoming is restored."

> We invented the concept 'purpose'; in reality purpose is *lacking*: one is necessary, one is a piece of fate, one belongs to the whole, one is *in* the whole—there exists nothing that could judge, measure, compare, condemn our being, for that would be to judge, measure, condemn the whole. . . . But *nothing exists apart from the whole*.[41]

Nietzsche later speaks of Goethe as the last German before whom he feels reverence, for Goethe attained the liberation Nietzsche teaches:

> A spirit thus emancipated stands in the midst of the universe with a joyful and trusting fatalism, in the *faith* that only what is separate and individual may be rejected, that in the totality everything is redeemed and affirmed—*he no longer denies*. . . . But such a faith is the highest of all possible faiths: I have baptized it with the name *Dionysos*.[42]

But who are, who can be, the adherents of this faith? In the next aphorism Nietzsche tells the reader that in a sense the nineteenth century's striving was the same as Goethe's, and yet the result was "a chaos, a nihilistic sigh, a not knowing which way to turn," and he asks whether it is not possible that Goethe was "not only for Germany, but for all Europe, merely an episode, a beautiful 'in vain'?" He concludes with a remark that could be put next to Heidegger's description of Socrates:

> But one misunderstands great human beings, if one views them from the paltry perspective of public utility. That one does not know how to make use of it *perhaps even pertains* to greatness.[43]

CHAPTER 6

The Room for Political Philosophy: Strauss on Heidegger's Political Thought

I

In the essay that is his final extended statement on Heidegger, Strauss defines political philosophy as the inquiry "concerned with the best or just political order which is by nature best or just everywhere and always" and observes that "in the last two generations political philosophy has lost its credibility."[1] In a remarkable change this inquiry has "lost its credibility in proportion as politics itself has become more philosophic than ever in a sense" for "throughout its whole history political philosophy was universal while politics was particular." Political events are now globally connected, such that unrest in an American city "has repercussions in Moscow, Peking, Johannesburg, Hanoi, London, and other far away places." Politics has become universal, or at least it cannot be as wholly focused as in earlier times on "the being and well-being of this or that particular society (a polis, a nation, an empire)." Implicit in Strauss's observation is the global transformation of politics in the modern era by political philosophy of Western origin with a universal purpose. Philosophy in the modern era became more active and charitable (and less contemplative and proud) as it undertook a universal practical project: "the relief of man's estate" by science and technology, the promotion of prosperity and the rights of man, the creation of a league of free and equal nations.[2] Accordingly it thought that its highest philosophical ends could be adequately realized in the realm of practice. By contrast premodern political philosophy reflected on what is "by nature best" but accepted with resignation the unlikelihood of its achievement in any particular society. Politics as a practical art, although enlightened by philosophers, acknowledged this limitation and pursued the best possible as allowed by the local conditions and character of given societies.

The present situation contains a profound paradox insofar as universalist politics, the product of universalist political philosophy, is no longer supported by belief in the principles of modern political philosophy or indeed any political philosophy. Strauss characterizes this situation as the "crisis of the West," which is above all a crisis of political philosophy.[3] Political philosophy has been discredited by two powerful forms of thought, positivism and existentialism, according to which "the validation of sound value judgments" is impossible. Positivism holds that only scientific knowledge is genuine knowledge, and such knowledge is unable to validate or invalidate any value judgments. Existentialism holds that "all principles of understanding and of action are historical, i.e., have no other ground than groundless human decision or fateful dispensation."[4] According to existentialism, science has no claim to be more "than one form of viewing the world among many of viewing the world," and what is more, its separation of fact from value is untenable. This however does not mean that existentialism provides a nonarbitrary grounding of values, since for existential thought any supposition of a universal value is a mere prejudice.

The opening paragraph of Strauss's essay lays out in compressed fashion what is probably his best-known account of political philosophy and of the contemporary modes of thought opposing it. According to this account, political philosophy is an inquiry with a practical orientation or purpose (knowledge of the order of society that is by nature best), although in the classical version Strauss advocates, this inquiry has limited practical ambitions. It serves political life (and by extension morality) through uncovering absolute, universally valid notions of virtue, justice, and natural right, or by the "validation of sound value judgments." Its principles, while universal in character (the object of *scientia* in the premodern sense), always have particular applications that cannot dispense with prudence. Positivism and existentialism oppose the possibility of such science with "relativistic" accounts of "values," and accordingly the first task in the recovery of the possibility of classical political philosophy is to expose the fallacies of relativistic thought and to open the way at least for the discovery of absolute notions of virtue, justice, and right.

This foreground account of his intentions, which Strauss surely intends to be widely taken as the true account, is misleading about his ultimate theoretical concerns. (In the essay under consideration Strauss says that "all outstanding thinkers" are misunderstood by their critics and their followers.) For the latter one must look at Strauss's account of Socrates's turn to the study of the human things as the core of philosophy or the "first philosophy," whereby "the political things, or the human things, are the key to understanding all things."[5] Political philosophy as Socrates founded it has a practically oriented side, giving counsel and beneficial teachings to statesman and politically ambitious young men, but at the highest level the inquiry into political matters is to lead to the philosophic life and specifically to a way of philosophizing in which those political matters reveal something fundamental about the nature of the whole. Political philosophy is not merely one discipline among a number of philosophic disciplines, as it appears to be for Aristotle and as it certainly is in the Christian Aristotelian tradition. In a striking reversal of this traditional approach, Strauss argues that through reflection on the prephilosophic experience of political life, which everywhere puts on exhibit the particulars of political life (as in the great political histories of Thucydides and Xenophon), human thought has its only access to the universals, and indeed only in the form of "fundamental problems." Strauss, it must be said, has little hope of reversing the contemporary crisis of liberal political philosophy, and even credits Heidegger with exposing the failure of liberal rationalism. Through Heidegger "all rational liberal philosophic positions have lost their significance and power. One may deplore this, but I for one cannot bring myself to clinging to philosophic positions which have been shown to be inadequate."[6] Strauss all the same proposes an alternative to Heidegger's philosophy, his account of Socratic political philosophy. This will not supply the absolute standards or principles needed to buttress Western democratic rationalism, but in some fashion it replies to "radical historicism." Several questions press on the reader at this point. If there is a link, as Strauss asserts on several occasions, between that historicism and Heidegger's support of Nazism, where is the guidance in Socratic thought toward a nontyrannical politics? What is the standard for political choices that replaces "history" if it is not knowledge of moral-political absolutes?

One can begin with an argument Strauss makes in the present essay and elsewhere, that historicist thought makes a comprehensive, transhistorical claim about all thought as conditioned by history. The claim cannot be saved as coherent unless it arises through an "absolute moment" in which the essential character of all thought becomes transparent, by an insight that no future changes of thought could render obsolete.[7] There is a Hegelian version of the absolute moment, in which the solution to the fundamental problems is revealed through the completion of the experience of history as a rational process, and there is Heidegger's version in which "the insoluble character of the fundamental riddles has become fully manifest."[8] It seems at first as though Strauss needs to refute the insolubility thesis in order to oppose historicism. "Historicism, however, stands or falls by the denial of the possibility of theoretical metaphysics and of philosophic ethics or natural right; it stands or falls by the denial of the solubility of the fundamental riddles." And yet he swiftly changes the ground of attack and asserts: "But one might realize the insoluble character of the fundamental riddles and still continue to see in the understanding of these riddles the task of philosophy; one would thus merely replace a non-historicist and dogmatic philosophy by a non-historicist and skeptical philosophy." Historicism goes beyond skepticism in regarding the "attempt to replace opinions about the whole by knowledge of the whole" as "not only incapable of reaching its goal but absurd," because that attempt rests on dogmatic premises that are only historical and relative. The skeptic, on the other hand, regards philosophy as possible in that it can replace opinions about the fundamental problems with knowledge of them. It does so without a theoretical metaphysics, philosophic ethics, or philosophy of natural right. Contrary to the claims of historicism, classical philosophy is not "based on the unwarranted belief that the whole is intelligible," for the "prototype of the philosopher in the classical sense was Socrates, who knew that he knew nothing, who therewith admitted that the whole is not intelligible, who merely wondered whether by saying that the whole is not intelligible we do not admit to having some understanding of the whole." He adds that "man as man necessarily has some awareness of the whole."[9] I venture to restate this another way: Human thought can grasp that life in the political realm or the "cave" necessarily discloses itself as incomplete, as defective, and pointing beyond itself to the "whole" of which it is a part, and conversely it can understand that the only way knowledge of the whole can be pursued is by starting in the political realm and reflecting on its character. (In this sentence a crucial word, found twice, is "that.") These insights constitute some understanding of the whole without the assumption that the whole is intelligible.

Heidegger's position that all thought is dependent on fate or an unforeseeable dispensation of Being is attractive to contemporaries, Strauss notes, since it denies that history is a rational process.[10] It is appealing for its seemingly nondogmatic character. All the same, it is a dogmatic thesis proposing a comprehensive account of the nature and limits of thought. Heidegger was aware of this difficulty, Strauss notes, and found it necessary to go beyond the early "existential" standpoint wherein all comprehensive views are projects or ideals grounded in resolute willing, in order to expound an account of the history of Being as offering an "eschatological prospect." Thereby his thought acquired a structure recalling the accounts of history in Hegel, Marx, and Nietzsche.[11] In a manner that can strike one as paradoxical, Strauss regards political

philosophy as offering an antidote to the implicit dogmatism of these philosophies that variously call for a disclosure of a final truth in history. At the same
time, it accepts as a comprehensive claim the thesis that the whole is not intelligible. Socratic political philosophy rests on the insight into a permanent rift in
the human condition between philosophic *eros* and the requirements of political life that renders impossible a comprehensive account of thought as either
limited to the disclosures of history or, alternatively, as wholly at home in the
political realm. This insight, although it constitutes another comprehensive
claim about a limitation of human thought, is not a self-refuting one, Strauss
claims, for it articulates a permanent problem in the human approach to the
whole without proposing an absolute thesis about the grounds that condition
all thinking.

Strauss's response to Heidegger combines a version of Heidegger's claim
that the whole is not intelligible with an exposure of his dogmatic premise
concerning the historical character of any possible thought. This unwarranted
premise is actually an unwarranted hope. Heidegger's thought on history
expresses the hope of full coincidence between the strivings of philosophic
questioning and the site or place (the local habitation and time) of the philosophic questioner. To the contrary, Strauss asserts, philosophic questioning,
as knowledge of ignorance, inevitably finds its own place and time questionable. It necessarily rejects the tyrannical claims of the present moment. It is
Heidegger's impossible hope that gives rise to the problem of relativism by its
affirmation of the fate of the present merely because it is the fate of the present.
Relativism is the symptom of the deeper philosophic error that is, at the same
time, the ultimate source of his tendency toward extremist politics.

II

Strauss famously made numerous comments on Heidegger's "radical historicism" as directly linked to his endorsement of National Socialism in 1933 as
rector of the University of Freiburg. It should be clear by now, though, that his
valuation of Heidegger is complex and by no means a mere reduction of his
philosophy to a version of National Socialist ideology. Even on a practical and
political plane Strauss shows guarded respect for Heidegger, insofar as Strauss
indicates some sympathy for his criticism of modernity. Yet Strauss wholly rejects all extremist political responses to the problems of modernity.[12] Whereas
philosophical inquiry by nature calls for radicality in questioning, politics
(which includes the political actions of philosophers as teachers and writers)
by its nature requires moderation and prudence.[13] In his various statements

on Heidegger, Strauss is centrally concerned with showing the connections in Heidegger's thought between his radical historicism, his failure to grasp the nature of politics (or of the relation of philosophy to politics), and his leanings toward extremist and transformationist (or "visionary") politics. Strauss also seeks to expose the roots of these tendencies in earlier modern thought, that is, in modern understandings of the relation of philosophy to politics (or "practice" more broadly). Thus, against Heidegger's self-understanding, Strauss regards him as the heir and culmination of modern philosophy and believes that the comprehension of his thought, especially in its fully developed later form, is indispensable for any effort to free oneself from modernity.[14] In this regard Strauss's philosophic-historical inquiries can be seen as a continuation of Heidegger's *Destruktion* that includes Heidegger in its critique, through uncovering the hidden roots of the modern historical consciousness whose validity Heidegger presupposes. Also in accord with the centrality of Heidegger for Strauss's self-understanding, Heidegger could be seen as the greatest living example of the general problem of the relation of philosophy to practical life—of the inherent dangers posed by philosophy to practice and the recurrent seductions offered by practice to philosophy.

Strauss claims he found an unacceptable moral teaching in Heidegger in the 1920s, "despite his disclaimer he had such a teaching." Heidegger called for "resoluteness without any indication of what are the proper objects of resoluteness. There is a straight line that leads from Heidegger's resoluteness to his siding with the so-called Nazis in 1933."[15] Yet, as we have seen, Strauss also saw Heidegger more positively in a larger intellectual context, namely, the widespread dissatisfaction following the First World War with the Enlightenment and modern rationalism, and the "new thinking" that supported the renewal of faith and orthodoxy in opposition to the liberal critique of tradition. Yet Heidegger's version of the critique of rationalism, in contrast to Rosenzweig's, "led far away from any charity as well as any humanity."[16] Deeply engaged with the thought of Kierkegaard and Nietzsche, Heidegger revealed the inadequacy of the established academic positions, including the dominant Neo-Kantianism (Ernst Cassirer), and offered a sense of hopeful renewal amid the Spenglerian gloom of the time. Heidegger "gave expression to the prevailing unrest and dissatisfaction because he had clarity and certainty, if not about the whole way, at least about the first and decisive steps."[17] Yet the hopefulness he inspired was, Strauss claims, ungrounded in responsible reflection on the practical possibilities. It is in this sense that Strauss asserts that Heidegger was "intellectually the counterpart to what Hitler was politically."[18] To note a kinship of Heidegger's thinking with the most radically antidemocratic and antimodern movement of the era is not to assert that Heidegger was committed to all the doctrines and programs (such as biological racism) of this movement. At the heart of the matter for Strauss is Heidegger's combination of a call to action (authentically rejecting the political-cultural status quo) and a denial of the possibility of ethics owing to the "revolting disproportion between the idea of ethics and those phenomena that ethics pretended to articulate."[19] Heidegger's doubts about the foundations of ethics were, in other words, not accompanied by a fitting skepticism about action. Indeed Heidegger longed for a sanctioning of action from a supra-ethical source, from "destiny."

The thought of the early Heidegger, culminating philosophically in *Being and Time* (1927) and politically in Heidegger's actions as rector, is quite interestingly not the primary focus of Strauss's thoughts. His most extended statements on Heidegger's political thought dwell on the significance of the later thinking of Heidegger after his disillusionment with the Nazi regime.[20] The theme of these treatments, stated very succinctly, is Heidegger's replacement of philosophic reflection on politics and ethics with the fateful dispensation of Being or the gods. Thus the resolute and activist stance of the early Heidegger and the later stance of meditative awaiting of a new dispensation of Being are connected by the absence of political philosophy, as Strauss understands that term. "There is no room for political philosophy in Heidegger's work, and this may well be due to the fact that the room in question is occupied by gods or the gods."[21] Strauss underlines this connection even as he avers that Heidegger's thought grows in depth after 1933-34, and particularly during the seminars on Nietzsche in the period 1936-40.[22] But although Strauss sees an "intimate connection between the core" of Heidegger's philosophic thought and his early support and later (post-1945) praise of the "inner truth and greatness" of the National Socialist revolution, these facts "afford too small a basis for the proper understanding of his thought."

As noted above, Strauss indicates that the core of Heidegger's thought is not historicism simply but a particular eschatological version of historical thinking emerging fully in the mature account of the history of Being (*Seinsgeschichte*) and linked to the eschatological visions of Hegel, Marx, and Nietzsche. In Heidegger's case the eschatological moment corresponds to the moment of the disclosure of the historicity of Being, or the mortality and transience of the grounds of human thought and existence. Strauss understands Heidegger's account of the historicity of Being as akin to the responses to Hegel on the part of Marx and Nietzsche, who see in the Hegelian completion of history only the inhuman reconciliation with bourgeois life (Marx) or the end of humanity in the advent of the last man without nobility and greatness (Nietzsche).

Strauss claims that Heidegger is much closer to Nietzsche than to Marx, in that "both thinkers regard as decisive the nihilism which according to them began in Plato (or before) . . . and whose ultimate consequence is the present decay."[23] Both see the present age as an "infinitely dangerous moment" and at the same time the moment when philosophy can prepare the ground for a new kind of greatness, "danger and salvation belonging together." Yet Heidegger after an initial attraction abjured Nietzsche's call for a new nobility exercising planetary rule (travestied by Nazism), and thus the later Heidegger "severs the connection of the [eschatological] vision with politics more radically than either Marx or Nietzsche. One is inclined to say that Heidegger learned the lesson of 1933 more thoroughly than any other man. Surely he leaves no place whatever for political philosophy."[24] Heidegger after 1933 denies that political action can overcome the flattening of the spirit in the technological world night and proposes instead that philosophy can prepare a novel kind of *Bodenständigkeit* (rootedness in a homeland) as the condition for human greatness, through initiating a dialogue between the most profound thinkers of the Occident and those of the Orient "accompanied or followed by a return of the gods." Strauss's statements do not imply that Heidegger on the plane of political action ever favored any movement other than National Socialism. Indeed Heidegger "never praised any other contemporary political effort."[25] Nor do Strauss's formulations imply that Heidegger's turning way from politics and his learning "the lesson of 1933" establish that his later reflections constitute a worthy philosophic project. Even so, the phrase "the lesson of 1933" suggests a partial agreement with the later Heidegger, namely, the rejection of political projects of overcoming modernity. But in the case of Strauss that rejection retains a place for political philosophy—in the special sense that term has for Strauss—and does not substitute new gods for rational inquiry into politics.

Strauss develops a similar estimate of Heidegger in his 1956 lecture on existentialism, where he notes "the kinship in temper and direction between Heidegger's thought and the Nazis," citing "the contempt for reasonableness and the praise of resoluteness." But this kinship does not provide grounds for dismissing Heidegger as philosopher. Indeed Strauss indicates some sympathy with Heidegger's views on the shortcomings of democracy (in which there is "no reminder of man's absolute duty and exalted destiny") and even claims (as noted above) that through Heidegger's critique of the tradition "all rational liberal philosophic positions have lost their significance and power."[26] In this lecture Strauss more explicitly links Heidegger's welcoming of Hitler's rise in 1933 to "Nietzsche's hope of a united Europe ruling the planet," and relates Heidegger's disappointment and withdrawal from active engagement in politics to the discovery that this hope "had proved to be a delusion."[27] Yet by replacing political action with a reflection that prepares a new world religion uniting the deepest elements of the West and the East, Heidegger maintains with Nietzsche the conception that "the philosopher of the future, as distinct from the classical philosopher, will be concerned with the holy." The new philosophic thinking, or the thinking that replaces philosophy, is essentially religious and is the heir of the Bible.[28] In undertaking the preparatory inquiry for a new world religion, Heidegger reveals himself as "the only man who has an inkling of the dimension of the problem of a world society."[29] In spite of this praise Strauss regards Heidegger's enterprise as involving "fantastic hopes, more to be expected from visionaries than philosophers."[30]

Strauss's judgment on Heidegger is subtle and understated, offering only hints of the extent and nature of Strauss's affinities and debts.[31] But it is clear that the target of Strauss's critique is only secondarily the moral and political consequences of Heidegger's thought and is more centrally the conception of philosophy that results in those consequences. In that conception philosophy is synthesized with religion and takes on the largest responsibilities for human welfare. That synthesis, in turn, arises first in the early modern period, when "the gulf between philosophy and the city was bridged" by the twin innovations of identifying the ends of the philosopher and the nonphilosopher, "because philosophy is in the service of the relief of man's estate, or 'science for the sake of power,'" and of fulfilling this new function by diffusion of the results of philosophy among nonphilosophers.[32] These innovations are the source, in Strauss's analysis, of the modern historical consciousness, in which the highest object of philosophic reflection is human action and its products, with the ultimate outcome of obliviousness to the superhuman and eternal. Philosophy, abandoning the primacy of contemplation in seeking to make man wholly at home in the city, loses sight of the suprapolitical. At the same time political life becomes the site of philosophically based transformative projects that it cannot sustain.[33] Whereas in early modernity such projects take the form of the Enlightenment's attack on faith and orthodoxy, in late modernity they become the effort to restore the nobility and metaphysical depth that were sacrificed on the altar of rational progress. Even when this effort loses any connection with direct action in politics, as it does in the thought of Heidegger after 1933, the distinctively modern conception of philosophy as inseparably fused with practical life is retained. The failures of the deepest and most ambitious versions of the ennobling effort, those of Nietzsche and Heidegger, confirmed in Strauss's view the rightness of his "concentration on the tension between philosophy and the *polis*, i.e., on the highest theme of *political* philosophy."[34]

* 3 *

Construction of Modernity

Words are not like landmarks, so sacred as never to be removed. Customs are changed, and even statutes silently repealed, when the reason changes for which they were enacted.

JOHN DRYDEN, *Fables Ancient and Modern*

On the Roots of Rationalism: Strauss's *Natural Right and History* as Response to Heidegger

But it is the essence of prudence that one know when to speak and when to be silent. Knowing this very well, Locke had the good sense to quote only the right kind of writers and to be silent about the wrong kind, although he had more in common, in the last analysis, with the wrong kind than with the right.

LEO STRAUSS, *Natural Right and History*

I. THE UNNAMED OPPONENT

Leo Strauss's *Natural Right and History* (1953) is an introduction to political philosophy through a historical treatment of natural right. "Natural right claims to be a right that is discernible by human reason and is universally acknowledged" (9).[1] Strauss seeks to restore knowledge of "the problem of natural right," which is "today a matter of recollection rather than actual knowledge"(7). He is careful not to identify the philosophy of natural right with political philosophy as such or even classical political philosophy. Political philosophy itself is older than any doctrine of natural right and indeed "seems to begin" with arguing for "the conventional character of all right" (10). But for the classical political philosophers, both adherents and opponents of natural right, "the distinction between nature and convention is fundamental. For this idea is implied in the idea of philosophy"(11).[2]

The modern "historical consciousness" denies "the premise that nature is of higher dignity than any works of man" (11), and in assuming that all human thought is historical, rejects "the idea of philosophy as the attempt to grasp the eternal," which is the fundamental premise of ancient conventionalism as well as of natural right doctrines (12). Strauss asserts that "our most urgent need" is to understand the issue between historicism and nonhistoricist philosophy (33),[3] for historicism in its philosophical form questions the possibility of philosophy, a possibility that is "the necessary and not sufficient condition of natural right" (35). What Strauss calls "radical historicism" (also " 'existentialist' historicism," 32) assumes that

> philosophy in the full and original sense of the word, as the attempt to replace opinions about the whole with knowledge of the whole, is not only incapable of reaching its goal, but absurd, because the very idea of philosophy rests on dogmatic, that is arbitrary, premises or, more specifically, on premises that are only 'historical and relative.' (30)

The first chapter ("Natural Right and the Historical Approach") contains a summary (30–31) of "the most influential attempts to establish the dogmatic and hence arbitrary or historically relative character of philosophy." According to this thinking, the tradition of philosophy dogmatically assumes that the whole is intelligible, and consequently identifies the whole as it is in itself with the whole in so far as it is intelligible. It thereby assumes the equation of "being" with "object," that is, with what can be "mastered by the subject." Further, the whole is thought to be unchangeable on the basis of "the dogmatic identification of 'to be' in the highest sense with 'to be always.'" Against these dogmatic assumptions and claims, radical historicist thinking puts forward the discovery of the historicity of the whole: the changing, incompletable, unpredictable character of the whole and the essential dependence, accordingly, of human thought on "something that cannot be anticipated or that can never be an object" mastered by the human subject. Thus " 'to be' in the highest sense cannot mean—or, at any rate, it does not necessarily mean—'to be always'" (31).

Informed readers today cannot fail to see that Strauss's summary is an account, albeit in some ways peculiar, of the thought of Martin Heidegger, none of whose works is cited and whose name is not once mentioned in the book. Strauss disavows any engagement in the present discussion with the unnamed author or authors of the doctrine compressed into a few pages; he claims that "we cannot even attempt to discuss" the most fundamental theses of radical historicism (31). When Strauss wrote his book Heidegger was barely known as a thinker in this country but was already notorious for his endorsement of Nazism while rector of the University of Freiburg and on occasions thereafter. The argument of *Natural Right and History*, in its foreground and not only there, is oriented toward the contemporary social sciences and a public-spirited discussion of the foundations of morality and law (8). Strauss had more than one ground for thinking he could not afford Heidegger a comfortable and well-lit abode in this setting. Even so, his first chapter exposes the elements—in Strauss's manner of laconic and mostly implicit argumentation—of a philosophical critique of Heidegger that is developed through the rest of the book. Taken as a whole the book lays the basis for a full confrontation with the thinker whom Strauss regarded as the one great philosopher of the twentieth century.[4] I will offer some observations about those elements and make some suggestions about the larger argument about Heidegger to which they point.

II. HISTORICISM'S UNSTABLE PREMISES

The radical historicist challenge to philosophy emerged when historicism "suddenly appeared in our lifetime in its mature form" as a "critique of human thought as such"; nevertheless an earlier historicist critique of natural right played an important role in radical historicism's formation (12–13). The crisis of natural right in the eighteenth century, from which emerged the historical school of jurisprudence, led ultimately to radical historicism (34). Strauss would show that the "experience of history," which the historical school claimed to discover, is still assumed, without examination, by radical historicist thought (22, 32–33).[5] In particular, radical historicism has not examined whether the said "experience" is not the outcome of two beliefs, the first of which it avowedly rejects: the belief in necessary progress and the belief in the supreme value of diversity or uniqueness (22). Strauss says we need an "an understanding of the genesis of historicism that does not take for granted the soundness of historicism" (33). He argues, in effect, that radical historicism is undermined by its failure to have adequate historical awareness of its own premises. It fails by the very standard of analysis it respects, knowledge of historical origins. What it especially fails to uncover is the shaping of the "experience of history" by the "politicization of philosophy" since the seventeenth century, an event that is the presupposition for the fact that a crisis in political philosophy (the crisis of natural right) "could become a crisis in philosophy as such" (34).[6]

The thought of the historical school is taken as a "convenient" starting point for this critique (13), but its philosophical sources—sources comparable in theoretical weight to Heidegger—are Strauss's chief concern. Two are prominently mentioned, more or less corresponding to the two beliefs that combine in the "experience of history": Rousseau as questioning the naturalness of the universal in the name of individuality (14–15), and Hume and Kant as criticizing theoretical metaphysics for the sake of the final securing of practical life against speculative subversion (19–20). Historicism shares with "the tendency of men like Rousseau" the view of the higher value of the local and temporal, and with Hume and Kant it shares the effort to define the limits of human knowledge within which certainty can be found. Historicist thought combines these in its nonskeptical position that all thought has a nonarbitrary basis in particular historical conditions (20). Like the modern critique of metaphysics it is directed against transcendence (15); historicism's claim to have discovered an "experience" that discloses the emptiness of all transcendence is explicitly or implicitly a proclamation of the superiority of the thought of the present to all previous thought. Yet this claim is inherently transhistorical and can be consistently incorporated within the historical experience only if interpreted as a nontheoretical commitment (26) or as "an unforeseeable gift or an unfathomable fate" (28). In this way the crisis of early historicism resulted in radical historicism. Yet historicism is from start to finish connected with "divination" (12, 33) and not with *theoria*.

One already discerns the outlines of a genealogical critique of Heidegger that unfolds in later chapters. The "critique of reason" as the search for certainty within well-defined limits proceeds from Hobbes's grounding of the "dogmatism based on skepticism" entailing the primacy of practice over contemplation (177n, 319–20). Strauss is centrally concerned with how the Hobbesian move sets the stage for German Idealist philosophy (173–77, 248–49, 272–82); the longest passage of the book on a German philosopher mentioned by name is a discussion of Hegel near the end of chapter 6 (319–21). The primacy of the practical is not overcome but only intensified when Hegel, with some resemblance to Burke, regards human action and its products, rather than the superhuman whole, as the highest theme of philosophy (319–20; cf. 29). The metaphysics of practice, in order to be a completed science, has to contemplate action as completed; history achieves its final *telos* in absolute knowledge of the logic of history. The Hegelian notion of completed practice introduces a motive for existentialism's attack on theoretical science (in Kierkegaard and Nietzsche) and for radical historicism's critique of the metaphysical tradition: the recovery of practice as concern with *agenda* in a "significant and undetermined future" (320). This is a motive that cannot be derived solely from the problems of the historical school.

The passage on Hegel in chapter 6 thus directs the reader back to the passage on radical historicism in chapter 1, wherein Hegel plays a larger role than seems the case on first reading. The radical historicist account of the history of philosophy runs as follows: metaphysics, as rooted in Greek thinking about Being (and culminating in Hegel, one may now add on second reading), assumes that the future of the whole can be predicted or that the whole is complete. This view of the whole is a consequence of the Greek identification of "to be" with "to be always," an identification made in accordance with a hidden presupposition in Greek thinking that disregards anything that cannot be an "object" mastered by the human "subject" (30–31). But the incompletability and unpredictability of human action belie this view of the whole: "the whole is actually always incomplete and therefore not truly a whole" (30–31, 320–21). Radical historicism claims to surpass both modernity and modernity's roots in antiquity; its attack on modern speculative philosophy of history is not a return to the premodern view of history as a sphere of contingencies, for it retains the modern assumption of the superiority of practice to *theoria*. And without *theoria*, or the grasp of the universal transcending the present, there can be no prudence (321).

Thus radical historicism, in treating the realm of contingent and incompletable practice—what it calls "the temporality of *Dasein*"—as the "horizon" from which Being is to be understood,[7] carries forward the modern limitation of human thought to the practical, with a deeper attack on theoretical metaphysics. Its account of theoretical metaphysics is profoundly informed by Hegel, both negatively (opposing his "completion of practice") and positively (practice remains the highest theme of philosophy).[8] It therefore is akin to the historical school, which has no substantial critique of metaphysics, but which all the same "acted as if it intended to make men absolutely at home in the world" (15) and rejected universal principles as making men "strangers on the earth" (14). However, radical historicism's effort to establish earthly temporality as the sole human dwelling is unstable, since it has absorbed the Rousseauian thought that the authentic individual cannot be at home in any social world (255, 260–61, 290). Nietzsche, in this regard recalling Rousseau, might have considered the possibility of restoring the Platonic notion of the esoteric character of theoretical analysis, thus rejecting the subservience of thought to life or fate. Strauss observes: "If not Nietzsche himself, at any rate his successors" adopted the alternative of subservience (26). Yet in Heidegger's thought historical fate at once calls for the rootedness in the particular and for the radical transcending of it: "The attempt to make man absolutely at home in this world ended in man's becoming absolutely homeless" (18). I shall return to this tension in Heidegger between the longing to be at home and the rejection of all being at home.[9]

III. THE MYSTERIOUS WHOLE: TWO VERSIONS

The critique sketched above, however, offers few inklings of Heidegger's full significance for Strauss. His account elsewhere of his early attendance at

Heidegger's lectures, and their shattering effect on him and his contemporaries, is hardly compatible with a view of Heidegger as dogmatic antiphilosopher.[10] Indeed central to *Natural Right and History* is a well-hidden positive relation to Heidegger, which may offer the most crucial ground for not mentioning him, and which lends a deeply ironical character to a book concerned precisely with exposing unexamined historical premises. The thought of a certain "Martin Heidegger" seems to be the unexamined premise of the argument directed against a figure who uncannily resembles him.[11]

Heidegger questioned in unparalleled fashion the soundness of the tradition of Western rationalism. Such questioning is wholly different from a willful rejection of the tradition.

> Certain it is that no one questioned the premise of philosophy as radically as Heidegger. . . . [Jacob] Klein alone saw why Heidegger is truly important; by uprooting and not merely rejecting the tradition of philosophy, he made it possible for the first time after many centuries—one hesitates to say how many—to see the roots of the tradition as they are. . . . Above all, his intention was to uproot Aristotle: he thus was compelled to disinter the roots, to bring them to light, to look at them with wonder.[12]

In a practical sense Heidegger, like many of his contemporaries, began from a certain experience: an overwhelming sense of the collapse of the Western tradition, *der Untergang des Abendlandes*. But no one else sought for the roots of this collapse with as much analytic power and philological mastery. Surely Heidegger made a case for an essential defect in the Western tradition that had to be taken seriously. When Strauss writes, "I began, therefore, to wonder whether the self-destruction of reason was not the inevitable outcome of modern rationalism as distinguished from pre-modern rationalism,"[13] his expression of "wonder" implies that the source of self-destruction seemed to him at first to be located plausibly elsewhere—perhaps at the Greek beginnings or in rationalism as such. Heidegger above all others had incited such reflections.[14] Strauss later found another way to reflect on the cause of the collapse when he "concluded that the case of the moderns against the ancients must be reopened,"[15] whereas Heidegger had concluded that modernity was just an extension of the "forgetting of Being" that had befallen the Greeks.

Therefore Heidegger's thought is not merely the most evident symptom of decline. Specifically Heidegger identified the fundamental presupposition of all rationalism as the axiom that "nothing comes into being out of nothing or through nothing"; he held that "the fundamental principle of philosophy is then the principle of causality, of intelligible necessity" (89).[16] In Socratic fashion Heidegger investigated this premise through an inquiry into that being, the human, which has access to Being or "which *is* in the most emphatic or authoritative way." The object of Heidegger's inquiry is therefore more adequately expressed as the question that inevitably arises for that being which finds itself "thrown" in the midst of beings: "Why are there beings rather than nothing at all?"[17] This question is not a cosmological question about the causal origination of beings out of other beings or the whole of beings. The question would persist even if it were known that the whole of beings is eternal. Therefore natural science can shed no light on the question. The true bearing of the question is on the questioner or, more precisely, on the questioning—on the possibility of questioning. All questioning about the beings presupposes an openness to beings as a whole, a fundamental disclosedness of beings, which cannot be grounded causally in any being or beings, including the highest or most perfect being. All attempts at such grounding suffer from a fatal circularity. Heidegger calls the fundamental disclosedness of beings *Sein* and claims that *Sein* so understood must be kept sharply separate from the theme of traditional metaphysics, being *qua* being or the being of beings (*Seienden*), which is concerned only with the causal constitution of beings or the cosmological question.[18] In Heidegger's view the highest themes of the metaphysical tradition—the Good, or the ideas, or *nous*—remain on the plane of the beings, or of *das Seiende*.[19]

Heidegger purported to uncover a thought that the entire tradition had neglected, and he alleged he was thinking beyond or, as he put it, behind the tradition. It expresses a common misunderstanding to say that Heidegger simply rejected rationalism or the Western tradition; to the end of his work Heidegger thought it necessary to think with and through this tradition, especially its Greek beginnings.[20] Furthermore, what he calls the "forgetting of Being" is not a mistake to be set aside but a tendency of thought inseparable from openness to the beings. Human thought cannot stay focused on the mystery of a disclosedness that eludes grounding, and thus there are the inevitable and related tendencies of grounding Being in a highest being (ontotheology) or in the human being (anthropocentrism or "humanism"). For Heidegger these two tendencies are at root the same. Such groundings are always alluring because Being, so far as we know, discloses itself to only *one* being among beings, the human. Strauss does not share the misunderstanding I mentioned, to be sure. What is more, there is evidence that he believed it necessary to participate in Heidegger's inquiry; Heidegger's question is a necessary one, and Strauss's inquiries are in a sense a continuation of Heidegger's (31, especially the sentence beginning "It compels us at the same time . . ."; cf. 89). The problems for Strauss arose in the implications Heidegger drew from his question, or the attitudes he adopted toward it. These problems relate ultimately to the absence of political philosophy in Heidegger[21] and to the connected preference for pre-Socratic over Socratic philosophy.

I offer only a few indications that Strauss might have looked at the Greek philosophers and perhaps especially Socrates with Heidegger's question in view. Strauss writes:

> And Socrates was so far from being committed to a specific cosmology that his knowledge was knowledge of ignorance. Knowledge of ignorance is not ignorance. It is knowledge of the elusive character of the truth, of the whole. Socrates, then, viewed man in the light of the mysterious character of the whole. He held therefore that we are more familiar with the situation of man as man than with the ultimate causes of the situation.[22]

There is little basis, if any, in Strauss's writings for the view that he sought to recover a teleological natural philosophy, or that he thought such recovery a necessary condition for philosophy in its classical form. He thought that the philosopher must come to terms with the unavailability of such cosmology; in the modern era, this means coming to terms with modern science's failure to provide an account of the human (8).[23] Essentially Socrates faced the same problem with the failure of the cosmologies he knew; his response to that difficulty was his "second sailing," the dialectical ascent from opinions (122–25). To understand philosophy this way means to acknowledge its unfinishable or aporetic nature (125–26, 29–30).[24] And perhaps, contrary to the first impression Strauss gives the reader, Strauss holds that Aristotle conceived philosophy in the same way. (Compare the text at *NRH* 8 with the citations of Aristotle's *Physics* in the note.)[25] One also should recall the passing remark in the Hobbes section of *Natural Right and History* about "the difficulty with which every teleological physics is beset" (172). In sum, I venture to say that Heidegger provoked Strauss (with some mediation by Jacob Klein) to approach Greek philosophy with the suspension of the traditional expectation of finding therein a teleological physics and cosmology. The belief that classical philosophy is inseparable from an "antiquated cosmology" had been a principal barrier against taking it seriously—a belief that Strauss came to see as a misreading of the Socratics.[26] Of course, the human must be understood teleologically insofar as it is oriented toward knowledge of the whole, or toward the question of the ground of the whole.[27] But this in turn means that the human orientation is toward fundamental and insoluble problems. And thus the philosopher, who is distinguished among humans by the awareness of these problems, is the being that preeminently reflects the character of Being as a whole. "To articulate the problem of cosmology means to answer the question of what philosophy is or what a philosopher is."[28] With suitable changes in language, this is granted by Heidegger. But in Strauss's estimation the awareness of the fundamental problems liberates the mind from its historical limitations and legitimizes philosophy in its original, Socratic sense (32)—a nonhistoricist sense that Heidegger regards as a falling away from a higher kind of thinking. How does one account for this difference?

IV. PHILOSOPHICAL SEDIMENT

It bears on this question to observe that Strauss draws a subtle distinction between the fundamental problems and "the fundamental alternatives regarding their solution." In one passage he says simply that both are "coeval with human thought" (32), but a few pages later he adds after "fundamental alternatives" the phrase "which are, in principle, coeval with human thought" (35). This seemingly small change points to the heart of the argument of Strauss with Heidegger.

In the first passage Strauss already modifies his quoted stance on solutions with a remark on "however variable or provisional all human solutions to these problems may be" (32). If solutions are thus variable it is doubtful that they are "coeval with human thought"—although "in principle" they could be. Indeed the "experience of history" derives some of its strongest support from the manifold evidence of this variability. Strauss in fact is quite open to the view that human experience is with respect to the proposal of solutions unpredictable and incompletable. He mentions the possibility that great thinkers might arise in the future—"perhaps in 2200 in Burma"—for whose thought we are quite unprepared. "For who are we to believe that we have found out the limits of human possibilities?"[29] It seems to be in a related sense that Heidegger sees human history as unfinishable—in opposition to Hegel—insofar as the perplexity of Being is without end, as long as there is man. This would give support to the claim that "there can be *entia* while there is no *esse*," on the assumption that *esse* or *Sein* means the perplexity of *esse* or *Sein*. Strauss mentions the assertion of Heidegger with skeptical reservation, it seems, yet without any criticism (32). But for Strauss the permanence of fundamental perplexities is the strongest argument for regarding the whole as complete in the decisive respect: the problems, rather than their solutions, are permanent and not variable. This wholeness, however, is available only on the level of *theoria*, which grasps the problems as problems (32); insofar as one remains on the level of practice, or of attempted solutions, variability and impermanence must be the dominant experience.

I suggest that in Strauss's view Heidegger does not distinguish the awareness of the fundamental problem from the historical efforts at solutions to it. Hence for Heidegger the question of Being—which always manifests itself in particular "dispensations"—has itself a historical and variable character, even though he also describes this question as determining the essence of man.[30] One could say that Heidegger is oriented toward the fundamental question with the intention of showing how the question as question can provide the practical solution to the problems of human existence; thus he speaks of thinking as piety. Or to put this another way, Heidegger's remarkable "path of thinking" conflates philosophical reflection on the problematic character of existence with nonphilosophic human concerns for being at home in the world—the world defined by particular languages, customs, poetry, and the gods. In Strauss's view this necessarily conflates the suprahistorical with the historical, or the philosopher's being at home in the whole with various ways of being at home in human affairs, in which the philosopher can never be entirely at home. For Strauss this entails that Heidegger does not recognize the natural duality of the human—the duality that Strauss sees as the permanent condition of the human (151–52).[31] According to Strauss, that duality will come to light only through an analysis of the "natural world" of the prescientific understanding—an analysis that must start with the phenomena of political life as they concern political actors and as they present themselves prior to their transformation by the philosophic and scientific tradition (78–81).[32] In his disinterment of the roots of philosophy, Heidegger neglected that analysis by starting with the question of Being and only with that question.[33] Heidegger passed over the primary sources for the required analysis of prephilosophic life, namely, the reflections on political life in the classical authors (79–80). But accordingly Heidegger's *Destruktion* of the tradition was, from Strauss's standpoint, radically incomplete.

The heart of Heidegger's thought is a longing for the overcoming of the duality of philosophic thinking and of being at home in human affairs, or for an unheard-of transformation of human life. In this hope of transformation Heidegger's thought seeks to relate itself to the traditions of revelation and to the thought of the East.[34] Strauss suggests that even in its later form, in which the resolute willing of *Being and Time* has been replaced by the patient receptivity (*Gelassenheit*) in which man is appropriated by Being,[35] Heidegger's thought is based on an act of believing or willing, a stance that is "fatal to any philosophy."[36] This is Strauss's most fundamental criticism of Heidegger, but it barely surfaces in *Natural Right and History*.[37] Perhaps it cannot be fully articulated without exposing the extent of Strauss's affinity with Heidegger on the aporetic nature of philosophy. All the same, Strauss's account in *Natural Right and History* of the origin of the idea of natural right in the prephilosophic situation—of the "discovery of nature" within the context of the ancestral *nomos*—provides the indispensable foundation for the criticism (81–119). Indeed this account provides an alternative to Heidegger's uncovering of the pre-Socratic roots of the tradition. Without the investigation of the political and moral context of the appearance of philosophy, such as Strauss undertakes, the full import of the "question of Being" cannot come to light. The absence of such inquiry in Heidegger necessitates that his conception of the philosophic life is "sedimented," to use a term of the phenomenologists.

Strauss regards the conflation of philosophic reflection and being at home in the world in Heidegger as typical of modern philosophy as a whole. Near the end of his reply to Alexandre Kojève's critique of his commentary on Xenophon's *Hiero*, Strauss describes this feature as follows:

> On the basis of Kojève's presupposition, unqualified attachment to human concerns becomes the source of philosophic understanding: man must be absolutely at home on the earth, if not a citizen of a part of the inhabitable earth. On the basis of the classical presupposition, philosophy requires a radical detachment from human concerns: man must not be absolutely at home on earth, he must be a citizen of the whole.[38]

What Strauss here ascribes to the Kojèvian-Hegelian philosopher is a motive that, like the historical school's rejection of revolutionary efforts at "transcendence," leads to the identification of the source and the condition of thought (or in the case of Heidegger, of aporia and answer). In *Natural Right and History* Strauss traces this back to Hobbes and, ultimately, Machiavelli.[39] I review now a few points in this account. Strauss understands Hobbes's new natural philosophy, based on the unification of Epicurean materialism and Platonic mathematicism, as allowing the construction of an island of human intelligibility "exempt from the flux of blind and aimless causation" (173) and, therewith, from skeptical attack on its foundations. A certain wisdom seems capable of permanent actualization, because the question of cosmic support from the larger whole in which the human exists can be viewed as superseded (169–77).[40] This self-limitation of thought is the ground of Hobbes's holding an "expectation from political philosophy [that] is incomparably greater than the expectation of the classics" (177).[41] Strauss points to the direct link between this Hobbesian innovation (which has parallels in Bacon and Descartes) and the turn to History as well as the idealist accounts of freedom (for the latter cf. 279, 281):

> But "History" limits our vision in exactly the same way in which the conscious constructs limited the vision of Hobbes. "History," too, fulfills the function of enhancing the status of man and his "world" by making him oblivious of the whole or of eternity. In its final stage the typically modern limitation expresses itself in the suggestion that the highest principle, which, as such, has no relation to any possible cause or causes of the whole, is the mysterious ground of "History" and, being wedded to man and man alone, is so far from being eternal that it is coeval with human history. (176)

This comment, obviously referring to Heidegger, leads to the question of how a conception of the whole as defined by "fundamental problems coeval with human thought" (Strauss) can be much different from a conception of "the mysterious ground . . . coeval with human history" and not relatable to higher causes (Heidegger). But as we have seen, Heidegger treats the manifestations of the problems (or the problem) as identical with history, whereas Strauss, who indeed seems to provide no account of how to attain knowledge of the eternal, regards the problems as suprahistorical. The confidence in this suprahistorical dimension derives from reason's unchangeable need to concede that the human situation could be grounded in some higher and eternal "possible cause"—although one unavailable to human reason. This further means that for Strauss it is essential for reason or philosophy to reflect on the possibility of that of which revelation speaks, although barring itself from ever speaking of it affirmatively. It is Strauss's judgment that by remaining mindful of the problem of the ultimate but unknowable ground, philosophy preserves an awareness of the permanent—as permanent perplexity—that emancipates it from the vagaries of history and lends enduring vitality to its thought.[42]

CHAPTER 8

Is Modernity an Unnatural Construct?

I

In a 1952 retrospect on the genesis of his 1936 Hobbes study, Leo Strauss comments on one of the most controversial and least understood aspects of his thought. "I had seen that the modern mind had lost its self-confidence or its certainty of having made decisive progress beyond pre-modern thought, and I saw that it was turning to nihilism, or what is in practice the same thing, fanatical obscurantism."[1] A German refugee living in 1930s England, he was hardly alone in noting the collapse of belief in the liberal-progressive Enlightenment. His response was not to take up a cause, either in defense or in criticism of the liberal democracies, but to reexamine the modern philosophical premises and arguments and to confront them with the premises and arguments they replaced. Strauss does not say here that he sought to revive ancient political practice (and it is hard to grasp what that could mean) or even to return to ancient political philosophy. "I concluded that the case of the moderns against the ancients must be reopened, without any regard to cherished opinions or convictions, *sine ira et sine studio*." To reopen "the case of the moderns against the ancients" was the indispensable task for one seeking the truth about the current crisis, since all principles were now in question. It might or might not result in a new defense of the moderns. (It did result in a kind of defense, as I shall argue.) In the course of his examination Strauss arrived at something quite different from either simple defense or simple criticism of philosophical doctrines: at an unorthodox understanding of the term "political philosophy," to elaborate which became his life's labor. With this term Strauss did not mean a political program or even a theoretical doctrine about politics, but a way of beginning to philosophize. He pursued the question "How does one begin in

philosophy?" through commentaries on a remarkable range of figures. He rejected the notion that philosophy can be a science since philosophy as activity
and way of life is irreducible to any set of theses, arguments, and conclusions.

Strauss famously arrived at the conviction of a certain superiority of ancient
philosophy, one due in large part to the accident of its historical position. The
ancients, being unburdened by an existing philosophic tradition, could see the
phenomena more directly.[2] Strauss said he learned from Husserl and Heidegger
the need to question the inherited philosophic tradition in order to recover the
original experiences of philosophizing that produced it. For Strauss this meant
turning to the ancient authors above all, for with their aid one could disclose the
"natural understanding"—the standpoint from which later thought, especially
modern philosophy, made a break.[3] That natural standpoint was not a doctrine
or a set of prephilosophic opinions but a way of questioning that exposes "the
fundamental problems and the fundamental alternatives regarding their solution."[4] This formulation causes difficulties for some of Strauss's readers. If the
later, especially modern, tradition breaks with the natural understanding, could
Strauss say that the tradition as a whole treats fundamental problems and alternatives that are "in principle coeval with human thought"?[5] Were the natural
and enduring problems available and appreciated only during certain historical epochs? Are the moderns, in their break with nature, thinking in a merely
artificial or historical fashion? Indeed it would seem that modern philosophers
might be denied the right to the title "philosopher," having lost contact with
the primary issues. Strauss wrote of modern thought—the popularization of
modern philosophy—as a "cave beneath the cave" from which one must free
oneself by an archaeology of textual interpretation. Were the modern philosophers themselves only cave-dwellers? If so, was the cave paradoxically of their
own making? If it was not of their own making, who made it, and why did they
not leave it? Stanley Rosen and Robert Pippin have raised such questions about
Strauss's thought in particularly incisive ways.

Strauss, however, suggested another side to the story. He affirmed that the
moderns, including the builders of "systems," such as Hegel, are philosophic,
even if they do not practice "the primary and necessary form of philosophy."[6]
Surely there can be no "quarrel" unless the parties share problems and questions, and in the present case those are philosophic. One suspects that Strauss's
seemingly unqualified preference for the ancients and his assessment of modern thought as unnatural involve some deliberate rhetorical overstatement, even
bordering on self-contradiction, in order to induce perplexity and arouse the
desire to grasp what is at stake in the "quarrel between the ancients and the
moderns." Strauss's readers and students were (and are), after all, likely to begin

with attachments to cherished modern projects and goals, and to be formed by the popularizations of modern philosophy, and it was necessary to create doubts about modernity as a whole and thereby a sense of urgency about a theoretical return to the beginnings. Indeed at one point Strauss was specific about a philosophic issue common to ancients and moderns and as such central to philosophy. Strauss once pronounced that the quarrel "concerns eventually, and perhaps even from the beginning, the status of 'individuality.' "[7]

It could be the case, accordingly, that the modern philosophers maintained a grasp of some fundamental questions that we cannot easily see, and if we have a blindness perhaps this blindness is in good measure due, rather paradoxically, to the effectiveness of their thought. Strauss held that all philosophers as philosophers acknowledge the existence of a fundamental tension between the good of political life (or "the city") and the good of the individual. Law and justice or morality understood as law-abidingness inevitably claim to be, and just as inevitably fail to be, the complete human good. Ancient and modern philosophers agree that "political life derives its dignity from something that transcends political life,"[8] since the claim of the city's laws to be the whole good is exposed to the problem of the disproportion between the general requirements of law and the good of individuals, or "the difficulty created by the misery of the just and the prosperity of the wicked."[9] The ancients stress that the individual attains a higher good in the perfection of the intellect, that "the individual is capable of a perfection of which the city is not capable."[10] The moderns, objecting to the supreme place accorded to philosophic virtue, found that "traditional political philosophy aimed too high," and beginning with Machiavelli they grounded political life and human endeavor generally in passions that are always effective.[11] Yet in Strauss's view the political success at which the modern philosophers were aiming was not merely convenience and efficiency but "the actualization of the ideal." In other terms, they purported to establish something that was considered desirable but unattainable by earlier philosophy, the adequate political defense of philosophy against its natural enemies.[12] In this regard the ancients had lower expectations from politics, while aiming at higher forms of philosophic, transpolitical excellence. The modern approach required a transformation of the meaning and goal of philosophy, wherein the ends of politics and philosophy are fused.

Thus the moderns reformulated philosophy's purpose as humanitarian, the "relief of man's estate," and inaugurated the project of freeing humanity from servitude to stepmotherly nature.[13] Yet this can be understood as radicalizing the ancient insight into the deficiency of law and politics, insofar as the new project universalizes the individual's transcendence of law. In place of *theoria* or philosophic virtue as the basis for that transcendence, one now stresses something that every human possesses regardless of natural gifts or virtue, the rights of man.[14] The political emancipation of the individual is based on the philosophic liberation of the human from natural teleology and from all ways of thinking that measure the human by some superhuman standard.[15] It is hoped that this liberation will secure general peace (the end of civil and sectarian conflicts about the ultimate good) and the gratitude of ordinary citizens for the new kind of philosophy, which no longer strives for knowledge of the superhuman but instead ministers to universal human needs. At first glance Strauss's account seems to characterize this modern project (or Enlightenment) as radically antinatural. Indeed he argued that Hobbes in pursuit of human liberation from natural ends conceived the human good as something grounded solely in a constructive will. Positing that nature in itself is unintelligible, Hobbes placed all intelligibility in what man makes and saw the political order as a man-made "island of intelligibility" within the cosmic darkness. Strauss surely overstated the case that for the moderns in general "we know only what we make."[16] All the same, the problem that the modern philosophers try to solve is natural—the natural tension between desire and justice, it could be called, with allowance for both subpolitical and suprapolitical forms of desire or *eros*.

I I

Here I insert a general observation about a deep and common misreading of Strauss. Contrary to the judgment of many of his readers (this includes many of his students), Strauss did not claim that this tension was hidden from all eyes until the philosophers brought it to light. It is the primary theme of the poets, in his account, and they differ from the philosophers in supposing that the human conflict admits of only comic and tragic—that is, imperfect—solutions, whereas philosophy arrives at a solution transcending both comedy and tragedy. "Yet by articulating the cardinal problem of human life as it comes to sight within the nonphilosophic life, poetry prepares for the philosophic life."[17] Hence Plato's Socrates should not be read literally when in the *Republic* he takes the side of the laws, which suppress the erotic, against the poets. Strauss did not hold that the poets should or could be only prophets or spokesmen for the gods and the laws, and he claimed that for Plato the alternative to "Platonic philosophy is not any other philosophy, be it that of the pre-Socratics or Aristotle ... the alternative is poetry," especially the profoundly innovative, and hardly pious, poetry of Aristophanes.[18] Strauss pointed to the significance of

Nietzsche's revival of the Aristophanic criticism of Socrates, and a subterranean theme in Strauss (one developed superbly by his student Seth Benardete) is what one could call the poetic discovery of nature.[19]

Such reflections, if carried further, allow one to see that Strauss was far from supposing that liberal politics, and modernity more widely, are only unnatural constructs. As I suggest, he pointed to their having roots in a poetic wisdom that exposes the complexity of human life while resisting lofty but specious solutions to life's enduring conflicts. Thus Strauss wrote of "the poetry underlying modern prose" with reference to Montesquieu, and he stressed the importance of the comic-poetic element in Machiavelli's vision.[20] Indeed from this natural basis modernity has derived its remarkable strength and resilience, it could be said. Strauss warmly endorsed liberal democracy's defense of individual rights in its struggles with totalitarian enemies, not merely out of some self-regarding or even civic-minded prudence, but because the liberal-democratic regime permits the possibility of recalling how individual perfection transcends the political.

What is the problem with liberal modernity? It is precisely its success in reducing the tensions and therewith its tendency to undermine the higher forms of the transpolitical life. Liberalism, in other words, promotes forgetfulness of the problems that are the ground of its own goodness. The shift from natural duties and obligations to natural rights promotes an "individualism" of self-absorption wherein the "ego is the center and origin of the moral world."[21] One could affirm (perhaps more than Strauss did) that the founders of the liberal democratic order did not intend their principles to produce human beings indifferent to civic life and unaware of its conditions. Yet this type is an abundant result of the prosperity and security of the liberal regime. Strauss therefore regarded with some sympathy the philosophic critics of liberalism from Rousseau and Hegel to Nietzsche and Heidegger, who attempted in various ways to invoke superhuman standards and aspirations through the ideas of freedom as autonomy, the historical process, the creative will, and the disclosure of Being. But their projects failed since the fundamental tensions cannot be resolved in higher syntheses on the plane of politics and history. Later modernity, in spite of its classical inspirations, departed further from classical thought by raising the expectations for human transformation, whereas liberalism's moderate approach is closer to the classical view of the permanence of the human problems.[22] In this regard it should not have to be said, but all the same it must be said, that Strauss was far from supposing that philosophic rule could overcome the shortcomings of liberalism.

Strauss's concern was with renewing philosophy within the liberal order, and such is the true meaning of his reflection on "political philosophy." This was a kind of reenactment of Socrates's turning to political life for the starting point for philosophy. For Socrates political life offered "the link between the highest and the lowest," between mind and body, and therefore was "the clue to all things, to the whole of nature." In Strauss's provocative readings of Plato and Xenophon, the Socratic innovation of looking to speeches or "ideas" for uncovering the "noetic heterogeneity" of the beings was the same as the discovery of the cosmological significance of the political.[23] Socrates sought to unfold the complexities of the dual existence of the human as moral-political being—a being who is both bound to the city and its laws and open to the whole of Being. Strauss states that morality has "two radically different roots" and asks, "how can there be a unity of morality, how can there be a unity of man ...?" The human exists as the dualism of "being a part of the whole while open to the whole, and therefore in a sense being the whole itself." It is only as this dual or in-between being that the human can philosophize, and thus the account of how philosophy is possible must begin with investigating how human beings attempt, by means of the laws and morality, to address the problem of the unity of man.[24] Strauss saw in this approach to philosophy's starting point a response to the leading modern critics of the rationalist tradition. Here, too, there is evidence of a favorable approach to modernity, insofar as Strauss avowed a debt to the most thorough and searching version of that criticism, Heidegger's "radical historicism," since "it compels us ... to realize the need for unbiased reconsideration of the most elementary premises whose validity is presupposed by philosophy."[25]

III

I conclude with some comments on the importance of this Heideggerian moment, and also return to my starting point of the ambiguity of Strauss's account of nature and history. It is tempting to understand the significance of Heidegger for Strauss as only negative, such that Heidegger's thought, as the "highest self-consciousness" of modern philosophy, is simply the extreme point of unnaturalness in the antinatural project of modernity, or the necessary self-destructive result of modernity's arbitrary starting point.[26] That Strauss was far from viewing Heidegger's thought as merely nihilistic is evident from the assertion that "by uprooting and not merely rejecting the tradition of philosophy, [Heidegger] made it possible for the first time after many centuries . . . to see the roots of the tradition as they are."[27] Thus Strauss made the remarkable claim that *after a certain historical development* a kind of thinking was not possible until the appearance of Heidegger, and he thereby points to a philosophic dependence on Heidegger, the appearance of whom constitutes something akin to the absolute moment in history, a theme that Strauss took up in accounts of Hegel, Marx, and Nietzsche.[28] (Strauss wrote of the theoretical advantage of the "crisis of our time," in which the "shaking of traditions" enables one to understand things "in an untraditional or fresh manner.")[29] On one level, the most superficial, this means that Heidegger undertook a *Destruktion* of modern thought that allowed one to see the defectiveness of the modern philosophic tradition's understanding of classical philosophy. But more deeply, Heidegger sought to uncover the Greek philosophic beginnings as free of the traditional Aristotelian interpretation of those beginnings, an effort Strauss avowed was crucial for his own thinking.[30]

For both Heidegger (more so the early Heidegger) and Strauss, Aristotle instituted the account of philosophy in which metaphysics and cosmology are sciences independent of the primary experiences of the whole or Being for man as practical or concernful being. Strauss understood that the primary experience is political and saw Heidegger's neglect of politics as the great lacuna in his thinking, relating to (or being the same as) his lack of practical moderation.[31] Yet the common thought of the two thinkers—a thought Strauss thought he saw in the Socrates of Xenophon and Plato and, with due regard to differences, in certain Greek poets and historians—is that without the human openness or striving toward the whole (which Strauss viewed as the erotic striving beyond law or *nomos*), there would be no articulation of Being, and for that reason "the whole is not a whole without man."[32] The only possible account of the whole or Being is through the human as finite, incomplete, erotic, and thus as confronting the tensions of political life. In Strauss's reading, Aristotle departed from this insight insofar as he founded political science as an independent discipline ("one discipline, and by no means the most fundamental or the highest discipline, among a number of disciplines"). Thus in contrast to Plato's cosmology, Aristotle's cosmology is "unqualifiedly separable from the quest for the best political order," from which one might be tempted to conclude that for Aristotle the whole is still a whole without man. "Aristotelian philosophizing has no longer to the same degree and in the same way as Socratic philosophizing the character of ascent."[33]

As Strauss was led to his interpretation of the Socratics through Heidegger, he was led to it through modernity. The experience of modernity proves to be a necessary condition not for the original Socratic thought, of course, but for its recovery in a form more reserved than the original, even disillusioned, and as such no longer preparing the ground for the later traditions, classical and modern (and one might add Christian) that emerged from it. Strauss indicated that his Socratism is essentially a reversal of the philosophic tradition by his paradoxical and polemical use of the post-Platonic term "political philosophy" to designate the true first philosophy of pre-Aristotelian Socratism. Therefore Strauss departed even from Plato, insofar as his presentation of the core Platonic thought departs from Plato's presentation, which gave birth to a metaphysical tradition. In reopening the "case of the moderns against the ancients" Strauss was not simply seeking a return to the ancients but radicalizing the critique of the classical metaphysical (Platonic-Aristotelian) tradition with the intent of rethinking the roots of ancient philosophy. This was a bold venture, undertaken with the assumption that derivative forms of rationalism—both the classical metaphysical forms and modern antimetaphysical forms—*could not,* after this *refounding* of philosophy, be viewed as the true fulfillment of those roots. (Hence a revival of the classical origins without a repetition of the history that followed is possible—with no call for Nietzsche's willing of "eternal recurrence"!)

I shall attempt a brief, certainly inadequate, summary of Strauss's relation to history in the light of these last remarks. The modern philosophic tradition is a combination of the natural and the unnatural or contranatural. In an effort to solve definitively the natural problem of the city and the individual, modern philosophy has recourse to artificial constructs that, however, ultimately obscure their natural starting point. Only by removing this obstruction, i.e., the modern solutions of the natural problem, can one recover the problem. The shaking of traditions, undertaken by Heidegger, was crucial to removing the obstruction. What is more, something was learned from the modern experience leading to Heidegger. Strauss indicated that one must employ for philosophic ends the modern constructs much as Socrates used a poetic construct—the idea of a perfect city—to lead his interlocutors out of the cave. The natural was not immediately available to them, as it is not to us. The modern "cave" has unique features, acquired in the unique history of Western thought, since this "cave," unlike any other, was (in part) conceived in philosophic liberty and dedicated to philosophic propositions. Hence Strauss used the *Republic*'s figure of the "three waves" to describe the phases of the self-dismantling of the modern ideal city. In this way history has provided not just a poetic speech but a realized philosophic poem—a poem retold by Strauss with certain Platonic distortions—as an indispensable vehicle for the disclosure of nature. Furthermore, this realized poem of modernity, as refashioned by Strauss, provides the philosophers of the future with a perspective on nature not vouchsafed by the poetic speeches of the ancient philosophers. For just as the cave from which one emerges at the end of modernity is not identical with the Socratic version, so the world beyond the cave now bears a different—indeed less exalted, more sobering—shape and aspect (*eidos*).

CHAPTER 9

Strauss on Individuality and Poetry

I

In the concluding paragraph of *Natural Right and History*, Leo Strauss claims that "the quarrel of the ancients and the modern concerns eventually, and perhaps even from the beginning, the status of 'individuality.'"[1] This utterance strikes one as surprising, not to say delphic, since individuality has not apparently figured as the point at issue in the preceding treatment of the ancient and modern accounts of natural right and natural law. "Individuality" does not appear to be what the modern founders have in view as the desideratum of their moral-political revolution. On the classical side, it seems beyond question that classical thought gives the individual or particular a lower status than the universal, and yet Strauss's statement suggests that the classics could at least contemplate giving it a different status. His assertion thus implies that these first appearances must be revisited.

I wish to relate this question to one about another central philosophical claim of Strauss, namely, that the modern revolution brings about a break with "the primary or natural understanding of the whole."[2] It is well known that the heart of his endeavor is to recover the natural understanding by means of historical inquiries, in order to restore to modern awareness the "fundamental problems and the fundamental alternatives regarding their solution."[3] Is the "status of individuality" one of these problems? Let us grant for the moment the existence of a permanent problem of individuality. How could a solution thereof—the modern solution—that "breaks with the natural understanding" be one of the "fundamental alternatives which are, in principle, coeval with human thought"?[4] As a willful rupture with nature, would not the modern account of human life—and thus its account of individuality—be only a historical particular? In that case, the "quarrel of the ancients and the moderns" would be a dispute wherein only one of the parties is natural and permanent. Would it not seem odd that something so basic and important for Strauss's thought—not to mention its importance for many other human beings—as the core of the revolution of modern thought cannot belong to the enduring human possibilities contemplated by philosophy?

On the other hand, would it indeed be odd, after all, if one or more of the fundamental possibilities is only—at least to our knowledge—a historical particular? Or if perhaps *all solutions*, no matter how long enduring and great, are only prudential negotiations of the basic tensions—solutions available to human beings under the circumstances that fate or fortune grants them?[5] In this case it would be difficult, if not impossible, to claim that the solutions are in some sense "coeval with human thought." The following remarks try to shed some light on these puzzles.

II

Let us start with the primary theme of the thought of Leo Strauss: "the city and man," the dualism that expresses the fundamental human condition. Strauss claims that classical political philosophy holds that "the individual is capable of a perfection of which the city is not capable."[6] "According to Plato and Aristotle, to the extent to which the human problem cannot be solved by political means it can be solved only by philosophy, by and through the philosophic way of life."[7] The city forbids an appeal beyond its laws with their divine sanctions, but philosophy appeals to nature, making a radical break with the laws in a way of life sustainable by only a few, remarkably self-reliant inquirers. Not obedience to law but free inquiry is the basis of true human perfection and happiness. "The transpolitical life is higher in dignity than the political life."[8] But far from removing all difficulties, this claim of the philosophers introduces a new set of problems relating to the tension between the philosophic individuals and the law-revering multitude. The first philosophers experienced this tension, but Socrates is the first philosopher to make it the central reflection of philosophy. With him the political things become "of decisive importance for understanding nature as a whole."[9] This is not because the political is the highest concern. Political life as the most urgent concern is the indispensable condition for the appearance of what is highest, "the form in which the highest principles first come to sight." The political things are "the link between the highest and the lowest" and as such "the clue to all things, to the whole of nature."[10] The understanding of this link proves elusive, and both theoretically and practically the relations of philosophy and the city remain problematic. The dualism of "the city and man" expresses the permanent human condition in the form of an insoluble problem. To the extent there is a solution, it is found in the way of life devoted to articulating the problem.[11]

According to Strauss, this Socratic or classical view of the tension between political life and philosophy constitutes "the primary or natural understanding of the whole" with which modern philosophy makes a radical break.[12] The break consists in the modern confidence that the tension can be definitively resolved as philosophy and politics unite forces in a common project, that of using philosophy and science to master nature for "the relief of man's estate." The success of this fusion or harmonization on a material plane obscures the sense that philosophic individuals, as pursuing the natural light of truth, inevitably experience dissatisfaction with life in the cave of opinion. The project creates a new "cave beneath the cave" from which a fundamental meaning of "individuality," its most adequate meaning, has disappeared. It is replaced by "individuality" as the universal emancipation of human beings on a subphilosophic plane. The modern accounts of nature that ground this emancipation are in rebellion against the natural understanding of the whole, but precisely for that reason they presuppose that understanding.[13] Subsequent generations of dwellers in the modern cave are increasingly remote from its foundations, as they regard the modern premises as the self-evident basis for the progress of civilization. The study of the founders of modern philosophy—Machiavelli, Bacon, Hobbes, Descartes, Locke, and Spinoza—can bring to light the motives and arguments for the break with the natural understanding. Only the philosophers make the break with full consciousness of it. Although political life is transformed so that the city's natural suspicion of philosophy and science is replaced by cooperation if not warm affection, on the popular level this means only a change of habit or attitude—not of understanding—brought about by philosophical reforms. What then compels the philosophers knowingly to break with nature? Is this a free choice, or something compelled by stepmotherly nature? According to Strauss, Aristotle was already aware of nature's stepmotherly character and did not consider the project of mastering her to be a fitting response.[14] By turning philosophy into the project of mastery, the moderns accept with full consciousness the "politicization" of philosophy.[15] They consciously make political life the ceiling above which the philosophic life will not rise as regards its ultimate ends.[16]

Strauss describes the modern revolution as "the secular movement which tries to guarantee the actualization of the ideal, or to prove the necessary coincidence of the rational and the real, or to get rid of that which transcends every possible human reality."[17] The movement begins with Machiavelli's judgment that "traditional political philosophy aimed too high" and that the grounds of political life must be placed in motives that are always effective: the primary natural urges or passions.[18] But in Strauss's account the modern intent is not just to aim at lower political results. Rather by such lowering it strives to actualize "the ideal" or the high—indeed to make its actualization necessary. In other terms, the project is to provide for the first time an adequate defense of philosophy by reconceiving it as a "humanitarian" activity, one that not incidentally frees humanity from the bonds of dogma and superstition. Again one asks: how is this project concerned with "individuality"? Liberation of individuality appears to be an outcome, or a means, in the project of actualization, but not its immediate object.

Let us note some passages where Strauss speaks of a direct link between modern "actualization" and a new account of individuality. In one passage he writes of Hobbes's transformation of ancient Epicureanism.[19] According to Epicurean doctrine the individual is by nature free of social bonds, since the natural good is identical with the pleasant, and law requires the restraint or denial of pleasure. Hobbes goes further to liberate the individual from natural ends as such; the good life is only a pattern devised by the will, it is not a natural pattern apprehended before it is willed. Hobbes's aim of constructing an "island of intelligibility" exempt from chance and superseding the question of the cosmic support of the human entails this liberation from teleology.[20] Again liberated individuality seems to be the effect, not the object, of the transformation. In Strauss's view, Locke continued Hobbes's project and "through the shift of emphasis from natural duties or obligations to natural rights, the individual, the ego, had become the center and origin of the moral world." Indeed Locke went even further than Hobbes in his doctrine of property, wherein "the work of man and not the gift of nature, is the origin of almost everything valuable."[21] The emancipation of the individual's productive acquisitiveness replaces restraint of appetite as the source of social bonds. In Rousseau's even more radical account of the original natural state, its complete indeterminacy makes it the "ideal vehicle of freedom," and freedom is understood as "a freedom from society which is not a freedom for something." Rousseau makes an appeal from society to "an ultimate sanctity of the individual as individual, unredeemed or unjustified."[22]

These philosophers present three versions of the modern effort to "get rid of that which transcends every possible human reality," efforts that liberate the individual from putative social and natural bonds transcending the individual's will. But individuality is liberated as the result of basing the human order on what human life makes for itself, without dependence on the transcendent. That dependence is the evil to be avoided; individuality is not the good to be attained. At least before Rousseau the life of the original, free individual is not good or desirable in itself. The natural state, being harsh, is only a negative *telos*. The treatment of free, original individuality as inherently good seems to be Rousseau's invention. But the quarrel between the ancients and the moderns concerning individuality cannot be limited to a quarrel between the ancients and Rousseau or the Rousseauians. What is more, Rousseau's "sanctification" of the individual is the result of his effort to remove difficulties he sees present in the earlier modern positions and so is not intelligible apart from his critique of early modern philosophy. It is thus a result, not a starting point.

It has to be observed that in all the modern philosophers, according to Strauss, the project of emancipation of the human from the superhuman is effected by means of a new account of knowledge that regards the intelligible as the object of human making. (In passing I note that Strauss's characterization here is much overstated, at least with regard to major moderns other than Hobbes, such as Bacon and Descartes, to say nothing of Leibniz, Kant, Hegel, et al.) This innovation is bound up with new conceptions of "method" as that which secures dogmatic certainty on the basis of prior skepticism about the appearances as given. Hobbes and the moderns depart from premodern nominalism, which "had faith in the natural working of the human mind," that is, belief in the natural origin of universals.[23] Rejection of that belief is an indispensable condition for replacing order grounded in the unreliability of stepmotherly nature with reliable man-made order. Strauss's reference to premodern nominalism points to his awareness of an earlier thinking in which the individual, not the universal, is the primary locus of the real. But such nominalism is defective for the moderns because it does not ground the possibility of scientific knowledge of beings, and scientific certainty (secured through a new account of "laws of nature") is required for "actualization" as the extension of human power and the overcoming of chance.[24] The modern sense of individuality arises from, and does not precede, that requirement.

III

But now I shall suddenly reverse myself and propose that a close look at Strauss's account shows that a certain reflection on the individual does indeed precede and condition the related modern demands for actualization, mastery of nature or chance, and the founding of new sciences. One must go back to the "presupposition" of the natural understanding of a natural tension between the individual and the political. This "presupposition" implies that moral and political life suffers from inherent defects, and these defects can be overcome only by a movement toward the "transpolitical." Perhaps the "politicization" of philosophy in modernity is then actually not a glorification of the political as the highest end, but a new response to its deficiency. A passage from the lectures entitled *The Problem of Socrates* can help with this. Observing that "political life derives its dignity from something which transcends political life," Strauss notes that "the essential limitation of the political can be understood in three ways":[25] the Socratic view that the transpolitical to which the political owes its dignity is philosophy (*theoria*), accessible only to good natures; the teaching of revelation that the transpolitical is accessible through faith, which depends on divine grace; and liberalism, according to which the transpolitical consists in something that every human being as such possesses, regardless of natural gifts or divine grace. According to the third way, political society exists for the sake of protecting the rights of man.[26] However, these remarks force one to raise the question: What is the nature of the limitation of the political, such that it needs a supplement beyond itself? It will be important to note that Strauss stresses that this limitation is not experienced only by philosophers.

I want to make another observation before pursuing that question. In the course of his account of the transpolitical in the lectures mentioned, Strauss tacitly replaces the third way of liberalism with another way, that of the poets, whereby he indicates that classical thought on the highest level (Aristophanes) proposes another way of thinking about the limitation, a way, Strauss claims, Plato regards as the most serious challenge to the philosophic way. I suggest— and this is now only a hypothesis—that he thereby indicates a (but perhaps not the only) natural root of liberalism, i.e., of the modern approach to individuality. The modern philosophers who sought to emancipate the political from the superhuman recognized that the political points to the transpolitical and does so in diverse and competing ways. In seeking the final reconciliation of philosophy with politics, they introduced the modern notion of the individual as defined by freedom rather than by natural teleology. Individuals so understood are the citizens of the liberal state, which does not rest on the superhuman. Such citizens are the grateful recipients of a new philosophy that aims not at knowledge of the superhuman but at ministering to universal human needs.

Here is my hypothesis: From the classical standpoint, this dual transformation of philosophy and political life, redirecting the human away from what superhumanly transcends political life, is indeed an extreme project. But there is an insight granted by the poets—the poetic account of *eros*—that provides a basis for viewing the individual as possessing a form of the transpolitical that is neither the life of *theoria* nor faith in revelation. What the poets show is that all human beings possess through certain merely human experiences some awareness of the limitation of the political, that is to say, of law. The modern project has a natural basis: it grounds political life in a universal awareness of the transpolitical (or subpolitical) in the human, which allows politics to be independent of the transpolitical as superhuman (the cosmic or divine grounds). There may be something apparently paradoxical in the claim that philosophers make poetic accounts of human existence the preferred point of departure. All the same, it is a starting point with warrant from nature and experience. When Strauss asserts that the famous "quarrel" concerns "eventually, and perhaps even from the beginning, the status of individuality," he indicates that the modern notion of individuality emerges most clearly in the thought of later modernity. But it is in later modernity that philosophy turns explicitly to poetry to remedy the defects of rationalist philosophy, a development already evident in Rousseau and Burke.[27] Still "perhaps even from the beginning" the moderns, in some less manifest fashion, perform the turn to poetry as they introduce the modern notion of individuality.[28]

IV

Before turning to the thematic treatment of poetry in the lectures on Socrates, I look briefly at the lectures entitled *Progress or Return?* which contain pregnant formulations on the limitation of the political. Here Strauss analyzes the problem of modern rationalism in terms of the opposition of Greek philosophy and biblical revelation, and in the course of the analysis poetry receives a short but significant discussion. Strauss presents an account of the recent crisis of rationalism in terms of a general collapse of the belief in the necessary parallelism between social and intellectual progress.[29] He claims that it is now widely admitted that progress in material (economic, technological, etc.) terms does not guarantee progress in virtue and wisdom. Also, confidence in the authoritative status of scientific knowledge, the ground and engine of progress, has been shaken by the awareness of science's merely hypothetical character. (For this latter point Strauss provides no argument but defers to Nietzsche's judgment.)[30] The shattering of the fundamental tenets of modern rationalism forces us to reconsider the roots of the tradition.[31] The lectures are notable for arguing that the modern belief in progress—thus modern rationalism itself—can be understood as a hybrid of Greek philosophy and biblical revelation. The Greeks supposed that human beings have made progress from imperfect beginnings through arts and sciences, and even allowed for unlimited progress in some arts, but not in legislation, since the requirements of social life and intellectual life are radically different. Human progress is periodically undone by natural catastrophes in Greek thought, while biblical revelation offers the guarantee of an infinite future through a covenant with God, that is, divine grace. Revelation regards as proud and sinful the belief that the beginnings are less than perfect and that human art improves on them. To compress Strauss's account to its essential points: Modern rationalism offers the assurance of infinite progress based wholly on human advances in the arts and sciences (thus replacing the revealed guarantee) and understands progress as unlimited in both the intellectual and the moral realms (thus denying the Greek views on the difference between these realms, as well as on periodic catastrophes). The result is biblical morality without revelation and philosophy as practical mastery of nature without contemplation.[32]

Strauss offers here no account of how this hybrid, the modern doctrine of progress, was formed, but only asserts that it was formed by philosophical argument that consciously employed biblical elements, and not by an unconscious process called "secularization." He offers, however, some insight into how such a hybrid was thinkable in the first place. While commenting on the radical difference between Greek philosophy and the Bible on the "one thing needful" (autonomous understanding vs. loving obedience to the law), he also notes that "the disagreement presupposes some agreement" and spells out two fundamental agreements of the two sources: morality consists in justice as obedience to law supported by divine sanctions, and morality is insufficient and in need of completion.[33] The two sources differ on what transcends and completes justice or morality, although both sources regard justice as problematic in light of the "difficulty created by the misery of the just and the prosperity of the wicked." The problem of justice is actually the problem of divine justice, since the primary sense of justice is observance of the divinely sanctioned law. The problem might be restated as the question of how the individual good relates to the common good, or how the individual relates to the universal or the whole.

Strauss regards both sources as able to formulate objections to the authority of law, and in that regard both allow for a fundamental exercise of reason in exposing its problem. But the two sources solve the problem "in a diametrically opposed manner."[34] The Greek philosophic solution regards law grounded in ancestral custom as inherently inferior to law based on rational inquiry; in sum, it discovers the idea of universal nature as standard and exposes the accidental character of laws of particular societies. But the authority to which it ascends, nature, is an impersonal necessity that replaces the personal gods.[35]

Strauss notes, however, that the Bible differs from all "myth"—and so is akin to philosophy—in its awareness of the problem caused by the variety of divine laws. How is the whole to be conceived if only one particular tribe possesses the one true divine law? This surely raises the question of divine justice, of whether the divine will is just in its punishing and rewarding of the particular. The biblical solution grounds the particular and contingent law in a divine will that is wholly just, but to human reason wholly inscrutable, and it regards the quest for knowledge of the grounds of the law as a rebellion against God.[36] Yet both sources see the need to ascend from the moral and political to the transmoral and transpolitical, and thus can engage in a continuing argument that is the "secret of the vitality of Western civilization."[37]

It follows that any synthesis or "system" that later thought attempts to make with the two sources also addresses the problem of justice, and therefore acknowledges the need for the transpolitical. The modern fusion, however, offers an approach (the rights of man) that obfuscates the two original transpolitical alternatives. Strikingly central to Strauss's analysis is the claim that awareness of the problem of justice is not the preserve of philosophy alone. Indeed he discusses prephilosophic forms of that awareness not only in the Bible but in Greek thought, using texts of Aristotle: the magnanimous man of the *Nicomachean Ethics* and the account of tragic poetry in the *Poetics*. The magnanimous man is not humbly obedient to the law but habitually claims great honors for himself. By regarding magnanimity as one of two foci of moral virtue (the other being justice), Aristotle presupposes that "man is capable of being virtuous thanks to his own efforts."[38] The identification of virtue with obedience to law receives a yet greater challenge from tragic poetry, for the tragedians (at least as Aristotle reads them) are concerned with the arousal and purgation of the passions that "seem to be the root of religion": fear and pity, which are related to guilt, the feeling of disobedience to divine law. Tragic art seeks to liberate the better type of man from all morbidity so that he can dedicate himself to noble action, whereby it prepares for philosophy by pointing to an account of the divine as not concerned with human goodness.[39] In these remarks on Aristotle, Strauss acknowledges sotto voce that the Western tradition contains another source of thinking about the problem of justice, which differs from both philosophy and revealed truth, and hence that there is another great "quarrel" in the tradition: between philosophy and poetry. By pointing to a way of thinking about the problem of justice—the relation of the individual to the whole—that is natural and yet not philosophic, he points to a possible natural root of what he expressly calls the "third" approach to the transpolitical (liberalism).

Two brief but important addenda on these lectures: Strauss notes that the meaning of philosophy is obscured above all by the identification of philosophy with "the completed philosophic system" already in the Middle Ages and "certainly with Hegel in modern times."[40] Such philosophy "is one very special form of philosophy; it is not the primary and necessary form." In the latter form (knowledge of ignorance) Socrates wondered whether "by saying that the whole is not intelligible we do not admit to having some understanding of the whole."[41] The Socratic philosophic life, in articulating that insight, "cannot possibly lead up to the insight that another way of life is the right one."[42] These remarks make clear that Strauss regards the modern syntheses or "systems" as still philosophic, albeit imperfectly, and that he does not leave the argument between reason and revelation at an impasse for both parties.[43]

V

A primary theme of the lecture series *The Problem of Socrates* is "the secular contest between poetry and philosophy of which Plato speaks at the beginning of the tenth book of the *Republic*," and the Platonic view that this quarrel is the decisive context for understanding the meaning of Socratic political philosophy.[44] "One could venture to say that the alternative to philosophy, to Platonic philosophy, is not any other philosophy . . . ; the alternative is poetry."[45] Strauss, as in the *Progress or Return?* lectures, states that the contemporary collapse of rationalism requires us to consider the origins of rationalism. "For a number of reasons this question can be identified with the problem of Socrates, or the problem of classical political philosophy in general." In these lectures, however, the problem for philosophy is not the challenge from revelation. The problem that classical political philosophy tried to solve and the obstacle it tried to overcome "appeared clearly in Aristophanes's presentation of Socrates."[46] Aristophanes's *The Clouds* "is the most important statement of the case for poetry" against philosophy.[47] The title *The Problem of Socrates* carries unmistakable overtones of the thought of Nietzsche. In the introduction to his book on Socrates and Aristophanes, Strauss makes that connection explicit. Nietzsche's attack on Socrates or Plato is the culmination of the radical questioning of the tradition that compels a return to the tradition's origins.[48] Nietzsche revives the Aristophanic critique of the young Socrates, which he uses "as if it had been meant as a critique of the Platonic Socrates."[49] Strauss implies that the Platonic Socrates, who defends justice and piety unlike the young Socrates of *The Clouds*, provides a response to both Aristophanes and Nietzsche. The examination of Plato's account of the quarrel between poetry and philosophy is a crucial element therefore in the response to Nietzsche's attack on rationalism (an attack that Strauss argues was initiated by Rousseau).[50] It discloses an "erotic" Socrates and an "erotic" Plato who are in crucial ways closer to the poets than later thinkers—including Nietzsche—had seen.

Aristophanes's poetry, although informed by philosophic thought, sees philosophy as a problem for civic life. His poetry is informed by the philosophic idea of nature, for it presents an account of the natural life as the enjoyment of the private and retired pleasures of family life, in tension with the just and the noble that are only conventional.[51] The family is more natural than the city. Yet Aristophanes launches a defense of noble convention rooted in the ancestral against philosophy, since human life cannot dispense with convention, which has a precarious middle status between the body and the mind. Socrates in the Aristophanic satire cannot grasp the requirements of civic life and lacks self-knowledge about his problematic relation to convention; he is amusical and apolitical.[52] But Aristophanes's defense of *nomos* is itself novel, and his restoration of sound, prephilosophic politics is incompatible with the ancestral polity.[53] The comic poet gives expression to the fundamental tension between the individual good and *nomos* and at the same time portrays the folly of not recognizing the limits of rational efforts to liberate human beings from convention. Xenophon and Plato in their defenses of Socrates present him as regarding politics and human things as worthy of serious study and show him aware of the limits of reason and especially of the limits of the philosopher's ability to persuade the multitude.[54] Indeed Socrates was the first philosopher to grasp that understanding political life is decisive for knowledge of the whole.[55] His reflection on the spirited aspect of the soul, or *thumos*, as providing the link between the higher and the lower, between mind and body, and as that which gives man unity, is central to this inquiry.[56] Spiritedness appears to be the characteristically human passion; in any case it is the political passion. In the *Republic* it is radically distinguished from *eros*.[57]

In practical terms Socrates sees the need of philosophy to enlist the thumotic rhetoric of Thrasymachus if the philosopher is to have any hope of founding and governing a city. Theoretically Socrates has full awareness the tension between reason's search for the universal and the inherently particular and exclusive character of society.[58] *Thumos* seems capable of resolving the tension. The construction in speech of the best city in the *Republic* rests on the thumotic demand for the parallel between the individual and the city: that the justice of the city (each part performing well one and only one task for the sake of the whole) and that of the individual are the same. The parallel breaks down, since when each part of the individual's soul performs its task well the individual attains a higher justice than the city's: a perfection that is possible in any city, and desirable for its own sake.[59] The spirited identification of the individual and the city can be carried out only through a radical suppression of the body and *eros*. Spiritedness indeed has a questionable relation to the human good; in its indeterminacy it is obedient to any end, whether of the mind or the body. The laws that *thumos* enforces (and without *thumos* there could be no law) have no necessary relation to the mind or the good. The standpoint of spiritedness and law is abstraction from the individual case; wisdom that does reflect on the individual case must transcend the standpoint of law and have a flexibility that law lacks. The problem faced by wise individuals is to translate their judgment into a form effective with the multitude. "The unlimited rule of undiluted wisdom must be replaced by the rule of wisdom diluted by consent," i.e., indirect rule by means of laws "on the making of which the wise have had some influence."[60]

Spiritedness for the most part, except when under the control of the wise, is the opponent of the highest human good; it produces spurious human unity. But spiritedness belongs inescapably to the context of human life and thus to that of philosophy as well; philosophic *eros* cannot ignore it, and not solely for practical reasons. Indeed the Socratic turn to political philosophy is centrally a recognition that being is heterogeneous, articulated into knowable classes or kinds; this awareness of "noetic heterogeneity" is above all the recognition of the distinctiveness of the political.[61] The political is a realm between body and mind, partaking of both; its heterogeneity from the rest of nature depends on the source of its precarious unity: *thumos*. The Socratic turn to the ideas is first of all a turn to the significance of *thumos* as the ground of a decisive heterogeneity in being. The intrinsic relation between *eidos* and *thumos*, in other terms, consists in the fact that the core of Socrates's philosophic revolution is the uncovering of the distinctiveness of the political as an *eidos* or class.[62] How then could *thumos* be only an obstacle to philosophic understanding? On the contrary, political life with its spirited foundation is necessarily the first way that human unity comes to sight, or necessarily the first way that the higher becomes visible in and to the lower.[63] Morality or law is the primary way in which the human exists as the dualism "of being a part [of the whole] while open to the whole, and therefore in a sense being the whole itself."[64] Political life is the chief way that the individual rises above and beyond himself, dedicating himself to a whole beyond himself: "All nobility consists in such rising above and beyond oneself." Politics is the clue not only to a fundamental heterogeneity but also to the possible unification of the heterogeneous. The unity precariously achieved by morality points to a more genuine unity.

In what way is the turn to political philosophy an answer to the poetic critique? To address this one needs an account of what the poet regards as his
distinctive wisdom. It happens to be quite close to the Socratic-Platonic philosophy just described. Strauss goes so far as to say that subject matter and
treatment are "fundamentally of the same character" in both poetry and philosophy.[65] The Platonic dialogue and poetry both have as subject matter the
variety of souls or human types (the heterogeneity of being), and both proceed
by imitation.[66] "Poetry does justice to the two sides of life by splitting itself, as
it were, into comedy and tragedy, and precisely Plato says that the true poet is
both a tragic and a comic poet."[67] Yet the dramatic poet's need to imitate many
kinds of people makes his art questionable from the standpoint of the legislation of the best city, which requires complete dedication of the citizen to one
job.[68] Plato's own procedure is of course to imitate many types and to produce
a work of poetry that speaks with many voices. Philosophy and poetry are alike
in bringing to light what the law forbids, a range of experiences and thoughts
at odds with the demands of conventional or demotic justice. Poetic imitation
creates the illusion of presenting real beings as wholes; in fact it heightens
something essential by disregarding something essential.[69] It thereby uncovers
the essential in various states of soul or characters, but thus raises the question
of whether there is a unity behind this multiplicity. It exposes the problem of
the unity of human life, a problem that it is the business of spiritedness to suppress or solve by force. Poetry is more closely related to the pleasant and erotic
than to the noble, even if (or because) *thumos* and the noble are indispensable
themes of poetry (as in the tradition founded by Homer).[70] Furthermore poetic
imitation, unlike a treatise, treats human beings as moved by passions and not
as pure intellects; poetic imitation is the appropriate vehicle for presenting
philosophy as a way of life.[71] Strauss writes that "what undergoes various kinds
of fate in treatises is not human beings, but *logoi*," and "Plato refers frequently
to this life and fate of the *logoi*, most clearly perhaps in the *Phaedo*. . . . Yet the
primary theme of the *Phaedo* is not the death of Socrates' *logoi* but the death
of Socrates himself."[72]

The difference between poetry and philosophy in Strauss's presentation
comes down to one point: the poets show only inferior ways of life, those that
fail to solve the problems of life in a satisfactory way. Autonomous poetry
presents nonphilosophic life as autonomous, and so remains drastically incomplete. "Yet by articulating the cardinal problem of human life as it comes
to sight within the nonphilosophic life, poetry prepares for the philosophic
life."[73] Legitimate poetry is ministerial to the life of understanding.

VI

I conclude with a few remarks on the meaning of the apparent disregard of poetry in Strauss's account of the sources of liberalism. Poetry's openness to the problematic character of life shows it to be more akin to philosophy's *eros* than to law and ancestral piety. Plato's presentation of a musical Socrates, aware of the complexity of the human passions and thus possessing an essential ingredient of prudence, counters the charge of the poets that philosophy is unerotic. Poetry has its source in a universal human capacity to experience the complexity of the passions and the limitations of law on a prephilosophic level. In the hands of capable poets, poetic imitation articulates this experience to disclose the structure of primary human tensions and problems. Poetry's failure consists in not making available by argument or example the thinker and the life of thought as the most satisfactory way of life, as neither tragic nor comic. In this way it prefigures the liberal account of the human in terms of freedom: the human capacity to pursue a variety of ends, without the judgment of a natural hierarchy of ends. In later modern philosophy, this becomes the celebration of diversity, or the preference for the local and particular over the universal.[74] Strauss indicates that Nietzsche's preference for the tragic life over the theoretical life is related to his adoption of the "fundamental premise of the historical school," namely, not the belief in necessary progress but "the belief in the supreme value of diversity or uniqueness."[75] Strauss's presentation of the origins and development of modernity as an artificial, willful project seems to commit a deliberate abstraction from this poetic element, which has its counterpart, if not its source, in ancient poetry. He thus enlarges the gulf between ancient and modern, even as, in a countervailing movement, he distances Socrates in his provocative reading from traditional rationalism and uncovers a Plato who can converse with Nietzsche and Heidegger to show philosophic respect for human particularity as only poetry can disclose it. His procedure, however, might be considered a Platonic abstraction: Just as the *Republic*'s "three waves" of founding first inspire enthusiasm, then lead to disappointment about the prospects for political idealism, so Strauss's account of modernity—banishing the poets with as much irony as Socrates—detaches the better natures from modern political hopes and awakens the philosophic need to return to the beginnings.

Dwelling and Exile

Only since the philosophy of German Idealism is there a *history* of philosophy wherein history itself becomes a path of absolute knowing to itself. History is now no longer the past that one has left behind oneself and is over with, but is rather the constant form of becoming of the spirit itself [*Werdeform des Geistes selbst*]. First in German Idealism is history grasped metaphysically. Until that time it is something unavoidable and unintelligible, a burden or a miracle, an error or a purposeful arrangement, a witch's dance or the teacher of "life," but in any case always something that one interprets directly on the basis of quotidian experience and its aims.

MARTIN HEIDEGGER, *Schelling: Vom Wesen der menschlichen Freiheit*

The Greeks, and therewith in particular Socrates and Plato, lacked the awareness of history, the historical consciousness. . . . But perhaps History is a problematic *interpretation* of phenomena which could be interpreted differently, which *were* interpreted differently in former times and especially by Socrates and his descendants. I will illustrate the fact starting from a simple example. Xenophon, a pupil of Socrates, wrote a history called *Hellenica*, Greek history. This work begins abruptly with the expression "Thereafter.". . . More importantly: the *Hellenica* also *ends* with Thereafter, what we call History is for Xenophon a sequence of Thereafters, in each of which *tarache* (confusion) rules.

LEO STRAUSS, "The Problem of Socrates"

I

History is a theme central to the thought of Heidegger and Strauss as late modern philosophers. Both see themselves as living in a time of exhaustion and collapse of the tradition, which calls for a new beginning, but their conceptions of history and of philosophy's role in it are otherwise starkly different. It is as important for Strauss to reject the German metaphysical approach to history as a meaningful process as it is for Heidegger to endorse a version of it. This is not to say that Strauss simply returns to the Greek account of history as a "sequence of Thereafters," since Strauss cannot claim that he is unaware of history in the modern sense or of the historical consciousness. For a late modern philosopher, the recovery of the nonmetaphysical approach requires a conscious effort of overcoming the inheritance of the historical consciousness. "The *distinction* between philosophic and historical cannot be avoided, but distinction is not total *separation*: one cannot study the philosophic problem without having made up one's mind on the historical problem and one cannot study the historical problem without having made up one's mind implicitly on the philosophical problem."[1] The rejection of history as a meaningful or "metaphysical" process is based not on a comprehensive alternative metaphysical doctrine but rather on skepticism about the possibilities of the political sphere. That the latter can only be a "cave" of conflicting opinion and not a true whole is the experience from which Strauss begins. To begin there "implicitly" is not the same as possessing final knowledge about the problem of history. The structure of the relation of philosophy to the city is an indeterminate dyad: philosophy must distinguish itself from the city but it cannot exist apart from the city. Strauss ascribes the same structure to the relation of the problem of philosophy to the problem of history, for the modern cave has been formed by historical thinking. Like all opinion in the cave, historical thinking has proved to be characterized by internal contradiction. That merely negative insight, far from constituting wisdom, is sufficient to ground a Socratic inquiry that denies its subservience to (or unity with) history while all the same not leaving behind the reflection on history.

Reflection on history cannot be abandoned after one has had the insight that philosophic questioning is subject to deformation as it becomes a tradition or as it becomes "history" with a negative teleological sense (growing forgetfulness). With this problem of history in mind, Strauss and Jacob Klein recovered the original meaning of the Platonic criticism of writing as in reality the achievement of a new form of writing that remains "alive" through requiring readers to question the doctrinal distortions of philosophy that the same writing seems to present as the truth of its own dialectic. In other words, Platonic writing anticipates its own fall into error (the tradition of the "doctrine of ideas"), which it enables close readers to avoid.[2] Although Heidegger did not read Plato in this way, he provided insights that enabled others to find this way, for he showed that Greek philosophy from the beginnings through Aristotle is moved by the aporia of Being (the question "of ancient times, and the question now and the question always," as Aristotle says), which specifically has the structure of tension between the apophantic disclosure of Being in *logos* and the attempt to give causal, genetic accounts of Being, which tend to occlude the original disclosure. In clear indebtedness to Heidegger, Jacob Klein took as the principal theme of his inquiries the twofold character of *eidos* as disclosure in *logos* (in stable intelligible structures) and as the causal-genetic ground of becoming. Klein wrote of "the one immense difficulty within ancient ontology, namely, to determine the relation between the 'being' of the object itself and the 'being' of the object in thought," and argued that this difficulty laid the basis for the modern approach in mathematics and physical science in which the solution to the aporia of Being is found in "the *symbolic* understanding of the object intended," or the identification of the actual object being studied (number, body) with the mere concept of the object (indeterminate magnitude, extension).[3] Referring to Klein's insights, Strauss argues that the new approach to knowledge as symbolic construction made possible the idea of progress, which "implies that the most elementary questions can be settled once and for all so that future generations can dispense with their further discussion, but can erect on the foundations once laid an ever-growing structure."[4] As the foundations were covered up by advances built upon them, philosophy, which requires lucidity about its proceeding, found it needed a special inquiry (the history of philosophy or science) "whose purpose it is to keep alive the recollection, and the problem, of the foundations hidden by progress."[5] Strauss, in accord with Heidegger and Klein, engages in such inquiry not in order to shore up the foundations but in order to expose the problem in them.

Heidegger made the ancient aporia accessible insofar as he showed that the question of Being begins with the prescientific disclosure of beings through human speaking and knowing as an engaged openness with the world, and made evident the presence of this understanding in ancient authors. Heidegger's intent was not merely to identify openness to Being with the practical handling of things as equipment (the ready-to-hand) but to uncover the presupposed horizon of this engagement ("world") as inherently elusive to discursive and causal accounts. At the same time he sought to show that the aporia of Being was under constant pressure of concealment by the tendencies toward "fallen" modes of discourse bound up with human existence, which is inauthentic and flees from genuine questioning, especially human "being-together" in anonymous, self-forgetting social life. It is an easy step from this analysis to the view that philosophizing is under constant threat from distortion in the form of tradition that arises from the social needs of teaching and communication. It is also not difficult to see that in spite of his vastly different appreciation of political life and philosophy's relation to it, Strauss's view of philosophy as radical openness to aporia that is in inherent tension with the requirements of law and political life was prepared by Heidegger's analysis. In other terms, Strauss's claim that the core of philosophy is political philosophy is equivalent to the claim that the primary theme of philosophic reflection is the forgetfulness of aporia, understood in nonhistoricist fashion.

II

Central to Strauss's nonhistoricist account of the problem of history is the transformation of the cave by revealed religion, or the religion of the book, which made possible the permanent subordination of philosophy to a doctrine that claimed to be comprehensive truth. In Strauss's account early modern philosophy attempted to reestablish the natural independence of philosophy from *nomos* but did so only through another subjection of philosophy to *nomos*: the practical, progressive, humanitarian project of Enlightenment that is grounded in universally accessible certainties. Philosophy lost its aporetic openness in order to secure civic freedom for itself and for all humanity, thereby becoming wholly at home in politics. Hobbes supplied the foundations of this project in the account of knowledge as construction, abstracting philosophy from ancient questions and controversies about causes. "The abandonment of the primacy of contemplation or theory in favor of the primacy of practice is the necessary consequence of the abandonment of the plane on which Platonism and Epicureanism have carried on their struggle. For the synthesis of Platonism and Epicureanism stands or falls with the view that to understand is to make."[6] The successors to the constructivism of Hobbes and Descartes are the various modern systems that claim to give a comprehensive structure of human knowledge that excludes the possibility of miracles and any revelation of a mysterious God. Of Spinoza Strauss writes: "There is therefore only one way of disposing of the possibility of revelation or miracles: one must prove that God is in no way mysterious, or that we have adequate knowledge of the essence of God. This step was taken by Spinoza." According to Spinoza "any knowledge of God we can have must be as clear and as distinct as that which we can have of the triangle," and his teaching "presents the most comprehensive, or the most ambitious, program of what *modern science* could be."[7] Although Strauss regards the contrast between ancient and modern philosophy on the question of the refutability of revelation as the key to their difference, his view on their positions is at times put cryptically. "A philosophy which believes that it can refute the possibility of revelation and a philosophy which does not believe that: *this* is the real meaning of la querelle des anciens et des modernes."[8] The ambiguity of the references in this sentence may be removed by recalling that Strauss expressly describes Spinoza as believing that he could refute the possibility of revelation. Since at least one major modern subscribes to refutability, it would seem to follow that the ancients have the more modest approach, although Strauss remarks on the "possibility of refutation implied in Platonic-Aristotelian philosophy. What their specific argument is, we cannot say before we have understood their whole teaching. Since I cannot claim to have achieved this, I must leave the issue open."[9]

Upon careful consideration, one sees that Strauss's view is that ancient philosophy as aporetic, as admitting that the whole is not intelligible, is in the stronger position for justifying its way of life as the most choiceworthy. But its strength does not depend on showing the refutability of revelation in a crucial sense, i.e., by offering a metaphysical account of the whole that establishes the impossibility of a mysterious, omnipotent first cause. He writes: "as far as I know, the present-day arguments in favor of revelation against philosophy are based on an inadequate understanding of classical philosophy," for "classical philosophy is said to be based on the unwarranted belief that the whole is intelligible." Countering this view, Strauss writes of Socrates as the philosopher "who knew that he knew nothing, who therewith admitted that the whole is not intelligible" although "he wondered whether by saying that the whole is not intelligible we do not admit to having some understanding of the whole."[10] In other words, Strauss thought that Socratic philosophy provides a sufficient grounding for the philosophic life that does not depend on knowing whether Plato and Aristotle had achieved refutations of the alternative of revealed truth. To be more precise, Socratic knowledge of ignorance provides a response to the *claim* of revelation to define the best life even if reason cannot prove the impossibility of a mysterious God. "The very insight into the *limitations* of philosophy is a victory of philosophy: because it is an *insight*."[11] This is a crucial point in Strauss (often misconstrued by interpreters), and it bears directly on Strauss's response to Heidegger, who in Strauss's estimation is quite "sensible" in avowing the mysteriousness of Being and of the origin of the human as bound up with Being. For Strauss the confrontation with that ultimate mystery leaves intact the possibility that reason has transhistorical knowledge of its limitations, or an insight that is not an *Ereignis,* a "gift of Being" or of some higher power, but derived from knowledge of the human dyadic openness and closedness of the "cave," which determines the human relation to the whole. Whereas Heidegger still agrees with the modern philosophers that the appearance of biblical revelation in the world changed the character of philosophy, presumably permanently, Strauss regards the insight into human duality as providing philosophy with a crucial means of transcending this historical contingency.

To restate Strauss's central insight: the *knowledge* of human dyadic openness to the whole, or the knowledge that access to the fundamental problems (including the problem that revelation claims to answer) is available only through an erotic ascent from the moral-political realm, is the root transhistorical insight. Hence "the political things and their corollaries are the form in which the highest principles first come to sight" and "they are the link between what is highest and lowest." The political things are the key to all things since man as political is the microcosm.[12]

Strauss could at the same time express sympathy with certain moments in modern philosophy that in an ancient spirit distance themselves from the authority of revelation, aiming at neither refutation nor subservience. Thus he praises Montesquieu who "tried to recover for statesmanship a latitude which had been considerably restricted by the Thomistic teaching. What Montesquieu's private thoughts were will always remain controversial. But it is safe to say that what he explicitly teaches, as a student of politics and as politically sound and right, is nearer to the spirit of the classics than to Thomas."[13] This statement makes evident that the "theologico-political problem" as Strauss sees it unfolds on the plane of politics insofar as reason has a claim to autonomy in practical matters, apart from the theoretical controversy between reason and revelation. Strauss evidently was confirmed in this view by the events of his own life. "The biggest event of 1933 would rather seem to have proved, if such proof was necessary, that man cannot abandon the question of the good society, and that he cannot free himself from the responsibility for answering it by deferring to History or to any other power different from his own reason."[14] Such statements call into question the view that Strauss regarded only philosophers as having a right to appeal to reason and that otherwise the lives of human beings are necessarily and properly guided only by revelation's demands for obedience or by "political theology."[15]

III

The focal thesis of the present study is that Strauss's criticism of the historicism of Heidegger's thought is not chiefly concerned with the skeptical and relativistic consequences of that thought, whereby Strauss would assert against it a set of moral absolutes, and that on the contrary, his judgment is that the appeal to History has the effect of concealing the skeptical and aporetic nature of philosophy as the critique of custom and law. This is the real meaning of Strauss's claim that Heidegger's thought has no room for political philosophy. Thus Heidegger is a profoundly paradoxical figure insofar as his questioning reopened the essential aporia of philosophy and at the same time it concealed from itself its own moral and political implications, distorting the nature of radical questioning by identifying it with the stance of grateful dwelling within worlds defined by particular languages and the poetic announcement of gods.

But if Strauss's true critique of Heidegger is commonly misunderstood, this has much to do with the paradoxical character of his own thought, since Strauss's skeptical overcoming of historicism involves a radical particularism of a special sort. In correspondence with Hans-Georg Gadamer concerning the latter's *Wahrheit und Methode*, Strauss writes: "Not only is my hermeneutical experience very limited . . . the experience I possess makes me doubtful whether a universal hermeneutics which is more than 'formal' or external is possible. I believe that the doubt arises irretrievably from the 'occasional' character of every worthwhile interpretation."[16] Strauss's mode of philosophizing by means of commentaries seeks to illuminate the diverse approaches of the great philosophers to the fundamental problems by placing their thought in dialogue.[17] It is not satisfied with an abstract and general account of those problems and their possible solutions, since the core of philosophy is the activity of addressing the tension between the theoretical life and its political-moral matrix. This entails a constant effort of ascent toward wisdom (knowledge of the whole) that is never completed, and every such ascent has unique features that are necessarily reflected in the individual philosopher's manner of writing. The study of a given philosopher involves becoming acquainted with his peculiar mode of speaking differently to philosophers and nonphilosophers, according to rhetorical strategies that seem to him required by his situation. His mode of rhetoric is inseparable from the substance of his thought, for it directly relates to how he conceives the philosophic life and its relation to political life. The highest subject of philosophy is the philosophic life itself, which is always lived as a particular effort to attain an end that is radically universal: to be at home in the whole.[18] The life and fate of *logoi* are thematic throughout the Platonic dialogues, "yet the primary theme of the *Phaedo* is not the death of Socrates' *logoi* but the death of Socrates himself."[19] The consequences of the philosophic life for facing mortality cannot be summed up in a formula or a theory but can fully emerge only in the actuality of that life.

It must be avowed that this conception of philosophy in which the substance of thinking is inseparable from the manner in which the philosopher conducts his life in his particular *nomos* accords an enormous weight to "history" in some sense. Strauss himself puts great emphasis on how philosophic rhetoric and therefore philosophizing in the context of the Jewish and Islamic revelations were shaped profoundly by their situation. One recurs at this point to Strauss's position that philosophy and history must be distinguished although they cannot be separated. What he means by "history" has no overall coherence or *telos*, is deficient in *logos* (as "cave"), yet is a necessary condition of philosophic *logos*. Philosophy necessarily begins with reflection on particulars that lead to awareness of the universal but are never wholly derivable from the universal.[20] No instance of the philosophic life is strictly speaking repeatable, given that it is always a particular life, engaged with particular circumstances, in erotic quest of the universal.[21] Löwith's formulation "repetition of antiquity at the peak of modernity" spoke to Strauss since it brings forward the essential novelty of what seems to be only a recurrence of the same. The boldness of repetition involves the daring of unorthodox readings. "Who can dare to say that Plato's doctrine of ideas as he intimated it, or Aristotle's doctrine of the *nous* that does nothing but think itself and is essentially related to the eternal visible universe, is the true teaching?"[22]

In opposing his recovery of tradition to both the tradition and his contemporaries, Strauss appeals to no authority but only his own insight. Philosophy as he conceives it is not a destiny or fate sent by history or Being as historical. Philosophers have a permanent, natural fate as exiles operating in the midst of the political realm that provides them with their questions and problems—a fate that can be experienced only by individuals, not by epochs or cultures.

ABBREVIATIONS

WORKS OF HEIDEGGER CITED

All references to *GA* below are to *Martin Heidegger: Gesamtausgabe* (Frankfurt am Main: V. Klostermann, 1975–).

EM: *Einführung in die Metaphysik*, 5th ed. (Tübingen: M. Niemeyer, 1987)

GA 3: *Kant und das Problem der Metaphysik*, ed. F.-W. von Herrmann, 1990

GA 8: *Was heißt Denken?* ed. P.-L. Coriando, 2002

GA 9: *Wegmarken*, ed. F.-W. von Herrmann, 1976

GA 16: *Reden und andere Zeugnisse eines Lebensweges: 1910–1976*, ed. H. Heidegger, 2000

GA 22: *Die Grundbegriffe der antiken Philosophie* (SS 1926), ed. F.-K. Blust, 1993

GA 29/30: *Die Grundbegriffe der Metaphysik: Welt-Endlichkeit-Einsamkeit* (WS 1929/30), ed. F.-W. von Herrmann, 1992

GA 36/37: *Sein und Wahrheit* (SS 1933, WS 1933/34), ed. H. Tietjen, 2001

GA 42: *Schelling: Vom Wesen der menschlichen Freiheit (1809)* (SS 1936), ed. I. Schuessler, 1988

GA 45: *Grundfragen der Philosophie* (WS 1937/38), F.-W. von Herrmann, 1984

GA 51: *Grundbegriffe* (SS 1941), ed. P. Jaeger, 1981

GA 54: *Parmenides* (WS 1942/43), ed. M. S. Frings, 1982

GA 62: *Phänomenologische Interpretationen ausgewählter Abhandlungen des Aristoteles zur Ontologie und Logik* (SS 1922), ed. G. Neumann, 2005

GA 65: *Beiträge zur Philosophie (Vom Ereignis)* (1936–38), ed. F.-W. Von Herrmann, 1988

GA 70: *Über den Anfang* (1941), ed. P.-L. Coriando, 2005

H: *Holzwege*, 4th ed. (Frankfurt am Main: V. Klostermann, 1963)

ID: *Identität und Differenz* (Pfullingen: G. Neske, 1957)

N: *Nietzsche*, 2nd ed. (Pfullingen: G. Neske, 1961)

SD: *Zur Sache des Denkens* (Tübingen: M. Niemeyer, 1969)

SDU: *Die Selbstbehauptung der deutschen Universität und Das Rektorat 1933/34*, 2nd ed., ed. H. Heidegger (Frankfurt am Main: V. Klostermann, 1990)

s z : *Sein und Zeit*, 19th ed. (Tübingen: M. Niemeyer, 2006)
v a : *Vorträge und Aufsätze* (Pfullingen: G. Neske, 1954)

WORKS OF STRAUSS

c c w m : "Correspondence with Hans-Georg Gadamer concerning *Wahrheit und Methode*," *Independent Journal of Philosophy* 2 (1978): 5-12.
c m : *The City and Man* (Chicago: Rand McNally, 1964)
e w : *The Early Writings (1921–32)*, trans. and ed. M. Zank (Albany: State University of New York Press, 2002)
g n : "German Nihilism," *Interpretation* 26, no. 3 (1999): 353-78.
c s : *Gesammelte Schriften*, vols. 1–3, ed. H. Meier (Stuttgart and Weimar: J. B. Metzler, 1996–2001)
h p p : *History of Political Philosophy*, with J. Cropsey, eds., 3rd ed. (Chicago: University of Chicago Press, 1987)
j p c m : *Jewish Philosophy and the Crisis of Modernity: Essays and Lectures in Modern Jewish* Thought, ed. K. H. Green (Albany: State University of New York Press, 1997)
l i g p p : "Living Issues of German Postwar Philosophy," in H. Meier, *Leo Strauss and the Theologico-Political Problem*, 115–39 (Cambridge: Cambridge University Press, 2006)
n r h : *Natural Right and History* (Chicago: University of Chicago Press, 1953)
o t : *On Tyranny: Revised and Expanded Edition, Including the Strauss-Kojève Correspondence*, ed. V. Gourevitch and M. S. Roth. (New York: Free Press, 1991)
p p : *Political Philosophy: Six Essays*, ed. H. Gildin (Indianapolis: Bobbs-Merrill, 1975)
p p h : *The Political Philosophy of Hobbes: Its Basis and Its Genesis*, trans. E. Sinclair, 2nd ed. (Chicago: University of Chicago Press, 1952)
p s : "The Problem of Socrates," *Interpretation* 22, no. 3 (1995): 319-38.
r c p r : *The Rebirth of Classical Political Rationalism: Essays and Lectures by Leo Strauss*, ed. T. Pangle (Chicago: University of Chicago Press, 1989)
r r : "Reason and Revelation," in H. Meier, *Leo Strauss and the Theologico-Political Problem*, 141–80 (Cambridge: Cambridge University Press, 2006)
s a : *Socrates and Aristophanes* (New York: Basic Books, 1966)
s c r : *Spinoza's Critique of Religion*, trans. E. Sinclair (New York: Schocken Books, 1965)
s p p p : *Studies in Platonic Political Philosophy* (Chicago: University of Chicago Press, 1983)
t m : *Thoughts on Machiavelli* (Glencoe, IL: Free Press, 1958)
w i p p : *What Is Political Philosophy? And Other Studies* (Glencoe, IL: Free Press, 1959)
x s : *Xenophon's Socrates* (Ithaca, NY: Cornell University Press, 1972)

NOTES

PARABASIS

1. *CM*, 9. The terms "crisis" and "critique" designate not just moments or possible stances in the history of philosophy but the condition of philosophizing as such. Philosophic thinking cannot "hasten forward with sanguine expectations, as though the path which it has traversed leads directly to the goal, and as though the accepted premises could be so securely relied upon that there can be no need of constantly returning to them and considering whether we may not, perhaps in the course of inferences, discover defects" (Kant, *Critique of Pure Reason*, A735/B763). In the forever-renewed search for beginnings, the center proves to be everywhere and the circumference nowhere. Interruption and crisis in the forward movement of thought are the distinctive signs of insight, therewith of "progress," in philosophic thought. In the drama of dialectic, parabasis is necessarily the principal action and theme. For an account of philosophy as "critical science" whose task is to make distinctions visible (*krinein*) in such a way that it "always puts itself under the most radical critique," see *GA*, 22: 7–11.

2. One should not overlook the great debt of both of these figures to Edmund Husserl precisely in the thematizing of "crisis" and in the phenomenological approach to its analysis. At the same time Heidegger and Strauss are more centrally concerned than Husserl with the uncovering of the origin of the tradition in the Greeks' radical openness to questioning, and with the tradition as the historical obscuring of this origin, although Husserl took up a related inquiry in his late *The Crisis of European Sciences and Transcendental Phenomenology*. See Hwa Yol Jung, "Two Critics of Scientism: Leo Strauss and Edmund Husserl," *Independent Journal of Philosophy* 2 (1978): 81–88, and the author's "Edmund Husserl," in *HPP*.

3. "Philosophy as Rigorous Science and Political Philosophy," *SPPP*, 29–37; first published in *Interpretation* 2, no. 1 (1971).

4. *SPPP*, 30. I am not concerned with whether Heidegger made such a statement or what he may have meant by it if he did make it. I am here concerned with Strauss's statement and what it reveals about his own relation to Heidegger. Indeed Strauss's authority for his view of Heidegger's opinion is obscure and not clearly traceable to Heidegger's express declaration ("As far as I can see . . .").

5. "An Introduction to Heideggerian Existentialism," lecture of 1956, *RCPR*, 29. A more authentic version of this lecture bearing Strauss's original title "Existentialism" appears in *Interpretation* 22, no. 3 (1995): 303–20. In the same lecture Strauss says, "prior to Heidegger's emergence the most outstanding German philosopher—I would say the only German philosopher—of the time was Edmund Husserl," *RCPR*, 28. This should lay to rest the question of whether Strauss thought of Heidegger as a philosopher. For literature treating both Strauss and Heidegger, see relevant essays or parts of the following: L. Batnitzky, *Leo Strauss and Emmanuel Levinas: Philosophy and the Politics of Revelation* (Cambridge: Cambridge University Press, 2006); S. Fleischacker, ed., *Heidegger's Jewish Followers* (Pittsburgh: Duquesne University Press, 2008); P. Kielmansegg, H. Mewes, and E. Glaser-Schmidt, *Hannah Arendt and Leo Strauss* (New York: Cambridge University Press, 1995); S. B. Smith, *Reading Leo Strauss: Politics, Philosophy, Judaism* (Chicago: University of Chicago Press, 2006); C. Zuckert, *Postmodern Platos* (Chicago: University of Chicago Press, 1996); C. Zuckert and M. Zuckert, *The Truth about Leo Strauss: Political Philosophy and American Democracy* (Chicago: University of Chicago Press, 2006).

6. See chapter 7 below.

7. Notable exceptions, besides the authors cited in note 5 above, are Jeffrey Barash, Mark Blitz, Michael Gillespie, Robert Pippin, Stanley Rosen, and Gregory Bruce Smith. Rosen is one of the few writers to address Strauss's concern with the possibility of philosophy. See "Wittgenstein, Strauss, and the Possibility of Philosophy," in *The Elusiveness of the Ordinary: Studies in the Possibility of Philosophy* (New Haven: Yale University Press, 2002).

8. *TM*, 13.

9. *SPPP*, 34–37; *WIPP*, 74–77; *RCPR*, 28–29. "Since the natural understanding is the presupposition of the scientific understanding, the analysis of science and the world of science presupposes the natural understanding, or the world of common sense." *NRH*, 79. See also chapters 3 and 4 below.

10. See chapters 2 and 3 below.

11. For Strauss's argument on this, see chapter 3 below.

12. *WIPP*, 39.

13. This is Strauss's interpretation of Socrates's account of his beginning philosophically with the direct approach to the causes of beings (his "pre-Socratic" phase), followed by his "second sailing" or his "taking refuge in speeches" as the approach to what the beings are. See *Phaedo* 95e–100b.

14. *RCPR*, 24–25, 38–42; *CM*, 2–3.

15. In "Nietzsche's Word 'God is Dead'" (1943), Heidegger writes: "Nietzsche himself interprets the course of Western history metaphysically, as the advent and development of nihilism. To think through Nietzsche's metaphysics becomes a matter of reflecting on the situation and place of contemporary men, whose destiny with respect to truth is still little experienced." *H*, 193–94. In "Religiöse Lage der Gegenwart" (1930), Strauss writes: "Through Nietzsche, tradition has been shaken to its *roots*. It has completely lost its self-evident truth. We are left in this world without any authority, any direction. Only now has the question *pos bioteon* again received its full edge. We *can* pose it again." *GS*, 2: 389, trans. *EW*, 32. See L. Lampert, *Leo Strauss and Nietzsche* (Chicago: University of Chicago Press, 1996), for an insightful discussion of Strauss's relation to Nietzsche focusing on Strauss's "Note on the Plan of Nietzsche's *Beyond Good and*

Evil." On Heidegger's appropriation of Nietzsche, see R. Pippin, "Nietzsche, Heidegger and the Metaphysics of Modernity," in *Nietzsche and Modern German Thought*, ed. K. Ansell-Pearson (New York: Routledge, 1991), and the contributions in A. Denker, M. Heinz, J. Sallis, et al., eds., *Heidegger und Nietzsche. Heidegger-Jahrbuch* 2, (Freiburg/Munich: Alber Verlag, 2005).

16. CCWM, 5–12.

17. See chapter 2 below.

18. For intellectual biographies of Strauss, see the studies by David Janssens, *Between Athens and Jerusalem: Philosophy, Prophecy and Politics in Leo Strauss's Early Thought* (Albany: State University of New York Press, 2008); Heinrich Meier, *Carl Schmitt and Leo Strauss: The Hidden Dialogue* (Chicago: University of Chicago Press, 1995); Eugene R. Sheppard, *Leo Strauss and the Politics of Exile: The Making of a Political Philosopher* (Waltham: Brandeis University Press, 2006); Daniel Tanguay, *Leo Strauss: An Intellectual Biography* (New Haven: Yale University Press, 2007); and the introduction in *EW*. Principal friends and correspondents of Strauss among Heidegger's students were Hans-Georg Gadamer, Hans Jonas, Jacob Klein, Gerhard Krüger, and Karl Löwith. The thought of another close correspondent, the Hegelian-Marxist Alexandre Kojève, is deeply engaged with Heidegger, although he was not Heidegger's student. For Kojève's relation to Heidegger, see E. Kleinberg, *Generation Existential: Heidegger's Philosophy in France, 1927–1961* (Ithaca: Cornell University Press, 2005).

19. "A Giving of Accounts," *JPCM*, 461. Heidegger's lecture course was *Phänomenologische Interpretationen ausgewählter Abhandlungen des Aristoteles zur Ontologie und Logik*, published in *GA*, 62. See also *RCPR*, 27–28. Heidegger states the fundamental intent of his interpretation of the *Metaphysics* in the following passage:

> The question now is: In what way is an inquiry into Being to be motivated? What is the object-sphere, what is the mode of access, from which the ground-meaning [*Grundsinn*] of Being emerges that is decisive for philosophic inquiry? . . . The determination of the meaning of Being which deals solely with the ground-meaning of Being in the sphere of objects, and which is of interest to philosophy, finds itself led back to the analysis of *Life*, human life in its specific-factic way and in its historical Being. . . . The question is: How is one in the first place to set about an investigation of the ontological- and object-meaning of life? For the concrete starting-point it is a matter of appropriating the material for such an inquiry through critique of philosophy. The starting-point must emerge out of history. . . . A genuine starting-point is possible only by going back to the decisive starting-points of philosophy, in the rubble of whose tradition we stand. On this basis every step of the interpretation and translation of Aristotle is determined. (*GA*, 62: 173–74)

For an incisive account of Heidegger's reading of Aristotle's *Nicomachean Ethics*, see S. Rosen, "Kant and Heidegger: Transcendental Alternatives to Aristotle," in *The Elusiveness of the Ordinary: Studies in the Possibility of Philosophy* (New Haven: Yale University Press, 2002).

20. *JPCM*, 462.

21. "An Unspoken Prologue to a Public Lecture at St. John's College in Honor of Jacob Klein," *JPCM*, 450.

22. *JPCM*, 462.

23. *JPCM*, 450.

24. *NRH*, 31. See chapter 7 below.

25. To my knowledge Strauss never characterizes Heidegger as a nihilist or his thought as nihilistic. He delivered a most interesting and revealing lecture in 1941 entitled "German Nihilism," in which he analyzes and criticizes the broad German tendency in the early twentieth century toward opposition to "civilization," understood as the Western democratic Enlightenment. See GN and corrections in *Interpretation* 28, no. 2 (fall 2000): 33–34, and also S. Shell's excellent essay on the lecture, "To Spare the Vanquished and Crush the Arrogant," in *The Cambridge Companion to Leo Strauss*, ed. Steven B. Smith (Cambridge: Cambridge University Press, 2009), 171–92. Surely Heidegger's thought has sympathies with this outlook, including a contempt for moderation that Strauss found in Heidegger's teaching before it became manifest in his praise of the Nazi movement (see chapter 6 below). All the same, Strauss does not reduce Heidegger's thinking, as genuinely philosophic, to the cultural tendencies of his time, and, if I am not mistaken, he regards nihilism as a subphilosophic phenomenon. For a thoughtful and careful study of how Heidegger's philosophy relates to National Socialist ideology and its sources, see C. Bambach, *Heidegger's Roots: Nietzsche, National Socialism and the Greeks* (Ithaca: Cornell University Press, 2003). Bambach writes of Heidegger's "philosophical attempt at geo-politics, a grand metaphysical vision of German destiny based on the notion of a singular German form of autochthony or rootedness in the earth: *Bodenständigkeit*" (xix–xx). As Bambach argues, Heidegger's concerns with "preserving and transforming the German *Volk* against the forces of industrialization, urbanization and the threat of foreign influence" linked him to Nazi ideology, but all the same Heidegger had philosophical concerns alien to Nazism, and his "ontological" account of German destiny brought him into explicit conflict with the biological racism and "political science" of Nazism. For accounts of Heidegger's political engagement that initiated the recent debate about Heidegger's Nazism, see V. Farias, *Heidegger and National Socialism*, trans. P. Burrell and G. Ricci (Philadelphia: Temple University Press, 1989), and H. Ott, *Martin Heidegger: A Political Life*, trans. A. Blunden (New York: Basic Books, 1993). See also H. Sluga, *Heidegger's Crisis* (Cambridge: Harvard University Press, 1993); J. F. Ward, *Heidegger's Political Thinking* (Amherst: University of Massachusetts Press, 1995); M. Zimmerman, *Heidegger's Confrontation with Modernity* (Bloomington: Indiana University Press, 1990); and most recently H. Zaborowski, *"Eine Frage von Irre und Schuld?" Martin Heidegger und der Nationalsozialismus* (Frankfurt am Main: Fischer Verlag, 2010), and the documents and interpretations collected in A. Denker and H. Zaborowski, eds., *Heidegger und der Nationalsozialismus. Heidegger-Jahrbuch*, vols. 4 and 5 (Munich: Karl Alber, 2009). For Heidegger's "idealist" concept of the *Volk*, see below, chapter 4.

26. *RCPR*, 37.

27. *NRH*, 122.

28. *CM*, 20.

29. *TM*, 19. See chapter 3 for more discussion of this and the previous two quotations.

30. Thus Steven Smith writes that there is "a set of common problems or questions that characterize Strauss's work: for example, the difference between ancients and moderns, the quarrel between philosophy and poetry, and of course the tension between reason and revelation. None of these problems can be said to have priority over the others nor do they cohere in anything as crude as a system. Whatever may be alleged, there is hardly a single thread that runs throughout these different interests." *Reading Leo Strauss*, 4. I have to disagree and say that the single thread running through Strauss's inquiries is the duality of the human as political and transcending the political, for which he uses the expression "the city and man."

31. 1 S. Smith, *Reading Leo Strauss*, 130.

32. *OT*, 212. I find it remarkable that Strauss implies that Kojève, the apologist for Stalin, has "the courage to face the issue of Tyranny" lacking in Heidegger, and that Strauss furthermore associates himself with Kojève in possessing such courage. This is especially odd in light of Strauss's critical remarks about Kojève's claiming that "all present-day tyrants are good tyrants in Xenophon's sense," which, as Strauss asserts, involves an allusion to Stalin, and also about Kojève's failure to grasp the meaning of Stalin's use of the NKVD and labor camps (*OT*, 188–89). Although Strauss's criticism seems to suggest the moral equivalence of Hitler and Stalin, Kojève's apology for Stalin did not earn from Strauss as much opprobrium as Heidegger's endorsement of Hitler. One could argue that Heidegger's action had greater practical consequences, lending authority to a new regime that was in need of legitimacy, whereas Kojève's favoring of Stalin came after the fact of Stalin's brutal accomplishments. But that would also make Kojève's apology more reprehensible as based on knowledge of the dictator's demonstrated capacity for inhuman cruelty such as Heidegger and others could not have concerning Hitler in 1933–34 at the peak of Heidegger's enthusiasm for the Führer. (Negative judgments of Hitler's character and of the Nazi program were of course certainly possible at that time.) Heidegger's philosophic superiority to Kojève conceivably plays a role in Strauss's stronger criticism of Heidegger. See the editors' introduction to *OT*, ix–xxii.

33. *SPPP*, 30.

34. "At any rate, it is ultimately because he means to justify philosophy before the tribunal of the political community, and hence on the level of political discussion, that the philosopher has to understand the political things exactly as they are understood in political life." See "On Classical Political Philosophy," *WIPP*, 94.

35. *JPCM*, 463. See chapter 6 below. Strauss's *Natural Right and History* is according to wide repute a defense of the America tradition of natural right, but only those who have not read the book could hold this opinion. Strauss refers to the Declaration of Independence with a one-line quotation and without analysis on the first two pages to establish the importance of the theme of natural right. (The University of Chicago Press in an astute marketing decision put the original Declaration on the cover of the paperback edition.) Strauss makes in the whole book just one brief reference to an American political thinker (Madison), and his treatment of the philosopher most closely associated with the American Founding, John Locke, is highly critical, arguing that the principles of Locke are ultimately barely distinguishable from those of Hobbes. At the same time, Strauss's genuine respect for the moderation and stability of the American founding principles and for the statesmanship that produced them entails qualification of a simply Hobbesian reading of American democracy.

36. Among the few statements of Strauss on foreign policy questions and the practical implications of political philosophy are two unpublished lectures from the early 1940s that appear with an introduction by Nathan Tarcov in the *Review of Politics* 69, no. 4 (fall 2007): 513–38: "What Can We Learn from Political Theory?" and "The Re-education of Axis Countries concerning the Jews." On the basis of these lectures, Tarcov remarks that "it turns out not only that Strauss's views do not seem to have inspired recent U.S. policy, but that they might have served as warnings against some of the missteps that have plagued U.S. policy in recent years." See N. Tarcov, "Will the Real Leo Strauss Please Stand Up?" *American Interest* online, September–October 2006.

37. *WIPP*, 16–17. One can think here of the three competing definitions of justice in Plato, *Republic*, book 1. See *CM*, 62–85.

38. Strauss was exposed to a version of this problem in his youth, before turning to philosophy, as he writes that he was "a young Jew born and raised in Germany who found himself in the grip of the theological-political predicament," *SCR*, 1–31. The arguments between Jewish orthodoxy and political Zionism brought him to question the Enlightenment critique of orthodoxy, after which he moved to the consideration of the difference between modern and premodern (Islamic and Jewish medieval, then ancient) accounts of the relation of philosophy to orthodoxy. See also chapter 2 below. I will not dwell on the prehistory of Strauss's discovery of Socratic philosophy, which has been closely examined by others, but only note that it shows that the theological-political was central to his own ascent to philosophy. See the writings in *EW*.

39. *WIPP*, 17.

40. See chapter 3 below. In anticipation of what is argued below, I will say that the theological-political problem concerns the fundamental duality of the human as political and transpolitical and that this problem is not about only the argument between philosophy and revelation, since it appears in various prephilosophic forms. Ordinary piety's turn to gods that reward and punish reflects a deficiency in morality as law-abidingness—in the meaning of morality most basic to political life. Ordinary piety already shows that the human is not constituted only by the law or the needs of political life, although it interprets the transpolitical goods in terms of support of the law (the happiness of the virtuous) and so it conceals the deficiency of the law from itself. See chapter 9 below. The flexible, nonpious action of statesmen is freer to disclose the deficiency of law as it reflects on the good of the whole political community. Philosophy is the most comprehensive and fundamental reflection on the duality, and thus it poses the profoundest challenge to piety as it pursues an end altogether transpolitical and would give an intelligible account of what piety is in terms of the duality. Strauss expresses this point with respect to biblical revelation: "For the Bible claims to present a solution to the very problem which gave rise to philosophy," and it offers a solution (obedience to the law of a mysterious God) diametrically opposed to philosophy's (the life of autonomous reason in quest of knowledge; see RR, 148–49). It does not follow that piety is the highest alternative to philosophy from philosophy's standpoint. (See Strauss's formulation: "If we assume on the basis of the Fall that *the* alternative for man is philosophy *or* obedience to God's revelation," RR, 142). Strauss argues that for Plato the great alternative to Socratic philosophy is the philosophic poetry of Aristophanes, as the most profound alternative to the Socratic approach to the fundamental duality (see chapter 9 below). Reflection on human duality provides Socrates and Socratic thinkers with a way of seeing how the philosophic quest for knowledge of the whole is made possible through an examination of the "political things." To that extent, indeed, the Socratic philosopher has grounds for being grateful for the existence of the city's gods. Accordingly Socrates may have a kind of theology, one peculiar to the philosopher.

41. Strauss uses the term "whole" with a problematic meaning that emerges contextually, as the whole, or the cosmos, of the problems faced by the human.

42. See chapters 1, 2, and 5 below.

43. See chapters 1, 4, and 5 below.

44. *JPCM*, 463.

45. See *EW*, 31–32.

46. *JPCM*, 463.

47. *OT*, 212. See chapter 7 below.

48. See chapters 3, 8, and 9 below.

49. *NRH*, 125–26.

50. *SZ*, 180–230; *Being and Time*, trans. J. Macquarrie and E. Robinson (New York: Harper & Row, 1962), 225–73.

51. A primary source for his suggestions on this is the Platonic trilogy *Theaetetus, Sophist,* and *Statesman.* See Strauss's treatment of the *Statesman* in "Plato," in *HPP*, and the comments on the trilogy in *WIPP*, 39–40. See also the letter to A. Kojève, 28.5.1957, in *OT*, 276–80 and chapters 2 and 3 below.

52. See *NRH*, chap. 3, and below, chapter 7.

53. Strauss on Socrates: "We may also say that he viewed man in the light of the unchangeable ideas, i.e., of the fundamental and permanent problems." *WIPP*, 39. Equivalently Strauss interprets the ideas in terms of Socratic knowledge of ignorance. "In other words, philosophy is possible only if man, while incapable of acquiring wisdom or full understanding of the whole, is capable of knowing what he does not know, that is to say, of grasping the fundamental problems and therewith the fundamental alternatives, which are, in principle, coeval with human thought." *NRH*, 35.

54. *NRH*, 81.

55. See chapter 9 below. I also mention (following a suggestion of Nathan Tarcov) the contest for rule within the soul in *Republic*, books 8–9, and in Nietzsche, *Beyond Good and Evil*, aph. 19, which contest between kinds of souls or "parts" of the soul has implications for political rule.

56. See chapter 7 below. The praising comment on Montesquieu at *NRH*, 164, makes plain that Strauss is not a proponent of doctrinaire natural right or natural law. See also the observation in "How to Begin to Study Medieval Philosophy," *RCPR*, 224: "The rules of conduct which are called by the Christian scholastics natural laws and by the *mutakallimun* rational laws are called by the Islamic-Jewish philosophers generally accepted opinions."

57. See Robert Pippin, "The Modern World of Leo Strauss," in *Idealism as Modernism: Hegelian Variations* (Cambridge: Cambridge University Press, 1997), and Rosen, "Wittgenstein, Strauss, and the Possibility of Philosophy." Although Strauss does not propose the notion of a natural life-world, he does argue for the existence of a natural problem—the tension between politics and philosophy—that comes to light for those who philosophize naturally. To the extent that Strauss suggests that the evidence for this problem arises from reflection on the alternatives of political life and philosophy as they once existed in their original, pure, and unmixed form—a reflection requiring historical studies for modern students—there is the possible theoretical difficulty that *knowing* that such reflection is a condition for the recovery of natural philosophizing presupposes somehow possessing already the grasp of the natural problem that needs to be recovered. (See chapter 2 below: Strauss's asserts to Karl Löwith, "We are natural beings . . ." but then adds, "The means of thinking by the natural understanding are lost to us.")

58. *WIPP*, 38: "To understand man in the light of the whole means for modern natural science to understand man in the light of the sub-human. But in that light man as man is wholly unintelligible."

59. *WIPP*, 55.

60. See chapters 4 and 5 below. Strauss also has a dual relation to Nietzsche, for on the one hand Nietzsche abandons nature for history, but on the other his thought points to the recovery of the classical account of the natural distinction between the philosopher and the nonphilosopher. See especially "Note on the Plan, etc." in *SPPP*.

61. *NRH*, 18. See chapters 6 and 7 below.

62. *NRH*, 176. See chapter 8 below.

63. *TM*, 294–96: Strauss cautions against "the error of denying the presence of philosophy in Machiavelli's thought" but also writes that "Machiavelli's philosophizing . . . remains on the whole within the limits set by the city qua closed to philosophy. Accepting the ends of the *demos* as beyond appeal, he seeks the best means conducive to those ends."

64. *PPH*, xv (preface to the American edition).

65. *RCPR*, 270.

66. See Nietzsche, *Beyond Good and Evil*, aphorisms 24, 59, 188, 230. See also Heidegger, *N*, vol. 1, "The Will to Power as Art," section 25, and Strauss, *SPPP*, 174–75, 182–83. One should however add that for Strauss the highest models of this art are the classical authors.

67. *RCPR*, 115–16. Strauss continues: "But we must note that what Hegel calls the triumph of subjectivity is achieved in the Aristophanic comedy only by virtue of the knowledge of nature, i.e., the opposite of self-consciousness." See also a letter to Hans-Georg Gadamer, 26.2.1961: "The deepest modern interpretation of Aristophanean comedy (Hegel's) is much less adequate than Plato's Aristophanizing presentation of Aristophanes in the *Symposium*." Strauss adds, "Heidegger is silent on comedy." CCWM, 7. See chapter 9 below as well. Hegel comments that "tragedy allows less scope for the free emergence of the poet's personal views than comedy does because there from the beginning the ruling principle is the contingency and caprice of subjective life," and notes the significance of Aristophanes's *parabases* as putting the author in relation to the Athenian public to whom he gives advice and discloses his political views. G. W. F. Hegel, *Aesthetics: Lectures on Fine Art*, trans. T. M. Knox (Oxford: Oxford University Press, 1975), 2: 1180–81.

68. Consider in this context the thought of Seth Benardete: "The stories of poetry center around foundational crimes, crimes that reveal what must not be violated if either man is to be man or the city is to be possible. The line between man's humanity and man's sociality, the poets seem to be saying, cannot be clearly drawn, for they show that the answer to the riddle of the Sphinx and Oedipus's incest and patricide are linked and that, in light of what Oedipus has done, Oedipus has to cease to be what he is. . . . The opposition, then, between philosophy and poetry seems straightforward enough. There is for philosophy a divide between man as man and man as political animal that poetry denies." *The Tragedy and Comedy of Life: Plato's Philebus*, trans. with commentary by S. Benardete (Chicago: University of Chicago Press, 1993), ix. At the same time Benardete observes that "the Socratic revolution seems to be coeval with Greek poetry, which had realized from the start, with its principle of telling lies like the truth, the relation of argument and action. Homer and Hesiod, then, would have to be recognized as already within the orbit of philosophy." With reference to Strauss's noting Homer's philosophic use of "nature," Benardete observes that "Strauss's recovery of Plato opened up the possibility of gathering into the fold of philosophy more than philosophy had ever dreamed of." *The Argument of the Action: Essays on Greek Poetry and Philosophy*, ed. R. Burger and M. Davis (Chicago:

University of Chicago Press, 2000), 415–16. Thus Benardete following Strauss understands the "quarrel" between philosophy and poetry as premised on a profound kinship as to the fundamental problem of the relation of nature to law (or the gods), which philosophy and poetry tend to resolve in different ways. Benardete's remarks, taken together, suggest that tragedy is less open to the idea of nature than epic poetry. See chapter 9 below.

    69. *NRH*, 323.

CHAPTER 1

    1. Nietzsche, *Werke in drei Bänden*, ed. K. Schlechta (Munich: Hanser, 1966) (henceforth *W*), 3: 464–65, and *The Will to Power*, trans. W. Kaufmann (New York: Random House, 1967) (henceforth *WP*), aph. 419.

    2. Ibid., aph. 419.

    3. *W*, 3: 765–67; *WP*, aph. 437.

    4. *W*, 3: 496; *WP*, aph. 416.

    5. *W*, 3: 756–58; *WP*, aph. 428.

    6. *W*, 3: 486: *WP*, aph. 410.

    7. *W*, 3: 479; *WP*, aph. 415.

    8. *W*, 3: 730; *WP*, aph. 429.

    9. *W*, 3: 771–72; *WP*, aph. 432.

    10. *W*, 3: 438; *WP*, aph. 407.

    11. *W*, 2: 957–58 (*Götzen-Dämmerung*, "Die 'Vernunft' in der Philosophie," 2).

    12. *W*, 3: 757; *WP*, aph. 428.

    13. *W*, 3: 912; *WP* aph. 417.

    14. *W*, 2: 1109–10 ("Warum ich so gute Bücher Schreibe").

    15. *W*, 2: 1110, citing *W*, 2: 1032 ("Was ich den Alten Verdanke," 5).

    16. *W*, 3: 496; *WP*, aph. 416.

    17. *W*, 2: 1111.

    18. *W*, 2: 1111.

    19. *W*, 2: 1111.

    20. *W*, 1: 131–32 (*Die Geburt der Tragödie*, sec. 24).

    21. *W*, 3: 912; *WP*, aph. 417.

    22. *W*, 3: 432; *WP*, aph. 958.

    23. *W*, 3: 912; *WP*, aph. 417.

    24. *W*, 3: 351–52 (*Die Philosophie im tragischen Zeitalter der Griechen*).

    25. *W*, 3: 353–54; cf. *Die Vorplatonischen Philosophen*, "Einführung" (Nietzsche's introduction), in *Nietzsche Werke*, ed. G. Colli and M. Montinari (Berlin: de Gruyter, 1995), pt. 2, vol. 4 (henceforth *VP*).

    26. *W*, 3: 358–60.

    27. *VP*, "Einführung."

    28. *W*, 3: 367–69.

    29. *W*, 3: 376–84.

    30. *SZ*, "Einleitung," 2–40.

31. *GA*, 65. For the relation of Heidegger's Nietzsche interpretation to the *Contributions*, see the essays by A. Vallega and D. Crownfield in *Companion to Heidegger's* Contributions to Philosophy, ed. C. Scott, S. Schoenbohm, D. Vallega-Neu, A. Vallega (Bloomington: Indiana University Press, 2001), and R. Polt, *The Emergency of Being: On Heidegger's* Contributions to Philosophy (Ithaca: Cornell University Press, 2006).

32. *SdU*, 24.

33. *SdU*, 25.

34. *SdU*, 12–13.

35. *GA*, 36/37: 11.

36. "Vom Wesen der Wahrheit," *GA*, 9: 190.

37. He does so in the Plato seminar mentioned and in a related essay, "Platons Lehre von der Wahrheit," published 1942 in a revised version; see *GA*, 9: 203–38. See W. Galston, "Heidegger's Plato: A Critique of *Plato's Doctrine of Truth*," *Philosophical Forum* 13, no. 4 (Summer 1982): 371–84, for an incisive discussion.

38. *GA*, 9: 233–34.

39. *GA*, 9: 234–36.

40. *GA*, 9: 237.

41. *H* 306, citing Nietzsche, *W*, 3: 895–96; *WP*, aph. 617: "To stamp becoming with the character of being—that is the *highest will to power*."

42. *GA*, 45: 126.

43. *VA*, 32.

44. *H*, 296–343.

45. *H*, 297–99; *GA*, 51: 105.

46. *H*, 305; *GA* 51: 99.

47. *GA*, 51: 123.

48. *H*, 300.

49. *H*, 300–302.

50. *H*, 307.

51. *H*, 310.

52. *H*, 311–12.

53. *EM*, 111, 145–46.

54. *H*, 336.

55. 40.

56. *GA*, 70: 140–42.

CHAPTER 2

1. See various letters cited in this chapter, and also the 1956 lecture "An Introduction to Heideggerian Existentialism," *RCPR*, 38–39. For discussion of Heidegger's thought before *Being and Time*, see T. Kisiel, *The Genesis of Heidegger's* Being and Time (Berkeley: University of California Press, 1993), and W. J. Richardson, *Heidegger: Through Phenomenology to Thought*, 3rd ed. (The Hague: Martinus Nijhoff, 1974). For the phases of Heidegger's developing criticism of Husserl's phenomenology, see D. Dahlstrom, *Heidegger's Concept of Truth* (Cambridge:

Cambridge University Press, 2001), and for the relation of Heidegger's thought to the "new thinking" of Rosenzweig, see P. E. Gordon, *Rosenzweig and Heidegger: Between Judaism and German Philosophy* (Berkeley: University of California Press, 2003).

2. See preface, *SCR*.

3. *JPCM*, 462. Strauss notes he was greatly assisted by Lessing in the study of Spinoza. "Lessing was always at my elbow. . . . As I came to see later, Lessing had said everything I had found out about the distinction between exoteric and esoteric speech and its grounds." See also Strauss, "Exoteric Teaching," *Interpretation* 14, no. 1 (1986): 51–59, and RR, 178–79, the comments on Lessing, "that man to whom I owe, so to say, everything I have been able to discern in the labyrinth of that grave question" of reason and revelation. "Lessing's attitude was characterized by an innate disgust against compromises in serious, i.e., theoretical, matters."

4. *SCR*, 30–31. For discussion see H. Meier, "How Strauss Became Strauss," in *Enlightening Revolutions: Essays in Honor of Ralph Lerner*, ed. S. Minkov (Lanham, MD: Rowman & Littlefield, 2006), 355–82.

5. See "Religöse Lage der Gegenwart" (1930), *GS*, 2: 377–91.

6. See note 20 below.

7. *JPCM*, 453.

8. 14.2.1934 in *GS*, 3: 494.

9. 17.11.1932, *GS*, 3: 406.

10. Plan for letter to Krüger, 12.12.1932, *GS*, 3: 415; see also *NRH*, 78. Strauss's remark on modern philosophy as an attempt to reclaim its natural basis can be compared with this passage of Jacob Klein on the new science of the seventeenth century: "It [the new science] conceives itself as again taking up and further developing Greek science, i.e., as a recovery and elaboration of 'natural' cognition. It sees itself not only as a science *of nature*, but as *'natural'* science—in opposition to *school* science. Whereas the 'naturalness' of Greek science is determined precisely by the fact that it arises out of 'natural' foundations . . . the naturalness of modern science is an expression of its *polemical attitude toward school science*. This special posture of the 'new' science fundamentally defines its horizon, delimits its methods, its general structure, and most important, determines the conceptual character of its concepts." Klein also notes that this reclaiming of naturalness is pursued rather paradoxically by a new elevation of practical arts in relation to theoretical sciences so that "*in general* the distinction between the *artes liberales* and the *artes mechanicae* is slowly obliterated." *Greek Mathematical Thought and the Origin of Algebra*, trans. E. Brann (Cambridge: MIT Press, 1968, German original published in 1934), 120, 125, and n. 132.

11. *GS*, 3: 414.

12. Letter to Krüger, 7.1.1930, *GS*, 3: 380.

13. Plan for letter to Krüger, 27.12.1932, *GS*, 3: 415; also the definitive letter of 27.12.1932, *GS*, 3: 420.

14. Letter of 27.12.1932, *GS*, 3: 420.

15. Plan for letter to Krüger, 27.12.1932, *GS*, 3: 414.

16. See Strauss, "Niccolo Machiavelli," *SPPP*, 210–11.

17. See *GS*, 3: 412, 414, 415, 420.

18. Letter to Krüger, 27.12.1932, *GS*, 3: 420.

19. Letter to Löwith, 2.2.1933, *GS*, 3: 620.

20. *GS*, 3: 621. Strauss gives this account of his discovery: "One day, when reading in a Latin translation of Avicenna's treatise *On the Division of the Sciences*, I came across the sentence (I quote from memory): the standard work on prophecy and revelation is Plato's *Laws*." This was the beginning of Strauss's understanding of esotericism in Maimonides and other medieval writers. *JPCM*, 463.

21. Letter of 23.6.1935, *GS*, 3: 648.

22. *GS*, 3: 649–50.

23. Letter to Löwith, 15.8.1946, *GS*, 3: 662.

24. *GS*, 3: 661.

25. Letter of 27.12.1932, *GS*, 3: 422.

26. These quotations are from a review of J. Ebbinghaus, *Über die Fortschritte der Metaphysik*, in *GS*, 2: 438–39, and from an autobiographical note of 1930–32. The Ebbinghaus review contains Strauss's first use of the figure "second cave" in print. Both are cited by H. Meier, *Leo Strauss and the Theologico-Political Problem* (Cambridge: Cambridge University Press, 2006), 57.

27. Letter of 17.11.1932, *GS*, 3: 406.

28. "Die geistige Lage der Gegenwart," lecture of 1932, in *GS*, 2: 456 and cited by Meier, *Leo Strauss and the Theologico-Political Problem*, 59–60.

29. Review of Ebbinghaus, cited by Meier, *Leo Strauss and the Theologico-Political Problem*, 57.

30. Letter of 1.8.1949, *GS*, 3: 598–99.

31. Strauss's comments may refer to the 1929 lecture "What Is Metaphysics?" which treats *das Nichts* and its relation to Being. A fifth printing with a new introduction appeared in 1949. Concerning the reference to the "unsolved Humean problem" in this letter: Martin Sitte recalls a conversation with Strauss in the spring of 1973 in which Strauss spoke of plans to write studies of Plato's *Gorgias* and Hume. Strauss died the following autumn and completed neither project.

32. These are translated as *Off the Beaten Track*, trans. J. Young and K. Haynes (Cambridge: Cambridge University Press, 2002), and *Nietzsche*, ed. D. Krell, 2 vols. (New York: Harper and Row, 1979–87). Although these two works are most prominently mentioned in the correspondence, Strauss read a number of other later writings, such as those cited at *SPPP*, 34, n. 3. The introduction to the fifth printing of "What Is Metaphysics?" (1949) would have given Strauss some indications of Heidegger's later thought. Consider the following: "The name 'existence' is used exclusively in *Being and Time* as the designation of the being of the human (*Dasein*). From 'existence' rightly understood is the 'essence' of *Dasein* to be thought, in whose openness Being itself announces and conceals itself, endures and withdraws, without the truth of Being exhausting itself in *Dasein* or indeed being placed in identity with it according to the metaphysical kind of proposition: all objectivity is as such subjectivity." *GA*, 9: 373–74.

33. Letter of 21.2.1950, *GS*, 3: 673.

34. Letter to Löwith, 23.2.1950, *GS*, 3: 674.

35. See chapter 7 below.

36. Letter to Löwith, 19.7.1951, *GS*, 3: 675.

37. Letter to Löwith, 21.12.1951, *GS*, 3: 676–77.

38. Letter to Löwith, 13.12.1960, *GS*, 3: 684–85. Strauss mentions that in addition to Löwith's book on Nietzsche he is reading *Der Satz vom Grund* and other writings by Heidegger. It should

be noted that in spite of his high estimation of the later work Strauss maintained deep reservations. One of his last utterances on Heidegger is in a letter to Gershom Scholem, 7.7.1973. "To me it is now clear after many years what is actually wrong in Heidegger: a phenomenal intellect inside a kitsch-soul; I can prove this. As I read a statement by him from the year 1934 about himself as a Black Forest peasant, I found the wish rising in me—in me!—to be or to become an intellectual." *GS*, 3: 769–70.

39. See Strauss's "Plato" essay in *HPP*, especially 69–70 in discussion of *The Statesman*, and *OT*, the letter of 28.5.1957 to Kojève, 279.

40. For more on Heidegger's reading of Plato see chapter 1 above. For Strauss on Plato see chapter 3 below.

41. Letter to Löwith, 15.3.1962, *GS*, 3: 685–87. Strauss also writes that "the profoundest interpreter and at the same time the profoundest *critic* of Nietzsche is Heidegger. He is Nietzsche's profoundest interpreter because he is the profoundest critic." PS, 324.

42. Letter to Strauss, 27.3.1962, *GS*, 3: 687.

43. Letter to Löwith, 2.4.1962, *GS*, 3: 688.

44. Letter to Löwith, 12.3.1970, *GS*, 3: 696.

45. See PS, 330.

46. Letter of 30.9.1971, *GS*, 3: 697. But strangely Strauss overlooks Heidegger's discussion of Hölderlin's thought on Christ as the brother of Hercules and Dionysus in *Was heißt Denken?* (*GA*, 8: 74), a work that Strauss cites elsewhere (*SPPP*, 34). See chapter 5 below.

47. See chapters 6 and 7 below.

48. PS, 324–30.

49. PS, 330.

50. PS, 329–30.

51. See chapter 4 below for Heidegger's reinterpretation of Kantian freedom.

52. In this regard consider the concluding sentences of "An Introduction to Heideggerian Existentialism": "Esse (Being) as Heidegger understands it may be described crudely and superficially and even misleadingly, but not altogether misleadingly, by saying it is a synthesis of Platonic ideas and the biblical God: it is as impersonal as the Platonic ideas and as elusive as the biblical God." *RCPR*, 46.

53. PS, 323.

54. PS, 333–34. On the other hand Xenophon in *Memorabilia* 1.2 shows that Alcibiades, the tyrant and friend of Socrates, raises this question in conversation with Pericles. See *XS*, 14–15. Strauss notes that Alcibiades is a Socratic and that his question is Socratic, although it is never raised by the Xenophonic Socrates. "This is another example of the limitation that Xenophon imposed on himself when writing his 'recollections.'"

55. PS, 329.

CHAPTER 3

1. "Living Issues in German Postwar Philosophy," LIGPP, 115–39.

2. LIGPP, 116.

3. *Beyond Good and Evil*, aph. 240. See the author's *Being after Rousseau: Philosophy and Culture in Question* (Chicago: University of Chicago Press, 2002).

4. LIGPP, 137.

5. LIGPP, 137–38.

6. LIGPP, 129. For an account of the separation of religious thought from political authority as the defining feature of modern Western life, see M. Lilla, *The Stillborn God: Religion, Politics and the Modern West* (New York: Alfred Knopf, 2007).

7. See sources cited in note 18 to Parabasis.

8. See *NRH*, 177.

9. LIGPP, 129–33.

10. LIGPP, 123. In this regard Strauss discerns a certain historical necessity in the course of modernity (though not in Western history as a whole) that allies him in a way (and not simply ironically) with Hegel. For Nietzsche's critique of the idea of culture in modern historical consciousness, see *SPPP*, 148–49.

11. See *PPH*, 79–107. In his first study of Hobbes (1936), Strauss underlines three aspects of Hobbes's new science of politics that prepare for the historical consciousness of later modern thought: the emphasis on applicability or effectiveness of principles, the rejection of the natural orientation in the world by speech in favor of mathematical method, and the account of knowing as a kind of making or construction.

12. LIGPP, 136–37. For remarks on Descartes's importance ("The rights of man are the moral equivalent of the *Ego cogitans*"), see *CM*, 42–45. Strauss's doctoral dissertation on F. H. Jacobi treats Jacobi's criticism of Cartesian rationalism as grounded on a spurious form of certainty that precludes a true confrontation with the mystery of the grounds of existence. One might claim that Strauss's lifelong concerns with the self-destructiveness of modern rationalism and the argument of reason versus faith have roots in his early work on Jacobi and the *Pantheismusstreit* that Jacobi initiated through his "exposure" of Lessing's Spinozism, and that Strauss discusses in the *Jubiläumsausgabe* of Moses Mendelssohn's writings. For discussions of these issues see Batnitzky, *Leo Strauss and Emmanuel Levinas*, and D. Janssens, "The Problem of Enlightenment: Strauss, Jacobi, and the Pantheism Controversy," *Review of Metaphysics* 56 (2003): 605–32.

13. See *SA*, 11–53, 311–14. See also chapter 9 below.

14. *CM*, 11; *WIPP*, 38; *RCPR*, 34.

15. Strauss writes that Husserl's analysis of the basic assumptions of modern science and philosophy, especially of the transformation of geometry underlying Galileo's physics, is of unsurpassed significance. LIGPP, 137; *RCPR*, 28–29; *SPPP*, 34–37.

16. LIGPP, 134.

17. LIGPP, 137.

18. *SPPP*, 29–37; *JPCM*, 457–66; and PS.

19. "An Unspoken Prologue," *JPCM*, 449–50.

20. *JPCM*, 464.

21. See chapter 7 below for Strauss on the genealogy of historicism.

22. *WIPP*, 26.

23. See chapter 6 below.

24. Letters to G. Krüger discussed in chapter 2 above and *SCR*, 9–11; *RCPR*, 28: Strauss notes that Ernst Cassirer had "silently dropped" ethics from H. Cohen's Kantian system and "had not *faced* the problem" of ethics. "*Heidegger did face the problem*. He declared that ethics

is impossible, and his whole being was permeated by the awareness that this fact opens up an abyss." See chapter 4 below for the Cassirer-Heidegger confrontation at Davos.

25. See the exchange of letters with K. Löwith in chapter 2 above.

26. The meaning of the *Kehre* or "turn" in Heidegger's thought in the 1930s is much debated. I hold the view that it involves no change in the fundamental question of Heidegger's thought (the question of Being or the *Seinsfrage*) but a change in the approach to the question. See chapter 1 above and chapter 5 below. For a discussion of Heidegger's later thought of *Ereignis* as the continuation of the inquiry into the "originary, fundamental, unifying meaning of Being," which is the single defining concern of Heidegger's path of thinking, see R. Capobianco, *Engaging Heidegger* (Toronto: University of Toronto Press, 2010), chap. 2.

27. *RCPR*, 27-46.

28. *RCPR*, 38-39.

29. Letter to Löwith, 15.3.1962, discussed above in chapter 2.

30. Letter to Löwith, 21.12.1951, discussed above in chapter 2.

31. *RCPR*, 29.

32. Letter to Löwith, 23.2.1950, discussed above in chapter 2; cf. *RCPR*, 34.

33. Letter to Löwith, 13.12.1960, discussed above in chapter 2; cf. *RCPR*, 42-44.

34. *WIPP*, 26: "Historicism rejects the question of the good society."

35. See chapter 2 above.

36. See *TM*, 78, for a statement on the defect of humanism: "Since man is a being that must try to transcend humanity, he must transcend humanity in the direction of the subhuman if he does not transcend it in the direction of the superhuman."

37. *NRH*, 122.

38. *CM*, 20.

39. *TM*, 19.

40. *NRH*, 122-24.

41. *CM*, 20.

42. *NRH*, 32.

43. *WIPP*, 38-39.

44. *WIPP*, 39.

45. *SA*, 314.

46. *NRH*, 79.

47. *NRH*, 32.

48. *CM*, 20.

49. *NRH*, 125.

50. Related to this stance is the suggestion that the philosophic life is simply based on a choice or an act of will.

51. *WIPP*, 39.

52. *RCPR*, 132.

53. *RCPR*, 132.

54. *RCPR*, 133.

55. Even so Strauss makes the well-known comment in the German edition of *PPH*, referring to his early studies of seventeenth-century biblical criticism, that "the theologico-political problem has since remained *the* theme of my studies." *GS*, 3: 7-8.

56. *RCPR*, 142.

57. *CM*, 127–28.

58. *CM*, 29.

59. *CM*, 138. S. Benardete admirably sums up the relation between Strauss's approach to reading Platonic dialogic imitation and Strauss's "linking up political philosophy with first philosophy" through the study of the soul: "Plato's psychology was Strauss' way to Plato's ideas: and Strauss' way was the way of the *Republic*. No single Platonic dialogue, however, can yield Plato's teaching about the soul; Strauss put great stress on Socrates' observation in the *Republic* that the problem of justice there precludes an exact account of the soul, even though the problem of justice seems to require such an account, inasmuch as the structure of the city is presumably in strict accordance with the structure of the soul. The *Republic* reveals the tension between the political and natural relation between *thumos* and *eros*. Such a tension needs to be represented or imitated. It is imitated through the action of the *Republic* that accompanies its argument. Strauss was the first, as far as we know, to give a coherent account of this double function. He showed that, how, and why the linking up of *logos* and *psyche*, which is dialectic, was of the essence of the Socratic revolution." "Strauss and the Ancients," memorial lecture delivered at the New School for Social Research, 1974.

60. "Without cities, no philosophers. They are the conditions." *JPCM*, 465.

61. *RCPR*, 164.

62. *Phaedo* 95e–100b. For outstanding discussions of the causal problem in this dialogue, see S. Benardete, "On Plato's *Phaedo*," in Burger and Davis, *Argument of the Action*, and R. Burger, *The "Phaedo": A Platonic Labyrinth* (New Haven: Yale University Press, 1984; rpt. South Bend, IN: St. Augustine's Press, 1999). The quest for cosmology encounters the problem of including the human soul and its problematic *telos* within an intelligible order. Yet the soul's problematic *telos* (bound up with its political nature) at the same time conditions inquiry about the cosmos as guided by the concerns with the beautiful, the good, and the just, and accordingly this inquiry cannot proceed except through examination of the soul's "pretheoretical" orientation by such concerns.

63. *WIPP*, 61. See also the letter of 28.5.1957 to Kojève in *OT*, 279, on Platonic cosmology: "The adequate division [of ideas] would presuppose that one could deduce all ideas, especially also the ideas of living; it would presuppose a 'rational biology'; this is impossible (see *Timaeus*); hence what is available is a dualism of a hypothetical mathematical physics and a non-hypothetical understanding of the human soul. The difference between Plato and Aristotle is that Aristotle believes that biology, as a mediation between knowledge of the inanimate and knowledge of man is available, or Aristotle believes in the availability of universal teleology, if not of the simplistic kind sketched in *Phaedo* 96b."

64. *NRH*, 172.

65. *R*, 260.

CHAPTER 4

1. See Herman Philipse, *Heidegger's Philosophy of Being: A Critical Interpretation* (Princeton: Princeton University Press, 2000), 256–66.

2. Philipse, *Heidegger's Philosophy of Being*, 223–29, 239–44.

3. Philipse, *Heidegger's Philosophy of Being*, 246–76.

4. Philipse, *Heidegger's Philosophy of Being*, 276: Heidegger's view of National Socialism is "never unambiguously negative." Philipse goes further. He characterizes the later theological thought as "spiritual Nazism" (270–72): grounded on the experience of the death of God as proclaimed by Nietzsche, and thus on the total withering of Christianity and its Platonic roots, this pious thinking awaits new gods who support the particular folk, the German folk, in its struggle with Western decadence. Heidegger's account of the history of the West gives no place to Judaism, even though its eschatological structure has unmistakably biblical sources. This is a special sort of Nazism to be sure: the greatness of the folk is based not on biology but on the spirit of language and poetry.

5. See *SPPP*, 34: "One is inclined to say that Heidegger has learned the lesson of 1933 more thoroughly than any other man."

6. See the account below of the Davos disputation with Cassirer, and the essay contemporary with it (1929), "Vom Wesen des Grundes," *GA*, 9: 161–62.

7. *SdU*, 6. These writings are reprinted in *GA*, 16, which contains many important things—speeches, lectures, official documents, exhortations to students and faculty—that make evident the full range and intensity of Heidegger's support of the new regime, even after his resignation from the rectorate in spring 1934.

8. See Philipse, *Heidegger's Philosophy of Being*, 248–49, whose chief source for biographical data is Hugo Ott, *Martin Heidegger: Unterwegs zu seiner Biographie* (Frankfurt: Campus Verlag, 1988).

9. *SdU*, 23.

10. *SdU*, 25.

11. To accusations that he harmed individuals, groups, the university, or Germany itself by his actions, Heidegger's response is one of full denial.

12. A start is made by Miguel de Beistegui, *Heidegger and the Political: Dystopias* (London: Routledge, 1988), 32–39.

13. See the author's *Freedom and the End of Reason: On the Moral Foundation of Kant's Critical Philosophy* (Chicago: University of Chicago Press, 1989).

14. *GA*, 42: 61–72, and Jeffrey A. Barash, *Martin Heidegger and the Problem of Historical Meaning* (Dordrecht: Martinus Nijhoff, 1988).

15. *GA*, 9, "Vom Wesen des Grundes," 133n.

16. In one notable self-accounting, Heidegger claims that his thought renews and deepens a concept of the essence of freedom emerging at the end of the eighteenth century: "Freedom now (in that period) has for the Germans a new sound and meaning. Freedom means: adherence to the law of the folk-spirit, that manifests itself preeminently in the works of poets, thinkers and statesmen.... Freedom: responsibility for the destiny of the folk." "Die deutsche Universität," in *GA*, 16: 291. This is two addresses, previously unpublished, that Heidegger gave in a "course for foreigners"—clearly a performance of public service—at the University of Freiburg in November 1934, after his resignation from the rectorate. Heidegger traces this new concept to all of the leading thinkers and poets of Germany of the age and claims that it was the principle behind the founding of the University of Berlin. This is one of Heidegger's most detailed statements

linking his thought to earlier German political thought, and it concretely ascribes a common root to his philosophy and National Socialism. Special praise is given to Friedrich Karl von Savigny, who "showed in relation to the essence of the state, that political freedom and unfreedom depend not on the form of state [*Staatsform*] but above all on whether the power of the state is rooted in the nature and history of a folk, or is entirely used up in the will of individual power holders and governments" (294). For the relation of Heidegger to the "historical school" of Savigny and Barthold Niebuhr, and to the romantic approach to history in general, see Barash, *Martin Heidegger and the Problem of Historical Meaning.*

17. Noteworthy in this regard are the seminar of winter 1927–28 on Kant's *Kritik der reinen Vernunft* (*GA*, 25) and that of summer 1930 on Kant's account of freedom in the Dialectic of the same work (*GA*, 31), bearing the title "Vom Wesen der menschlichen Freiheit. Einleitung in die Philosophie."

18. The Davos disputation is found in *GA*, 3: 274–96. I will not give page references for each passage cited and discussed in what follows, but refer the reader to the entire text. On the disputation see Strauss, *WIPP*, 245–46; J. A. Barash, ed., *The Symbolic Construction of Reality: The Legacy of Ernst* Cassirer (Chicago: University of Chicago Press, 2008), essays by J. A. Barash and M. Roubach; M. Friedman, *A Parting of the Ways: Carnap, Cassirer and Heidegger* (Chicago: Open Court, 2000); P. E. Gordon, *Continental Divide: Heidegger, Cassirer, Davos* (Cambridge: Harvard University Press, 2010). Strauss wrote his doctoral dissertation on F. H. Jacobi for Cassirer; Heidegger and Strauss both have academic beginnings in Neo-Kantianism.

19. In a lecture given at Davos during the same *Hochschulkurse* (third appendix in *GA*, 3), Heidegger put forth the famous thesis, argued in the book, that "Kant through his own radicality brought himself before a position from which he had to draw back in fear [*zurückschrecken*]. That is to say: destruction of the foundations theretofore of Western metaphysics (Spirit, Logos, Reason)" (*GA*, 3: 273).

20. In the fourth edition of this book (1973) Heidegger says that Kant was for him just a "refuge" (*Zuflucht*) whom he could treat as the spokesman for his own account of Being; he says that he misunderstood both his own question and Kant at that time. *GA*, 3: xiv. For learned and penetrating discussions of Heidegger's relation to Kant, see Stanley Rosen, *The Question of Being: A Reversal of Heidegger* (New Haven: Yale University Press, 1993), 192–211, and *The Elusiveness of the Ordinary: Studies in the Possibility of Philosophy* (New Haven: Yale University Press, 2002), 94–134. See also the references in note 43 below.

21. *SdU*, 21. "Was ist Metaphysik?" *GA*, 9: 103–22.

22. *Vom Wesen der Wahrheit: Zu Platons Höhlengleichnis und Theaetet, GA*, 34 (seminar winter 1931/32); "Vom Wesen der Wahrheit," *GA*, 9: 177–202; "Platons Lehre der Wahrheit," *GA*, 9: 203–38.

23. *SdU*, 22.

24. *SdU*, 24.

25. *SdU*, 13.

26. *SdU*, 25. Heidegger perhaps reads some thoughts of the later 1930s back into the period 1930–32. All the same, the memoir makes evident the persistence in Heidegger's thought of the "idealist" orientation.

27. *SdU*, 26.

28. *SdU*, 39.

29. *SdU*, 39.

30. For discussion of this passage, see Philipse, *Heidegger's Philosophy of Being*, 260–62.

31. *SdU*, 12.

32. *Einführung in die Metaphysik* (Tübingen: Niemeyer Verlag, 1953 and later editions), reprinted as *GA*, 40. I will cite the Niemeyer edition as *EM*.

33. *EM*, 7.

34. *EM*, 8.

35. *EM*, 9.

36. *EM*, 29, 34.

37. *EM*, 28; cf. 35.

38. *EM*, 35–37.

39. Hegel, preface to first edition of *Logik* (1812), cited at *GA*, 54: 148–49.

40. *GA*, 16: 294: "Savigny showed that right [*das Recht*] arises not solely and not primarily from the formal legal thinking of legislation [*Gesetzgebung*], but rather, as in the case of language, from the folk-spirit of the peoples [*Völker*], with their belief and their customs."

41. "Vom Wesen der Wahrheit," *GA*, 9: 190; see also *GA*, 42: 15; H, 340–41.

42. For a formulation that has explicit reference to the contemporary political situation (Germany's withdrawal from the League of Nations), see *GA*, 16: 333: "True historical freedom as the independence of the recognition of one folk by another has no need of the organized illusory community [*Scheingemeinschaft*] of a 'League of Nations.' . . . The true historical freedom of the peoples [*Völker*] of Europe is the *presupposition* for the West's returning once again spiritually-historically to *itself* and for its securing its destiny in the great decision of the earth against the *Asiatic*."

43. This perhaps emerges most forcefully from Heidegger's extensive conversation with great philosophers from Parmenides to Nietzsche. For accounts of his "dialogue" with Kant, see F. Schalow, *The Renewal of the Heidegger-Kant Dialogue: Action, Thought, and Responsibility* (Albany: State University of New York Press, 1992), and C. Sherover, *Heidegger, Kant and Time* (Bloomington: Indiana University Press, 1971).

CHAPTER 5

1. *H*, 340–41.

2. *GA*, 42: 21–22.

3. *GA*, 42: 15.

4. *GA*, 9: 187.

5. *GA*, 9: 188.

6. *GA*, 9: 190.

7. *GA*, 8: 60–61.

8. *GA*, 8: 70–71.

9. *GA*, 8: 71.

10. *GA*, 8: 71–72, citing *Götzen-Dämmerung*, "Streifzüge eines Unzeitgemässen," aph. 39.

11. *GA*, 8: 72–74.

12. *GA*, 8: 74.

13. Nietzsche, *Götzen-Dämmerung*, "Streifzüge," aph. 38.

14. Nietzsche, *Götzen-Dämmerung*, "Streifzüge," aph. 41.

15. *GA*, 8: 19.

16. *GA*, 8: 32.

17. *GA*, 8: 81.

18. *GA*, 8: 87.

19. *GA*, 8: 95. Heidegger's citation is from Schelling, *Werke*, I/7: 350.

20. *GA*, 8: 60.

21. *GA*, 3: 274–96. See also chapter 4, section III, above.

22. *GA*, 3: 274–96.

23. *GA*, 3: 274–96.

24. *SdU*, 24. See also chapter 4, section IV, above.

25. *SdU*, 25.

26. *SdU*, 12.

27. *EM*, 8.

28. *GA*, 54: 148–49.

29. *SdU*, 39.

30. *EM*, 9.

31. *EM*, 28–29, 34.

32. *EM*, 35–37.

33. *EM*, 32.

34. *EM*, 7.

35. *EM*, 117.

36. *EM*, 125.

37. *EM*, 96–97.

38. *GA*, 29/30: 109–10, citing *Der Wille zur Macht*, Musarion edition, 19: 360f., aph. 1050.

39. *GA*, 8: 75.

40. *GA*, 8: 20.

41. *Götzen-Dämmerung*, "Die vier grossen Irrtümer," aph. 8.

42. *Götzen-Dämmerung*, "Streifzüge," aph. 49.

43. *Götzen-Dämmerung*, "Streifzüge," aph. 50.

CHAPTER 6

1. "Philosophy as Rigorous Science and Political Philosophy," *SPPP*, 29.

2. *CM*, 3–4.

3. *CM*, 1–6.

4. *SPPP*, 30.

5. See chapter 3 above.

6. *RCPR*, 29. The passage continues: "I am afraid that we shall have to make a very great effort in order to find a solid basis for rational liberalism. Only a great thinker could help us in our intellectual plight. But here is the great trouble: the only great thinker in our time is Heidegger."

7. *SPPP*, 32–33, and *NRH*, 28–29.

8. *NRH*, 29–30.

9. *RCPR*, 262. The paragraph ends with this important comment: "As far as I know, the present-day arguments in favor of revelation against philosophy are based on an inadequate understanding of classical philosophy."

10. *SPPP*, 30.

11. *SPPP*, 32–33, and *RCPR*, 38–39.

12. This was not always the case. One cannot fail to mention in this connection Strauss's letter of 19.5.1933 to Karl Löwith, in which Strauss praises the principles of the right ("fascist, authoritarian, imperialist") by which he means the fascism of Mussolini, whereas he makes clear his contempt for the Nazis (*GS*, 2: 624–25). Werner Dannhauser comments: "we must admit that the young Strauss, not yet thirty-five at the time, was more reactionary than we might wish him to be." Dannhauser's whole discussion of the published correspondence of Strauss ("Leo Strauss in His Letters") deserves attention, in Minkov, *Enlightening Revolutions*, 355–61.

13. "Philosophy is the attempt to replace opinion by knowledge; but opinion is the element of the city, hence philosophy is subversive, hence the philosopher must write in such a way that he will improve rather than subvert the city. In other words the virtue of the philosopher's thought is a certain kind of *mania*, while the virtue of the philosopher's public speech is *sophrosune*." *JPCM*, 463. For a discussion of the deficiency of Heidegger's political judgment, Smith, *Reading Leo Strauss*, chap. 5. Smith takes issue with the claim of Luc Ferry that Strauss's return to Greek philosophy adopts wholesale Heidegger's critique of modernity and applies it in a revival of hierarchical, antiliberal politics.

14. See letter to Karl Löwith of 21.12.1951, *GS*, 3: 676–77.

15. *JPCM*, 461.

16. *JPCM*, 147.

17. *WIPP*, 246. Concerning the decay of the faith in progress after the First World War, Strauss writes, "Spengler's *Decline of the West* seemed to be much more credible [than the faith of the communists]. But one had to be inhuman to leave it at Spengler's prognosis. Is there no hope for Europe? And therewith for mankind? It was in the spirit of such hope that Heidegger perversely welcomed 1933." *RCPR*, 41.

18. *JPCM*, 450.

19. *WIPP*, 246.

20. *RCPR*, 27–46, and *SPPP*, 29–37.

21. *SPPP*, 30.

22. See letter to Karl Löwith, 15.3.1962 in *GS*, 3: 685–87: "But one may of course raise the question whether Nietzsche achieved what he intended . . . and then there is no possibility known to me superior to Heidegger's philosophic doctrine of which his interpretation of Nietzsche forms an integral part."

23. *SPPP*, 33.

24. *SPPP*, 34. In this same essay Strauss indicates that the lack of political philosophy in Heidegger may be partly explained by its absence from Husserl's conception of "philosophy as rigorous science." While praising Husserl's phenomenological criticism of the scientific understanding of the world, he notes that there is no reflection in Husserl until the very end of his life—"under the impact of events which could not be overlooked or overheard" in 1935—on the

possible adverse affects of philosophy as rigorous science upon those who need a worldview, and thus on the age-old antagonism between "those who are conservatively contented with the tradition and the circle of philosophic human beings." *SPPP*, 34-37.

25. *SPPP*, 30.

26. *RCPR*, 29-31. Surely Strauss has some sympathy for Heidegger's view of the technological world society as a "nightmare." "It means unity of the human race on the lowest level, complete emptiness of life, self-perpetuating doctrine without rhyme or reason; no leisure, no elevation, no withdrawal; nothing but work and recreation; no individuals and no peoples, but instead 'lonely crowds.'" *RCPR*, 42.

27. *RCPR*, 41.

28. *RCPR*, 41, 43-44; see *JPCM*, 150-51, 171-72.

29. *RCPR*, 43.

30. *SPPP*, 34.

31. Consider in this context the statement of Daniel Tanguay: "His [Strauss's] aim is to present the ancients' solution but without committing himself to a restoration of metaphysics or cosmologies incompatible with the proclamation of the radical limits of the human intellect and of the unintelligible and mysterious character of the Whole." Tanguay, *Leo Strauss: An Intellectual Biography*, 108.

32. *JPCM*, 463. For discussion of Strauss on "synthesis," see Tanguay, *Leo Strauss: An Intellectual Biography*; Zuckert, *Postmodern Platos*, 185-200.

33. *NRH*, 24-34, 176-77, 319-21; *WIPP*, 55; *OT*, 212. Relevant here is Leora Batnitzky's observation that "on Strauss's reading, Heidegger's and Levinas's error lies in a shared over-inflated sense of philosophy, which denies the distinction of theory and practice." Batnitzky, *Leo Strauss and Emmanuel Levinas*, 178.

34. *JPCM*, 464. The paragraph continues thus: "What distinguishes present-day philosophy in its highest form, in its Heideggerian form, from classical philosophy is its historical character; it presupposes the historical consciousness. It is therefore necessary to understand the partly hidden roots of that consciousness."

CHAPTER 7

1. Page numbers in text refer to *NRH*.

2. Moreover "the whole galaxy of political philosophers from Plato to Hegel, and certainly all adherents of natural right, assumed that the fundamental political problem is susceptible of a final solution. This assumption ultimately rested on the Socratic answer to the question of how man ought to live" (*NRH*, 35-36). As the reference to Hegel makes evident, there are political philosophers, both ancient and modern, who endorse the core idea of Socrates while not adhering to natural right. The central practical question of political philosophy, "the question of what the goal of wise action is," need not be framed in terms of natural right.

3. See also *WIPP*, 26-27, 57. Elsewhere Strauss states that historicism is "the serious antagonist of political philosophy" and that "positivism necessarily transforms itself into historicism" (*WIPP*, 25-26). In present-day social science the appeal to History and the appeal to the distinction between Facts and Values (positivism) are the two grounds for rejecting natural right

(*NRH*, 8). For a somewhat different approach to *Natural Right and History* as response to Heideggerian historicism, see Zuckert and Zuckert, *The Truth about Leo Strauss*, 91–102.

4. *RCPR*, 27–30.

5. See *GA*, 42, 83. In a significant pair of speeches given at the University of Freiburg in August 1934 ("Die deutsche Universität"), which certainly served state-approved political aims, Heidegger speaks of the importance of German romantic thought (Savigny is singled out for special praise) and its account of freedom as based in the *Volk*. Here Heidegger shows awareness of sources of his thought—and of current political realities—in the historical school (*GA*, 16: 285–307, esp. 289–97). All the same, Heidegger devotes little time to the sources of the modern historical consciousness in his teaching and writing.

6. A closely related point is made when Strauss notes that opposition to the doctrinaire early modern versions of natural right led to the stress on history in the effort to recover the distinction between theory and practice (*NRH*, 13–16, 319–20). The point helps one to see why Strauss investigates not simply "natural right" but "the problem of natural right."

7. *SZ*, 15–19; *GA*, 3: 20–35.

8. It is helpful to recall that the primary modern philosophic sources for the young Heidegger, apart from Husserl, were Kant, Hegel, Kierkegaard, Nietzsche, and Dilthey. See Otto Pöggeler, *Der Denkweg Martin Heideggers* (Pfullingen: Neske, 1963), 17–36, and Barash, *Martin Heidegger and the Problem of Historical Meaning*. For an important and revealing statement on Hegel see Heidegger, *ID*.

9. *SPPP*, 33–34.

10. *RCPR*, 27–30; *SCR*, 9–10; *WIPP*, 245–246; *JPCM*, 449–52, 460–62. See Steven B. Smith, "*Destruktion* or Recovery? Leo Strauss's Critique of Heidegger," in *Reading Leo Strauss*, for an account of Strauss's judgment of Heidegger's political-moral failure. See also Catherine Zuckert, *Postmodern Platos*, especially pp. 164–173.

11. One could think of the entire historical mode of presenting this critique of historicism as having ironic features. Strauss's one book directly engaging German thought is his most "German" in form. The account of historical inevitability in the progression of modern thinkers is surely overstated so as to give less attention to the dissent from modern progress by Rousseau and Nietzsche. Strauss's borrowing from Plato's *Republic* of the "three waves" figure to describe the history of modern political philosophy (*PP*, 81–98) also points to an intent both playful and serious: like Socrates's interlocutors, the reader must participate in the construction of the "ideal city" (in this case, Strauss's ideal construction of the modern development) in order to uncover the limitations of this account. And that construction itself exploits, in an inverted way, the modern belief in inevitable progress. See Heinrich Meier, *Die Denkbewegung von Leo Strauss* (Stuttgart: Metzler, 1996), for distortions inherent in Strauss's historical mode of argument.

12. *JPCM*, 450.

13. *SCR*, 31.

14. *SCR*, 9–10.

15. *PPH*, xv.

16. See also lecture version of *NRH*, 2: 3.

17. See especially *EM*, 1–39; "Was ist Metaphysik?" *GA*, 9: 103–22.

18. It is not possible here to enter into the subject of Heidegger's indebtedness to Husserl's phenomenological inquiry for the formulation of the ontological problem. But surely Husserl's central concern with showing that reason's openness to a world of objects or its "intentionality" is not explicable through causal-genetic accounts was decisive for Heidegger. See *SPPP*, 31, 34–37; the author, "Edmund Husserl," in *HPP*, 870–87. Strauss refers to Husserl (again without naming him) when he describes modern science as a "radical modification" of the natural understanding, rather than the "perfection" of it, and calls for an analysis of the natural understanding as the presupposition for an analysis of science, at 78–80. Jacob Klein was following both Husserl and Heidegger in his historical investigation of the origins of modern mathematics as "symbol-generating abstraction" and in his account of it as presupposing a natural understanding of number that the modern notion conceals. Strauss makes evident a debt to his work (*NRH*, 78; *PPH*, 142, 163; *JPCM*, 449–52, 457–66). See the epilogue below. But Klein was most beholden to Heidegger for the latter's analyses of Platonic-Aristotelian *eidos* as disclosing the world or as "apophantic." Heidegger stresses that the Greeks, and especially Aristotle, were the greatest of all phenomenologists in their thinking of truth (*aletheia*) as "the self-announcing of the phenomena . . . the unconcealment of what is present, its disclosure and self-showing" (*SD*, 87).

19. As Strauss puts it: "*Sein* cannot be explained by *das Seiende*, as causality cannot be explained causally" (*RCPR*, 44; also PS, 328).

20. *H*, 336–37.

21. *SPPP*, 33–34.

22. *WIPP*, 38–39.

23. See also *WIPP*, 39–40.

24. The foundation of classical political philosophy was "the quest for cosmology rather than a solution to the cosmological problem" (*WIPP*, 39).

25. In the text Strauss asserts that according to Aristotle "the issue between the mechanical and the teleological conception of the universe is decided by the manner in which the problem of the heavens, the heavenly bodies, and their motions, is solved." But the cited passages from the *Physics* (196a25ff., 199a3–5) argue that causality in the heavens is not "for the sake of an end" but necessary causation. Coming to be for the sake of an end is discovered from experience of terrestrial beings like ourselves, wherein chance is intermingled with final causation; the teleological nature of these beings is in no way deducible from the motion of the heavens. See also Rosen, *Elusiveness of the Ordinary*, 153–54.

26. *WIPP*, 38.

27. "Since man must understand himself in the light of the whole or of the origin of the whole which is not human, or since man is the being that must try to transcend humanity, he must transcend humanity in the direction of the subhuman if he does not transcend it in the direction of the superhuman" (*TM*, 78).

28. *WIPP*, 39.

29. *RCPR*, 30.

30. "Brief über den 'Humanismus,'" *GA*, 9: 313–64.

31. With this one touches on the source of what Strauss calls the lack of "any charity as well as . . . any humanity" in Heidegger's philosophy (*SCR*, 9).

32. See note 18 above.

33. *OT*, 212.

34. *RCPR*, 42–46; *SPPP*, 33–34.

35. *GA*, 9: 187–91; *N*, 2: 193–99.

36. *SCR*, 9–12, 29–30; cf. *NRH*, 26–27.

37. It is suggested in the note at 26 (Nietzsche's preference for the "tragic life" to the theoretical life) and the references to "divination" at 12 and 33 and the reference to "revelation" at 28.

38. *OT*, 212.

39. Cf. *WIPP*, 45–46.

40. See Richard Kennington, "Strauss's *Natural Right and History*," *Review of Metaphysics* 35, no. 1 (September 1981): 57–86, for a very insightful treatment of the theme of "metaphysical neutrality" in Strauss's account of modern philosophy. As Kennington points out, the emancipation of man from natural ends and from the whole is the root of the favoring of individuality, or of the individual's becoming "the center and origin of the moral world" (*NRH*, 248).

41. I take this to be the most decisive point of Strauss's critique of modern philosophy, and it is more central than his objections to "the lowering of the goals" in modern democratic politics. Indeed Strauss's criticism applies in a way more certainly to post-Rousseauian idealistic versions of modern politics dedicated to raising the goals. On this I differ with the approach to Strauss of Robert Pippin, "The Modern World of Leo Strauss."

42. *RCPR*, 270.

CHAPTER 8

1. *PPH*, 15.

2. *WIPP*, 27.

3. *NRH*, 78–80; *CM*, 43.

4. *NRH*, 32.

5. *NRH*, 34.

6. *RCPR*, 258.

7. *NRH*, 323.

8. *RCPR*, 161.

9. *RCPR*, 248.

10. *RCPR*, 161.

11. *WIPP*, 48.

12. *WIPP*, 51.

13. *CM*, 42–44.

14. *RCPR*, 162. Here one needs to have regard for the theological-political problem posed by revealed religion, especially the Christian form in which the promise of salvation transcends the law, and all believers partake of life in another kingdom as well as that of this world. Strauss saw this mixing of philosophy and "*nomos* tradition" as posing special problems not just for politics but for philosophy, which modern philosophy sought in its way to overcome. See chapter 2 above.

15. *NRH*, 279.

16. *NRH*, 172–77; *RCPR*, 243–44.

17. *RCPR*, 182. See chapter 9 below for further discussion of the points in this paragraph.

18. *RCPR*, 149–50, 125.

19. *RCPR*, 252; *NRH*, 90 n. 10; *SA*, 312.

20. *WIPP*, 50, 45.

21. *NRH*, 248.

22. *WIPP*, 50–55.

23. *RCPR*, 132–33, 142, 169; *WIPP*, 38–40. See chapter 3 above.

24. *RCPR*, 164.

25. *NRH*, 31.

26. *WIPP*, 55.

27. *JPCM*, 450.

28. *SPPP*, 32–34. Strauss's moment, however, has crucial differences from those of his German predecessors. The moment of insight for Strauss enables us to uncover the natural, transhistorical truths that tradition has overlaid, and this recovery does not involve, it seems, progress beyond the original form of the insights. Yet I add the cautionary "it seems" in light of the thoughts in the text that follows.

29. *CM*, 9.

30. *JPCM*, 450.

31. *SPPP*, 30–34.

32. *HPP*, 77.

33. *CM*, 21. Of course Aristotelian philosophizing is still an ascent, and Strauss's statements do not exclude the possibility that for Aristotle human *theoria*, as contemplation of nature apart from the political realm, is necessary for the completion of the whole or of nature. Platonic readings of Aristotle can be found in S. Benardete, "On Wisdom and Philosophy: The First Two Chapters of Aristotle's *Metaphysics A*," in *The Argument of the Action*; R. Burger, *Aristotle's Dialogue with Socrates: On the 'Nicomachean Ethics'* (Chicago: University of Chicago Press, 2008), and M. Davis, *The Politics of Philosophy: A Commentary on Aristotle's Politics* (Lanham, MD: Rowman and Littlefield, 1996).

CHAPTER 9

1. *NRH*, 323.

2. *CM*, 42; *NRH*, 78–80.

3. *NRH*, 32.

4. *NRH*, 35.

5. *HPP*, 74–75.

6. *RCPR*, 161.

7. *RCPR*, 182.

8. *RCPR*, 132.

9. *RCPR*, 126.

10. *RCPR*, 133.

11. *WIPP*, 38–40.

12. *CM*, 42–45.

13. *CM*, 43.

14. *CM*, 42.

15. *NRH*, 34.

16. *TM*, 296.

17. *WIPP*, 51.

18. *WIPP*, 40–50.

19. *NRH*, 279.

20. *NRH*, 169–77.

21. *NRH*, 248.

22. *NRH*, 294.

23. *NRH*, 174–75.

24. *NRH*, 176–77.

25. *RCPR*, 161. I shall frequently cite these lectures (*RCPR*, 103–83) in the remainder of this chapter. The version in *RCPR* omits the first of the original six lectures, which were delivered at the University of Chicago in fall 1958. A more authentic version of the lecture series appears in *Interpretation*, 23, no. 2 (1996): 129–207.

26. *RCPR*, 162.

27. *NRH*, 293, 312, 323.

28. See *WIPP*, 50, on "the poetry underlying modern prose" in Montesquieu, and *TM*, 289, 292.

29. *RCPR*, 238.

30. *RCPR*, 240–42.

31. *RCPR*, 245.

32. *RCPR*, 235–37.

33. *RCPR*, 246–48.

34. *RCPR*, 248.

35. *RCPR*, 252–56.

36. *RCPR*, 256–57.

37. *RCPR*, 271.

38. *RCPR*, 248–49.

39. *RCPR*, 250.

40. *RCPR*, 258.

41. *RCPR*, 262.

42. *RCPR*, 260.

43. Two views about Strauss are often found in the literature: that he held modern philosophy to be not genuinely philosophic, and that he regarded the argument between reason and revelation as leading only to an impasse. I have tried to show that both views of Strauss are erroneous. He did, however, argue that modern philosophy, as lacking the Socratic response to human ignorance of the whole, was less able than the Socratic to address the challenge of revelation. Strauss provides his own attempt to "deduce" biblical revelation (or its "idea") and writes, "the task of the philosopher is to understand how the original (mythical) idea of the *theios nomos* is modified by the radical understanding of the moral implication and thus transformed into the idea of revelation," but he also concludes his proposed "deduction" with objections. RR, 164–67. See also chapter 2 above and the epilogue below.

44. *RCPR*, 125.

45. *RCPR*, 149–50.

46. *RCPR*, 168–69.

47. *RCPR*, 125. See also CCWM, 7: "The greatest document of the case of poetry against philosophy is Aristophanes' *Clouds.*"

48. *SA*, 6. See also the first lecture of the series "The Problem of Socrates" in *Interpretation* 23, no. 2 (1996): 136–38.

49. *SA*, 8.

50. *NRH*, 252–53.

51. *RCPR*, 111, 115, 118.

52. *RCPR*, 125–26.

53. *RCPR*, 109, 112.

54. *RCPR*, 155–59.

55. *RCPR*, 126.

56. *RCPR*, 165.

57. *RCPR*, 165–66.

58. *RCPR*, 159.

59. *RCPR*, 161.

60. *RCPR*, 146.

61. *RCPR*, 132, 142, 169.

62. *RCPR*, 165; see the remark on *thumoeides.*

63. *RCPR*, 133.

64. *RCPR*, 164; thus man is the microcosm, 133.

65. *RCPR*, 180.

66. *RCPR*, 151, 154.

67. *RCPR*, 181.

68. *RCPR*, 174.

69. *RCPR*, 150.

70. *SA*, 173: "This entitles us perhaps to say that Aristophanes is not opposed to philosophy simply, but only to a philosophy that, disregarding Eros, has no link to poetry."

71. *RCPR*, 181.

72. *RCPR*, 180.

73. *RCPR*, 182.

74. *NRH*, 14, 22, 322–23.

75. *NRH*, 26 n. 9, 22.

EPILOGUE

1. PS, 335.

2. S. Benardete writes that the Platonic mode of imitation, "which never ceases to amaze, made it possible for Plato to preserve the Socrates who in never writing represents the truth that philosophy alone has no tradition within the perpetuation of philosophy in its necessary decline." He adds: "Strauss's deconstruction of philosophy is thus not Heidegger's, who hurried past Plato to Parmenides and Heraclitus, by-passing Socrates." *Argument of the Action*, 414.

3. Klein, *Greek Mathematical Thought and the Origins of Algebra*, 192. Klein proceeds to characterize this identification as a move in which "an object of an *intentio secunda* (second

intention), namely the concept as such, is turned into the object of an *intentio prima* (first intention)." Contrary to what is often said, Klein does not regard ancient ontological inquiries, which ascend from the "natural" experience of number and bodies, as simply superior to the modern approach, which allowed for the whole range of discoveries in modern science. It is rather that these modern discoveries have concealed the aporia of Being, which ancient philosophy exposed. Thus Klein on Aristotle writes of a "bifurcation in the direction in which the *eidos* [works]" (in the process of generation and in the process of understanding) as one that "threatens the integrity of Aristotle's philosophizing." Similarly there is a duality in the meaning of *arche* for Aristotle: "it is (a) the begetting, unchanging and imperishable power which works on a suitable material and it is (b) that pliable material which is being transformed by the begetting power into the natural thing." In both cases a stable principle of intelligibility has to relate to the elusive realm of change and becoming. See Klein, *Lectures and Essays* (Annapolis: St. John's Press, 1985), 185, 226. In the case of Plato, Klein gives an account of the "failure of *logos*" to "count" the arithmetical structure of Being (*on*) as the community (*koinonia*) of motion and rest in Plato's *Sophist*. See *Greek Mathematical Thought*, 94–95. I have profited from conversations about Klein's work with Paul Wilford.

4. *WIPP*, 76. Among Strauss's students Richard Kennington in particular developed a deep understanding of the relationship in early modern philosophy between new foundations of knowledge in "metaphysically neutral" principles and the new practical *telos* of mastery of nature. See R. Kennington, *On Modern Origins: Essays in Early Modern Philosophy*, ed. P. Kraus and F. Hunt (Lanham, MD: Lexington Books, 2004). Kennington saw the need to make some revision of Strauss's constructivist view ("to understand is to make") of the early modern accounts of knowledge.

5. *WIPP*, 76, and the entire essay "Political Philosophy and History," ibid., 56–77. Strauss refers in the essay to Klein's book on Greek mathematical thought and an essay, "Phenomenology and the History of Science," which was reprinted in Klein, *Lectures and Essays*, 65–84.

6. *NRH*, 177.

7. RR, 154–55. See also *SCR*, preface to the English translation, where Strauss describes Spinoza's account of nature and the whole as a version of constructivist thought.

8. RR, 177.

9. RR, 179. Strauss also mentions Kant's criticism of the identification of "being" with "evidently knowable" in Kant's critique of earlier philosophy and its approaches to theology. Earlier (classical) philosophy holds that "there is no revelation, because there can be no evident *knowledge* of the fact of revelation. The argument presupposes the tacit identification of 'being' with 'evidently knowable.' Philosophy is essentially 'idealistic.'. . . It is *this* fact which gave rise to Kant's Critique of Pure Reason, to his distinction between the phenomenon and the Thing-in-itself." My understanding of Kant's transcendental idealism is that it denies the possibility of revelation as the evident sign of supernatural events while admitting that God or being is not accessible through clear and distinct ideas. It is not altogether plain from the Strauss passage that he includes Kant among the moderns who deny the possibility of revelation. RR, 176–77. See *Critique of Pure Reason* A631/B659.

10. *RCPR*, 262. It is clear that Strauss does not mean that the whole is wholly unintelligible. "For of something of which we know absolutely nothing, we could not of course say anything." The whole's limited intelligibility is the intelligibility of the fundamental perplexities, the

knowledge of which Socrates calls knowledge of ignorance. In Strauss's view, Socrates sees the unavailability of wisdom as a permanent condition for man. Philosophy "is essentially a quest, because it is not able ever to become wisdom" (*RCPR*, 260). It is also clear that Strauss sees the knowledge of these perplexities as the basis of the goodness of the philosophic life and of its claim of superiority to revelation. "But the very uncertainty of all solutions, the very ignorance regarding the most important things, makes quest for knowledge the most important thing, and therefore makes a life devoted to it the right way of life" (*RCPR*, 260). Revelation would not be meaningful to human beings without the fundamental perplexities, of which only philosophy acquires *natural* knowledge—knowledge that is unavailable to revelation by its own principle. Strauss argues that both philosophy and revelation address the problem of justice, more specifically the insufficiency of justice as law (see chapter 9 above). Philosophy understands this as a permanent or natural problem without a perfect solution, whereas revelation offers the perfect solution of the mysterious omnipotent deity.

The penultimate paragraph in the lectures entitled *Progress or Return?* is often cited as presenting Strauss's final thought on the quandary of philosophy, which, having to admit the possibility of revelation, is "not evidently the right way of life," with the consequence that "the choice of philosophy is based on faith" (*RCPR*, 269). But Strauss goes on to say that "this difficulty underlies all present-day philosophizing," which finds itself "incapable of giving an account of its own necessity." He does not say it underlies all philosophy, and indeed in an earlier passage of the lecture (cited above) he describes philosophy "according to the original notion" as showing "why philosophy cannot possibly lead up to the insight that another way of life apart from the philosophic one is the right one" (*RCPR*, 260). There he speaks of classical philosophy, which he says is not adequately understood by present-day arguments in favor of revelation (*RCPR*, 262). Classical or Socratic philosophy seems capable of giving an account of its own necessity.

The penultimate paragraph, it should be noted, begins with an odd disclaimer of speaking "colloquially" and of making a point that Strauss can show "is not quite trivial," i.e., is somewhat trivial. He goes on to say that his use of the term "philosophy" is "in the common and vague sense of the term where it includes any rational orientation in the world, including science and what-have-you, common sense" (*RCPR*, 269). Clearly he is not speaking of philosophy "according to the original notion," and the present-day philosophizing that he adduces as unable to give an account of its own necessity is of a piece in this incapacity with science and common sense or "the vague sense" of philosophy.

11. RR, 174. Such statements make clear that Strauss's position does not rest on any form of natural theology. He writes of a "most serious difficulty" that arises for natural theology (RR, 154) and more widely for efforts to establish metaphysically that philosophy is the right way of life (*RCPR*, 260).

12. See chapter 3 above.

13. *NRH*, 164.

14. *WIPP*, 27.

15. Heinrich Meier is perhaps the leading representative of this reading. Since the authority of Plato and Aristotle may be the most effective in this regard, one should note that neither thinker presents the life of the pious observer of the sacred law as the highest and most serious alternative to the life of the philosopher. (One might add that nothing remotely suggesting this ranking is to be found in Shakespeare.)

16. CCWM, 5–6.

17. *RCPR*, 29–30.

18. Strauss does not give much attention to the indications in modern philosophers of concern with the philosophic life as a distinctive life, apart from some remarks on Machiavelli, Rousseau, and Nietzsche. This concern is surely underplayed in the rhetoric of the modern philosophers, but that does not entail its essential absence. In the end it is difficult to assess the extent to which Strauss's Platonic-Nietzschean device of dialectical overstatement controls his account of modern philosophy.

19. *RCPR*, 180. See discussion in chapter 9 above.

20. In his essay on Thucydides in *The City and Man*, Strauss writes that Thucydides as historian presents universals through his engagement with the particulars of the wars between Athens and Sparta, and therefore does something like what the poet does according to Aristotle. Thucydides can be vindicated as a historian who is not "less philosophic" than the poets, contrary to Aristotle's ranking of poetry and history. *CM*, 141–44.

21. Such observations relate to Strauss's Platonic claim that from the philosophic standpoint the true alternative to philosophy is poetry of a higher (Aristophanic) kind and *its* version of the problem of the individual and the city. See chapter 9 above.

22. *RCPR*, 34.

INDEX

Leibniz, Gottfried Wilhelm, 19
Lessing, Gotthold Ephraim, 44, 50,
177n3
"lesson of 1933," 117, 183n5
liberalism, 112, 133, 137–38, 147, 150, 155
Locke, John, 145, 171n35
logoi, 154, 162
logos, 35, 106, 107, 157, 162
Löwith, Karl, 4, 49, 55–59, 163; Nietzsche
and, 4, 49, 55–57, 178n38, 187n22
Lukács, Georg, 59

Machiavelli, Niccolò, 18, 131, 135, 145
Maimonides, 178n20
Marx, Karl, 59, 116–17
Meier, Heinrich, 196n15
Mendelssohn, Moses, 44
modern philosophy, 13, 16–20, 64–68,
193n43, 197n18; "unradicality" of, 43–61.
See also modernity
modernity, 17, 19, 47–48, 50–52, 56, 69, 125,
126, 147, 148, 155; crisis of, 48; critique of,
46, 99, 100, 114–15; Nietzsche and, 17, 29,
47, 50, 100; pre-Socratics in late, 27–42;
repetition of antiquity at the peak of, 49,
58, 163; technological nihilism of, 92, 105;
as unnatural construct, 133–41
Montesquieu, Charles-Louis de Secondat,
161, 173n56, 193n28
moral appraisal, 106
moral law, 87, 88
moral teleology. *See* teleology
morality, 31, 93, 150, 153; critique and justifications of, 29, 30, 60; freedom and, 88 (*see
also* freedom); Kant on, 86–89; Nietzsche
on, 28–31, 38, 39, 49; politics and, 65–66,
72–74, 86, 95, 138, 160–62; roots of, 77, 138,
149. *See also* ethics; transmorality
mysterious whole, 20, 78; two versions of,
125–29

National Socialism (Nazism): Heidegger's
disillusionment with, 116; Heidegger's

support of, 1, 10, 36, 54, 68, 83–85, 91, 93,
112, 114–17, 122, 170n25, 183n4
natural philosophy, 47, 48, 51, 52, 128, 131
Natural Right and History (Strauss), 14–15,
142, 171n35; Heidegger as unnamed opponent, 121–23; as response to Heidegger,
2, 121–23, 126, 128, 131
natural rights, 15, 121, 123
nature, problem of, 15–16, 58–59, 62–64. See
also *phusis* (nature)
Nietzsche, Friedrich Wilhelm, 4, 12, 31–33,
36–42, 46, 48–50, 52, 54, 55, 57, 60, 62,
64, 65, 69, 90, 116–18, 125, 137, 155,
179n41; Aristophanes and, 66, 137, 151–52;
attack on Enlightenment, 13; *The Birth
of Tragedy from the Spirit of Music*, 30;
Christianity and, 36, 47–49, 52, 56, 90; on
the "death" of God, 36, 37, 90, 103, 168n15,
183n4; doctrine of eternal recurrence,
31–32, 50 (*see also* eternal return); *Ecce
Homo*, 30; Enlightenment and, 13, 29, 101;
German philosophy, Germans, and, 19, 28,
29, 31, 39, 62–64, 108; on the Greeks, 19,
28–34; Heidegger on the higher freedom
and, 96–109; historicism and, 57, 62, 65,
66; Hobbes and, 49; idealism and, 29;
Karl Löwith and, 4, 49, 55–57, 178n38,
187n22; metaphysics, 36, 38, 90, 102, 103,
168n15; modernity and, 17, 29, 47, 50, 100;
on morality, 28–31, 38, 39, 49; natural philosophy and, 47, 48, 52, 74; nihilism and, 4,
36–37, 39, 102, 103, 105, 168n15; *Philosophy
in the Tragic Age of the Greeks*, 32, 33; Plato
and, 29–31, 49, 151–52, 155; rationalism
and, 60, 152; Socrates, Socratism, and,
29–31, 33, 37–38, 46, 47, 60, 65, 66, 151;
Xenophon and, 60. *See also* Socratism,
Strauss's post-Nietzschean; *Will to Power,
The* (Nietzsche)
nihilism, 35–37, 39, 91, 92, 102–5, 117, 133,
170n25; Nietzsche and, 4, 36–37, 39, 102,
103, 105, 168n15
nominalism, 146

Printed and bound by CPI Group (UK) Ltd, Croydon, CR0 4YY

09/06/2025

14685700-0001